Dedication

To my family and to the memory of the victims of the Holocaust.

Acknowledgements

I would like to thank Michael O'Brien and the editorial staff of
The O'Brien Press Ltd. for having the trust and patience in me to write
my memoir. Also I would like to thank my cousin, Chava Shelach, and my
brother, Miki, for helping me get the facts right. Thanks to the following for
their contributions: Chezi Reichental, Bandy Scheimovitz, Bill Morrison,
Robert (Bob) Spitz, Pavel Kučera, Susanne Seitz, Oskar Baranovič.
Thanks to Colette Colfer for help with typing my notes and Nicola Pierce for
helping me to write the book. Thanks also to Lynn Jackson and Gerry Gregg
for their support.

'I speak so that my past does not become
somebody's future.'
Elie Wiesel

With my best wishes

Contents

PART III   AFTER BELSEN ~ LATER LIFE

Introduction from the Holocaust Education Trust Ireland

After more than fifty years of almost complete silence about his incarceration as a young boy in Bergen-Belsen concentration camp, Tomi began to tell his story. When Holocaust Education Trust Ireland (HETI) was established in 2005, he became an enthusiastic member of the small group of Holocaust survivors committed to delivering one of HETI's schools programmes, *'Hearing a Survivor Speak'*.

Since then, Tomi has been speaking to senior-cycle students in post-primary schools throughout Ireland, making an indelible impression on all who hear him. During the school year, Tomi shares his personal experiences of the Holocaust with approximately four thousand students. The response from students, during Tomi's school visits and subsequent correspondence he receives, is powerful evidence of the impact of his story.

As the number of Holocaust survivors diminishes, Tomi is acutely aware that he is one of the final witnesses. He feels compelled to tell his story to young people so that they will know what happened in the Holocaust and he is dedicated to furthering Holocaust education. Tomi believes he owes it to the victims and he owes it also to the survivors, to ensure that this horrendous episode in European history is never forgotten.

In 2008 a documentary film, *Till the Tenth Generation,* supported by the Irish Film Board and transmitted by RTÉ 1, traced Tomi's story back through his childhood in Czechoslovakia, his capture and incarceration by the Nazis, his family's experience after liberation from Belsen, and his adult life, culminating in his arrival in Ireland in 1960. A DVD of the film is now available in every post-primary school in the Republic as part of an education pack, which also includes a Teacher's Guide and a CD of teaching materials. Now Tomi has written his autobiography, *I Was a Boy in Belsen*, and these two documents will ensure that Tomi's story is safeguarded in perpetuity.

It is a pleasure and an honour to know Tomi Reichental and to work with him. Holocaust Education Trust Ireland is indebted to him for giving so generously of his time and energy in supporting our programmes. The Trust wishes him every success with *I Was a Boy in Belsen* and many more years of fruitful activity and much fulfilment in the future.

Lynn Jackson
Chief Executive, Holocaust Education Trust Ireland

Introduction

'In Poland if the Jews did not work they were shot. If they could not work they had to succumb. They had to be treated like a tuberculosis bacillus, *with which a healthy body may become infected.*

'This was not cruel, if one remembers that even innocent creatures, such as hares and deer are killed so that no harm is caused by them. Why should the beasts ... be spared?

'Nations that did not rid themselves of the Jews perished.'

Adolf Hitler in conversation with Admiral Horthy
of Hungary, Klessheim Castle, April 1943

The Final Solution was the most audaciously evil endeavour undertaken in human history. The annihilation of every Jewish man, woman and child was the overarching priority of the National Socialist regime in Germany during World War II. The fact that the state that possessed the most advanced technological expertise, industrial resources and scientific knowledge in Europe mobilised these assets to kill millions on the basis of their race and religion will provoke people to reflect on the Holocaust for centuries to come.

Most of the island of Ireland was spared the carnage and horrors of the conflict Adolf Hitler launched to establish continental hegemony to last for a thousand years. The fate of Europe's Jewish population was not a matter of pressing concern to most Irish people before, during or after 'The Emergency'. The industrial slaughter of six million Jews from every corner of Nazi-occupied Europe was an almost incomprehensible revelation to those who saw the hellish newsreels of the liberation of Bergen-Belsen by the British Army in April 1945.

Tomi Reichental and his brother Miki were just some of the starving, haunted figures captured briefly in a filmed sequence of Jewish children waving at the moment of deliverance through barbed wire into the lens of a Bolex camera. The Reichental brothers were from the village of Merašice in what was once Czechoslovakia. They and millions like them were the people Neville Chamberlain had referred to as 'people from far away places' not worth fighting a war over. Instead, Hitler was appeased at Munich in 1938 and 'peace in our time' was achieved for the twelve months it took the Nazis to conquer the Czechs, hand Czechoslovakia over to the Fascist Monsignor Jozef Tiso and send the Wehrmacht into Poland in September 1939.

Tomi Reichental, his mother, father and brother would miraculously survive the Shoah (the Holocaust). But it would take him and many more like him many years to find the words to describe the ordeal. This book gives us a precious personal insight into what happened to these people in 'the far away places' Neville Chamberlain had sold down the river. From 1940 to 1945 the Reichentals and everyone like them became the continent-wide quarry of the merciless legions of Himmler's Gestapo.

When I first encountered Tomi in the summer of 2007 at the invitation of Oliver Donohoe from the Holocaust Education Trust, I was meeting not only my first Holocaust survivor but also the first person I can recall meeting who came from the vanished urbane sophisticated Jewish society of Central Europe. A world destroyed forever by the apocalyptic death squads of the Nazis and their accomplices.

To connect with that lost world I embarked on a painful creative journey with Tomi and a dedicated film crew, led by the inspirational cinematographer, Seamus Deasy. That odyssey into the darkest corners of modern European history culminated with the successful completion of the feature documentary film *Till the Tenth Generation* in 2008.

That film dramatically tells the story of how thirty-five of Tomi's closest relatives were gassed, guillotined, starved and worked to death at various Nazi killing sites in Poland, Czechoslovakia and Germany from 1942 to 1945. Remarkably, Tomi and his family cheated death against all the odds and went on to re-build their lives from the ashes in the new state of Israel in 1949.

In doing so, they escaped the renewal of state-sponsored anti-Semitism ushered in by the post-war communist regimes across the territories of Eastern Europe at the instigation of Josef Stalin. The Soviet Union's dictator marked down the Jews who had survived the Nazis as potential 'class enemies'. The new party line on Zionism was dogmatically implemented by local communists terrified to step out of line with Moscow. In these circumstances, it was a prudent move by the Reichentals to sell up and abandon their farm in Merašice and take their chances in the new Jewish state.

I'm delighted to see Tomi Reichental expand on his vivid personal account of his precious life in this volume. His autobiography will now stand as an enduring testament to both the diabolical scale of Hitler's extermination project and the resilience of the human spirit.

In 2010 in Listowel in North Kerry, Tomi and I were invited by Jimmy Deenihan, the local Dáil Deputy and Minister for Arts and Culture, to present the film at the impressive St John's Theatre in the market square in the town. Listowel is the only place in Ireland that has marked the Holocaust with a memorial. It is located on the banks of the river Feale in a shaded tranquil corner of the European Park.

The occasion happened to fall on 15 April. Sixty-five years earlier, to the day, Tomi Reichental had been liberated from the hell that was Bergen-Belsen concentration camp. In the audience that night in Listowel was Paddy FitzGibbon, the local man instrumental in the erection of the only memorial to the Shoah in the Irish Republic.

Both of us were delighted to see Paddy at the screening because we have often quoted his eternally incisive remarks when we introduce the film to audiences at many of the film festivals and commemorative events we have been invited to in recent times. FitzGibbon's said these words in 1995 when the Listowel memorial was unveiled to the public:

'*Go home from this place and tell your children and your grandchildren that you have looked into the eyes and shaken hands with people who have survived the greatest cataclysm mankind has unleashed on mankind. Tell them to tell their children and their children's children, because these people will be mourned and spoken about and wept over for 10,000 years. For if they aren't we are all done for.*'

When the reader has turned the last page of this book, he or she will have encountered and embraced the universal relevance of Tomi Reichental's story. Hopefully, also, they will be inspired by the sombre advice of Paddy Fitzgibbon and tell their children and their grandchildren to read it some day too.

Gerry Gregg, Dublin

Foreword

My childhood is divided into three very different phases: the carefree years before the onslaught of the anti-Jewish laws; the subsequent arrest and deportation of myself and my family to Bergen–Belsen concentration camp; and finally the struggle to return home to a tattered normality after our liberation. The first part seems the briefest of all.

It all started far away, outside our small village, Merašice in Czechoslovakia. It started with whispers, then abuse – and the final stage was murder …

Robbing the Jews to Make Them Poor

With the declaration of independent Slovakia on 14 March 1939 by the Catholic priest, Fr Josef Tiso, the Czechoslovakian Jewry experienced an ill wind of change in attitude. The radical and national elements in the new government clamoured for a solution to the 'Jewish Question', as defined by Nazi Germany. The first thing to be done was to exclude Jews from the economy. Therefore, the new state passed a law prohibiting Jews from manufacturing and selling Christian artefacts – which really didn't make much difference to anybody.

Something more stringent needed to be done.

A month later the government ordered all Jewish notaries to be sacked and out of the total practising Slovak solicitors and doctors only 4 percent were allowed to be Jewish (my Uncle Artur, a solicitor, and Uncle Desider, a doctor, were sacked too).

This was more like it!

These sorts of orders encouraged anti-Semitic Slovak nationalists to really let loose. Hadn't they been saying for years how the Jews prevented the advance of the intelligentsia because they occupied all the best professions? The expulsion of the Jews from national life continued with the order, on 21 June 1939, informing Jews that they no longer needed to serve in the national army.

Now it was time to get more personal, time to start looking at Jewish property and businesses with a view to transferring it all, as simply and efficiently as possible, into Christian hands. The only option, initially, for the innovative Jewish shopkeeper or factory owner was to elect to hand over half their business to a Christian, a process described by the authorities as 'voluntary Aryanisation'. This way, at least the Jew got to hold on to 50 percent of his livelihood. Meanwhile, the new partner received the very best training in preparation for running the whole business one day – in the not too distant future – without the need for state investment.

So it was, about twelve months later, that the new Prime Minister – the hugely anti-Semitic Dr Vojtech Tuka –

demanded a speeding up of the process. From now on, the Ministry of Finance would decide if a business was to be Aryanised or simply liquidated – like my grandfather's shop. In the years 1940 to 1941, a total of 2,223 Jewish businesses were transferred into Christian hands while 10,000 smaller businesses were liquidated. Jews could no longer sell or buy a business without official permission – which was as rare as it was obscenely expensive.

Restrictions on Jews stretched to determining how much of their own money they could withdraw from their own bank accounts. In April 1941 they could take out 500 crown a week; five months later they could only take 150 crown.

Then it got down to the nitty-gritty: all household valuables were to be handed in. Jewish people had to part with fur coats, cars, cameras, radios and even valuable books. My parents asked one of their farm-hands to hide their one-hundred-piece Rosenthal dinner set and keep it safe for them. When they went back for it, in 1945, the set, according to their trusted employee, had mysteriously vanished.

Lastly, Jews had to pay a special 20 percent flat tax on whatever they still owned. This was the last straw. By 1942, when the deportations were happening in earnest, most Jews were practically destitute. The nation was taught to regard them as useless parasites on social welfare, costing the country more money than they were worth.

It was time to take the next step.

Getting Rid of the Jews

The deportations began on 25 March 1942. From then on the deportation continued, first with young Jewish women and men, and later entire Jewish families were arrested and deported. Each transport contained between a thousand and 1500 people. There was panic throughout the community, with many families going into hiding and large numbers escaping to Hungary. Grandmother Rosalia, my mother's mother, was smuggled into Hungary and her son, Artur, also sneaked over the border with his wife and children. People were disappearing at an alarming rate; it was the only subject of conversation at this time.

The Germans, not wanting to lose control of thousands of Jews, had the first deportees send postcards home indicating that everything was just fine. Naturally, these cards were heavily censored to ensure against the awful truth being revealed. However, people soon found ingenious ways of spreading the news.

Your sister Sarah went to see your grandmother last week.

Maurice met his brother George some time ago.

The censors had no idea that the grandmother and George were dead. Here were the first confirmations that the rumours were true: the Jews were dying. Some deportees were made to post-date their cards, which meant they had already been murdered by the time their families were reading that they were safe and well. Quite a number of these postcards are preserved in Yad Vashem Museum in Jerusalem.

Meanwhile, Jewish people did all they could to evade deportation, using whatever connections they had to obtain exemption papers – although the permits were frequently disregarded since the Hlinka Guard, the Slovakian SS equivalent, had to a quota to fill and the numbers simply had to add up. So, really, everybody was in danger.

Today it is estimated that from a population of 90,000 Jews in Slovakia 70,000 were murdered (including thirty-five members of my family) and approximately 20,000 survived.

PART I
NORMAL LIFE CHANGES

Chapter 1
· · · · · ·

Our Home in Merašice

We lived in Merašice, a small, Slovak village in the region of Topolcany, that was home to just seven hundred people. It was a typical village, with the one pub and the Catholic Church providing the entire social life for the locals. My father frequented the pub in order to keep up-to-date with all the news. There were no newspapers, so information was best secured over a beer or a *slivovitz* (plum brandy). The pub owner, Mr Varga, usually sat and drank with his customers while his wife did all the work. Infrequent visitors, who were on their way elsewhere, were immediately offered food by Mrs Varga – she was a first-rate hostess. From what I remember, the pub was always open; there were no particular hours and the door was never locked. Anyone who passed by always nipped in for a drink and a chat. My father used to say, 'Even the horses have learnt to stop outside.'

News and gossip were also gleaned from the parish priest, who was a great friend of our family; my parents particularly enjoyed playing cards with him. The old church was probably the most striking building in the village, its simple Gothic interior dating all the way back to 1397, and the steeple was the first thing a visitor would see as they approached the village. Father Harangozo was a small, stout man, whose constant kindness and acts of charity – and partiality to enjoying a few drinks – made him very popular as a neighbour. He lived in a small house beside the church with his sister Marguerite, who acted as his housekeeper and secretary. Aside from his parochial duties, he also taught religion in the local school. A Hungarian, he was delighted with the fact that my educated parents could talk to him in his own language. Of course, his busiest day was Sunday when the church bells rang out summoning the relevant villagers to mass. They would emerge out of their houses in their best clothes. After mass the men headed in groups to the pub, while the women headed home to make the dinner.

My grandparents' shop was the only decent one for miles around. Far from big, the shop was basically a small room with a counter that separated the public from the small living area out back. It was a mixed hardware store that provided everything from flour, sugar, needles and thread to paper, glue and whatever the busy housewife needed to clean her house. If you wanted something more than this, maybe a new outfit or a pair of shoes, you had to take the single daily bus to the next town. My abiding memory of the shop is how every single item was accounted for and had its own special place. It was always pristine – the dust, imaginary or otherwise, being swept out the door several times a day. When, on the rare occasion that my grandfather, or *Opapa*, as we called him, was out of a particular product, he would solemnly promise the customer that he'd order it immediately and have it for them within the next couple of days. Never less than professional, he addressed every single customer, regardless of age and status, by their proper name. No slang words were uttered here, nor any kind of casual familiarity. *Opapa* was an efficient man and his business was a perfect reflection of his character.

He was rather strict, yet we were very fond of him, in spite of himself. My brother, Miki, and I would visit him at work in order to be given sweets, never more than one or two each, as a bribe to leaving him in peace. He only ever dressed in black from head to toe, including his black hat and black moustache. His strictness extended to his religion too. Accordingly, we had a local *shoket* (butcher), who served the Jewish community. He visited us every couple of weeks to kill our chickens and cows in the kosher way. On Friday nights for the Sabbath meal, the family would wait until *Opapa* took his seat first. Miki and I were always on our best behaviour because we simply had to be. There were no arguments or fooling around. Instead, our energy was focused on our prayers and our food. The meal had to be completely finished before we could leave the table, and even then we had to ask *Opapa* for permission first.

Our grandmother, *Omama*, was the exact opposite of her husband in appearance and manner. While he was tall and slim, she was small and plump, cutting an imperfect figure in thick layers of clothing that were protected by the frilly apron she wore every day. Her thick, wavy hair was silver grey and her double chin wobbled as she went about her chores. I remember her only as an old woman – she must have been in her sixties at least, but she never stopped working. She looked after the house, did all the cooking and baking, and then would look after the shop when *Opapa* went to get more supplies. My father was the only one of her nine children who lived in Merašice and, consequently, she spoiled Miki and me, stuffing us, much to my mother's dismay, with whatever she was baking: poppy-seed cake, cheesecake, jam sponge or apple tart. Sometimes I would visit her just to watch her make rye bread, a typical village fare with loaves the size of a small cartwheel. She'd always make two loaves, enough for several weeks. When she wasn't too busy she'd entertain me with stories, well-known ones like 'Little Red Riding Hood' and 'Hansel and Gretel'.

My mother was rather liberal in her opinions and only visited the synagogue on holy days. She often slipped us non-kosher food too, like salami or bacon, telling us to hide it from *Opapa*. She believed in children eating fatty foods during the cold, harsh months of winter. I was a fussy eater and was often sick with colds and frequent ear infections. My poor mother would be forced to spend her meal times trying to persuade me to eat my vegetables. My reasons for ignoring her requests were pretty erratic, and no doubt typical of a young child: 'I can't eat this spinach; it will make me green all over.'

My parents' marriage had been arranged – by whom I don't know – but it was a happy one. What I do know is that they married on 26 October 1930 when he was twenty-eight years old, five years older than her. They honeymooned in Venice, a rarity at the time. I assume the trip was a wedding present from the Scheimovitzes, my mother's family, who were all successful professionals, including her sister Margo, who was a dental technician and actually ran her own surgery, very unusual for the time. My father's side was none too shabby either. His siblings included a surgeon, an architect and an office manager. Father had attended a German college in Slovakia, where he studied commerce and agriculture. He could also speak several languages, but never showed any interest in pursuing a 'proper' professional career. When

Opapa opened his shop, deciding he was too old to farm, Father was more than content to take over the farm. So it was that Mother, a city girl from a well-to-do family, married a farmer and came to live in a tiny village. As could be expected, things were a bit difficult in the beginning; it took Mother a while to settle into her new life, but eventually she found her feet. It probably helped that she and Father had a lot in common. They were both big readers and also loved music, especially opera. Many evenings were spent around the radio, our only source of entertainment. My parents also enjoyed socialising and Father always had plenty of friends in all types of places. We never saw our parents arguing, but would sometimes notice them not talking to one another for a couple of days, though this didn't happen very often.

We had a maid who doted on my mother – in fact, they were the best of friends. Mariška, a Roman Catholic, had six children of her own, and her husband worked for a German family. She did the washing and ironing, allowing my mother to concentrate on cooking and baking.

We weren't the only family in the village to have a maid. There were a few wealthy families in Merašice, and the villagers believed us to be rich too, for various reasons. Firstly, there was the shop; secondly, there was my father's farm of 120 hectares that employed five local men; and thirdly, our house was just that bit bigger. All the houses around were whitewashed and built of mud, while our house was whitewashed but built of brick. There was also the fact that my mother didn't dress like the other women, who favoured lots of coloured skirts and headscarves – my mother's clothes were quieter in colour and neater in style. Meanwhile, my father went about wearing a tie, unlike everyone else too. He also had a 125cc motorbike, our only luxury. I loved to sit on the tank watching heads turn as they heard us approach.

At harvest time Father would lodge every penny he made in the bank and there it stayed until there was a proper need for it. Everything we ate was homemade: butter, jam, white cheese, pastry and bread. During the hot summers my mother made her own ice-cream. She also made liqueurs, boiling fresh fruit over the fire and pouring it into glass jars. In this way our visiting relatives had their pick of pear, plum or cherry liqueur, and even brandy. Between my mother and my grandmother, our family was thoroughly self-sufficient. This meant that there was never any actual money in the house. I'm not even sure that our maid was paid in coin; perhaps her payment was the food that my mother would give her.

So, yes, it was true that we had everything we needed, but it really wasn't that much. Since our house had only one bedroom, Miki slept on the small couch in the sitting-room while I slept at the bottom of my parents' bed. Furthermore, while our bed linen, Rosenthal dinner plates, glasses, cutlery and ornaments were undoubtedly all first-rate, they were all presents that my parents had received as newlyweds. Once a year I would be taken to town for new clothes.

We certainly didn't think of ourselves as being well off, but still, there was an invisible social barrier between our family and the locals, despite my father's extrovert nature. People only ever addressed my grandfather as *Stari Panko* (Old Sir), and my grandmother was *Stara Pani* (Old Mistress), while my Mother was *Mlada Pani* (Young Mistress) and Father was *Mladi Panko* (Young Sir).

I loved Merašice. Like its inhabitants, it was self-sufficient. Apart from the pub and the church, there was the school and a whole host of specialised tradesman. There was Mr Perutka, the carpenter, who made my skis and toboggan. He could turn his hand to anything, from a fancy cabinet to a sturdy wheel for a hard-working cart. I can't remember the name of the blacksmith, but I loved to watch him work as he folded iron like it was pastry. Mr Polackek was the mechanic; he worked on the steam engines that were rented for harvesting the fields, and could also fix motorcars, which were a rarity in the village. Fortunately, he could also repair the water pumps, as there were only three wells in Merašice. These sorts of skills stayed in the same family from generation to generation. If another family wished their son to learn a trade they had to pay the craftsman a hefty sum for the required three-year apprenticeship. Money was scarce, so that was a big undertaking.

Other tradesmen passed through, constantly moving from village to village, to where the work was: the glazier, the man who sharpened scissors and knives, and the man who repaired things like pots and pans. Nothing was ever thrown away, only sharpened and fixed. My parents were very welcoming to these travellers; my mother fed them and my father let them sleep in one of our barns.

There was a second prosperous business in Merašice, apart from farming, and that was the manufacturing of red bricks for the construction industry. The local factory was owned and run by two Germans, Mr Ploich and Mr Shultise. As with just about everyone else in the village, my father got on very well with these two, thanks to his fluency in German.

Our village was such an idyllic place and never more so when, during the summers, my cousins visited from the city, making me realise all over again what a paradise surrounded me. My mother would bring us scoops of her ice-cream in our very own tea house, the small, wooden structure in the back garden which contained a round table and bench upon which eight excited kids could just about fit. If we were still hungry, we had a variety of fruit to choose from — I needed only to stretch out my hand to grab cherries, grapes and gooseberries, and in autumn apples from the apple tree with its spidery branches that dangled low enough for us to help ourselves.

A little stream ran through the village where we'd swim and fish for hours on end. Then we'd return home with tiny fish in the palms of our hands, excitedly ambushing my mother at the door: 'You have to fry these because we want to eat them for dinner.'

Thanks to the warm weather I went barefoot all summer. I had to be careful, however, when the sun grew fierce as I would inevitably be forced to return indoors, suffering from heat-induced migraines. In between football matches and fishing for dinner, I loved to follow my father around, checking out the crops and then hanging out with the man who took the cows out to pasture. Because I was the boss's son, he made me whistles from the willow branches that dangled at either side of the stream.

Summer also meant the wondrous smell of fresh flowers in the air. A vast, colourful array of flora grew in and around the village. It's something that I'll never forget, that heady scent of perfume that persisted no matter where I stood, and attracted umpteen bees and flying insects. One of my favourite times of the year was harvest time when all of us children, usually half-naked under the blue sky, would run to the fields to watch the big, noisy steam engine work away – a welcome improvement on the horse and plough.

Winters were also special and meant just one thing: snow – and lots of it. It started to fall in November and would cut us off from everywhere else, blocking the roads and making it impossible to travel by bus or car. Even as a young child I appreciated the stillness of the village when the snow served as a sort of muffler against noise. The world seemed like such a softer place under the blanket of white. Then, during the day, it would begin to thaw, only to freeze anew at night, leaving hardened drips, or icicles, dangling from the roofs of the houses. My mother had the carpenter make us a fine toboggan which was bigger than everyone else's — Miki and I would follow her to the top of the hill, near the church, and then we would all climb on for the breathtaking descent.

Of course, winter also meant Christmas — not that Christmas was actually celebrated in our house. We had our own festival, *Chanukah*, the festival of the lights, which begins some time before 25 December and lasts eight days; each night an additional candle on the *chanukiah* is burnt to commemorate the rededication of the Holy Temple back in the second century BCE. However, Miki and I were more than happy to join in our neighbours' festivities too. The men in the village would dress up as Santa Claus or St Nicholas and come to the door bearing presents. On Christmas Eve we too cleaned our shoes like our neighbours' children and put them out on the windowsill. When we'd wake up the next morning, our shoes would be miraculously filled with sweets and little toys.

Life was little short of perfect in those fun-filled days, but it wasn't to last. If there had been any feelings of ambiguity towards the Reichentals because of our perceived wealth or because my grandfather was stern and not given to small talk, or because my father was a boss, these feelings were to be suddenly fuelled by perhaps the biggest difference of all between us and our neighbours — our religion.

Chapter 2

· · · · · ·

Žid! Žid! Žid!

We were the only Jewish family in Merašice. Well, that's not strictly true – we were one of three original Jewish families, but the other two converted to other religions. Fortunately, there were other Jewish families in the surrounding villages and we kept in contact with them. The Goldbergers were lifelong friends of my parents; they lived about a kilometre away from us, in Otrokovce, and we visited them quite often. Mr Goldberger was also a farmer, like my father. There were two children, a boy called Zoli, who was Miki's age, and his sister, Marta, who was mine. I loved visiting their house, especially in June on account of the generous fruit trees in their back garden. We would stuff ourselves on the ripe cherries – but always left room for the wonderful cakes that Mrs Goldberger baked in our honour.

Mr Goldberger would always give me the same joking advice that never failed to make everyone laugh: 'Now, listen to me. When you grow up you must learn how to be a glazier. Then, when you've done that, you get yourself a partner. Then, when you've done that, send him ahead into a village and tell him to break some windows. The next morning you arrive bright and early and declare yourself open for business. And that's how you make your fortune.'

East of Merašice was the village of Kapince, home to the Friedmans. Whenever we had to take the train, we would visit them as it stopped there. Their house was another source of tasty cakes and, therefore, another favourite of mine. South of Merašice was the little village of Galanova, which had a small synagogue. Our family walked here on the Sabbath and on holy days, to pray and meet up with our Jewish friends.

Sabbath began on Friday evening with the sight of the first visible star, although the cooking of the special foods would have started the previous night. For instance, *Sholet*, a thick bean soup, had to be cooked overnight, along with eggs in their shells. When the eggs were peeled, they'd be brown in colour and wonderfully tasty. Also the *Chala*, the special white plaited bread, had to be baked the day before. Our meals on Fridays and Saturdays would begin with *Opapa* reciting the blessing over the *Chala*: '*Baruch atah Adonai, Eloheinu Melech Ha-olam, hamotzi lechem min Ha-aretz*' (Blessed are you, Lord our God, King of the Universe, who brings forth bread from the earth).

After the blessing, we would be served up chicken soup, followed by *Sholet* and then cakes. Even though I had to be on my best behaviour and wear my best clothes, I enjoyed the festivities. All the family dressed up and ate together in perfect harmony.

Mariška always arrived especially early on Saturday mornings since we weren't allowed to do anything physical – from lighting the fire to switching on the lights, or even tearing paper. We couldn't run, write, do any chores, or listen to the radio. Instead, Miki and I either read or played quietly in the garden. In the evenings we played host to Jewish friends or else we went to visit them in their houses.

The Sabbath was a very special day, and still is, of course, but back then, in Merašice, it was the only day that I felt Jewish and thus different from our neighbours.

I can well imagine that the grown-ups did everything in their power to keep their growing worries from us but it was an impossible task. While I was unaware of the evil forces at work and heading our way, there were some things that I couldn't help noticing. Miki and I spent hours playing football with the other kids in the village square. I was usually the goalkeeper while Miki, a talented player, was a popular addition to any team. A passer-by would hear the excited shouts of 'Pass it, Miki, over here!' or 'Come on, Tomi, kick it out!' and assume we were all the same.

With the publication of the Jewish Codex in Slovakia in September 1941, things began to change. Jews were not allowed into public places such as parks, cinemas, theatres, swimming pools and so on; they were not allowed to fish, drive a car, ride a bicycle, own binoculars, a radio, camera; travel restrictions were strictly enforced; Jews had to wear the yellow star, and there were marriage restrictions between Jews and non-Jews. This document is probably the most horrific in Slovakian history. Inspired by the Nazi hatred of the Jewish people, the Codex was a massive sixty pages, crammed with 270 articles bent on restricting the social, professional and economic life of the Jews. From now on anyone passing by the impromptu football matches would still hear Miki and me being called on excitedly by our friends to pass the ball or whatever, only now we were more baldly addressed. No longer did Miki score goals; from now on it was, 'Hey, the Jew scored!', and no longer was a player urged to kick the ball to Tomi, it was, 'Give the ball to the Jew.'

Perhaps it was around this time that my parents warned Miki and me to be careful when we went to the toilet. If there were other children around we were to hide our circumcised penises from them. I don't remember having much to say about this – but, then, I never questioned my parents. When they sat us down to tell us that we'd have to start being care-ful, that we'd have to start hiding our 'Jewishness' from others, it was, for me, no different from them telling us that we had to mind our manners and always give up our seats to adults.

The new signs of the times, the new restrictions, were for-mally communicated to the Reichental family at large when my grandfather's shop was taken from him. On 31 May 1941 the little shop became just another miserable statistic when it was liquidated, along with ten thousand other small Jewish businesses. It was brutal shock to *Opapa*. The shop was his life, his line of communication to the village. He knew eve-rybody and never forgot to ask after a mother's child or a sick relative. His customers had always relied on him, not just for needles and thread or bars of soap, but also for his advice. If anyone needed a solicitor or a specialist doctor, they would ask *Stari Panko* for a personal recommendation. His shop gave him his unique standing in Merašice – and now it was gone. He never recovered from this humiliation, rarely leav-ing the house because, as he saw it, he no longer had much of a reason to do so.

It was only a little while later that my own idyllic home life came to an abrupt end. I was aged six at this time. According to the Codex, no Jewish child could attend a national school. In other words, Miki and I were no longer welcome in the local school. Therefore it was decided that we would be sent to live with my father's sister, Aunt Renka, in Nitra, where there was a large Jewish population, with more than one Jewish school to choose from. Mother began preparations immediately. Miki and I had to accompany her on a shopping expedition to the next town, where she bought us new clothes, including coats for winter, which wasn't too far away. It was she who did all our packing, including the generous amounts of food that she was bringing for our aunt: eggs, flour, bread and chicken.

We'd have to take the train from Kapince, and since Father couldn't leave the farm he had one of his men, Mr Duraj, take us there in the horse and carriage. On reaching Kapince, we visited our friends, the Friedmans, like we always did, for cake and coffee. I remember the worried faces of the grown-ups as they discussed the New Order, as heralded by the Jewish Codex, and what it meant for us Jews.

The train arrived on time. I had visited Nitra plenty of times before and the train journey was usually my favourite part, but that morning I felt torn between the excitement of watching the landscape flash by my window and the sadness I felt at leaving my father and Merašice behind. Furthermore, since our aunt's house was too small, our mother wouldn't be staying for that first night and I wasn't looking forward to saying goodbye to her. No one knew how long Miki and I would be staying. I felt it was better not to ask.

Nicknamed the 'Radošina train' because it came from Radošina town, the train took its time, stopping every ten minutes to pick up people from the numerous villages along the way. Finally, we reached Nitra station about an hour later and from there it was a twenty-minute walk on the cobblestoned path to Aunt Renka's house. She was at the door waiting for us, welcoming us in with fierce hugs as she simultaneously ushered us towards the table where she had prepared a fine dinner. As soon as the meal was over, there was only time to look at the room that Miki and I would be sharing before Mother had to leave for the train back to Kapince. Mr Duraj would meet her off the train and drive her home. Not surprisingly, there were many tears; it was the first time we had to part from her in our lives. Everything seemed to be happening so fast. Miki and I would begin classes at our new schools the very next morning – me in the junior school, Miki in the senior school. To keep us from thinking too much about it all, Aunt Renka helped us unpack our belongings, suggesting that we leave out the new clothes in preparation for the early start.

That evening she asked me to give her my coat as she needed to sew something on it. I was intrigued when she produced a yellow star.

'What is that, Auntie?' I asked.

She didn't exactly smile as she replied: 'You're a big boy now, Tomi, so this means that you've to wear this any time you leave the house. From now on all Jews over the age of five must have a yellow star.'

Her explanation satisfied me and I didn't give it another thought.

The following morning Aunt Renka took me by the hand and we set off for the junior school which was just down the road. I felt very confident in my new clothes and was pleased at how many people greeted my aunt with every step we took. She appeared to know just about everyone in this mostly Jewish neighbourhood. Any lingering unease I felt from listening to my mother and the Friedmans talking about the New Order was completely forgotten as I skipped along beside my aunt, seeing only friendly faces around me. At school I was introduced to the teachers and then placed in a class of ten children or so. As soon as I had settled in, Aunt Renka said goodbye: 'You know your way home, don't you? So I'll see you about a quarter past twelve, then, and I'll have your lunch ready for you. Be a good boy now.'

I remember I had an enjoyable morning. There were no proper lessons. Instead, our teachers taught us games, thereby helping us to get to know each other. When the bell rang at twelve o'clock we all put on our coats and, as soon as we were formally released, raced out the door to head for home. Proud that I could remember my way back to Aunt Renka's, I set off happily. As I neared her house I saw three boys about my age standing in front of the corner shop. There was something about them that made me nervous. I felt my chest tighten as the three of them, in silence, watched me approach. Then, as I passed them by, they muttered at me, '*Žid! Žid! Žid!*' (Jew! Jew! Jew!). Confused and suddenly very scared, I took off down the street, unable to stop until I reached Aunt Renka's front door. Even as I ran, I instantly knew what had made me nervous about the boys: they weren't wearing any yellow stars. That was probably the first time that I really felt different.

Of course, it would only get worse. It seems like every day after that I had to face being shouted at by more and more children whose coats weren't branded by the yellow Star of David. Cries of 'Dirty Jew', 'Smelly Jew', 'Pig' followed me as I sprinted home, always frightened. After a while I wasn't just shouted at; when they started spitting at me I was obliged to run across the road, and sometimes stones were fired after me as I ran. I was hated by these children and I'm not sure that I understood why. I was a nice person who only wanted to make friends. My parents and grandparents were always kind and helpful to everyone they met.

I suppose I did recognise that it had to do with my being a Jew. I remember feeling angry about being Jewish. Why couldn't I have been something else? It wasn't fair. My being Jewish was the reason I had to leave my parents and my home, and now it was causing these angry children to hate me, to spit at me and call me horrible names.

Perhaps the most depressing fact of all throughout this particular upsetting time was that the grown-ups in my life merely accepted my fate – *our* fate. Miki was experiencing the exact same thing. Aunt Renka could only trot out useless advice: 'Just do your best to avoid them. Try not to draw their attention.' It was the same at school. The teachers constantly looked stressed and worried, answering our complaints about the daily abuse with more useless advice: 'Avoid any kind of confrontation.' What we mightn't have appreciated was that they completely understood our fears since they were going through the same treatment themselves. Anyone wearing the yellow star was subject to harassment on the street, informal or otherwise. Teachers were frequently absent or delayed due to the fact they had been stopped for their papers by the police. Arrests were common if a Jew was perceived to be trying to hide their star by covering it up in some way.

Still, I feel they could have provided an explanation for the hatred. They could have talked to us about anti-Semitism and warned us about what was going on outside the school walls. But they didn't. Instead they told us absolutely nothing. Probably they didn't want to frighten us. We were only kids, after all.

So I spent the next couple of months trying to dodge the bullies and looking forward with all my might to Christmas. Our mother duly arrived in late December to take Miki and me back to Merašice for the holidays. I was overjoyed to see her and, once I had my fill of being hugged and doted upon, I was utterly impatient for the train to race me home, back to my father and the farm. Mr Duraj collected us from Kapince and drove us home in the horse and carriage, where our father was waiting for us. He hugged us both in delight and asked us plenty of questions about school. Then Miki and I ran next door to our grandparents, who were waiting impatiently to see us. We were ready to be spoilt and, sure enough, *Omama* had made us our favourite little cakes to celebrate our homecoming.

To my delight, the usual snow had fallen, the layer of pure white making the village look like a perfect Christmas card. I had been dreaming about this sight for weeks. Mother assured us that she'd take us tobogganing at our favourite spot, up the hill beside the church. True to her word, she took us almost every day of the holidays, and we worked up sharp appetites in the cold air as we climbed the hill as fast as we could so that we could slide down it again and again, screaming with fear and excitement. My brother and I were home for Christmas and all was as it should be. As usual, Miki and I also polished our shoes and put them on the windowsill so that Santa would fill them with goodies while we slept. How I had longed to escape the tension of Nitra, to take a break from the daily insults and threats, to forget the worry in my aunt's face and the weariness of my teachers.

Yet, as much as my mother acted like everything was perfectly okay, I knew it wasn't. The tension had accompanied us all the way back to our house. For one thing, the holiday was a lot quieter than usual, with absolutely no visits from uncles, aunts or cousins, which was very peculiar. Of course, this was as a result of the new travel restrictions, another feature of the Codex: Jewish people now needed a special permit to travel 50km or more, and naturally these permits were obtained only with great difficulty. My father's easygoing, sociable manner came in handy as he had to bribe an official to extend his travel permit, which was only ever valid for between one and three months. Our freedom to travel depended on his maintaining a good relationship with the offices of the interior ministry. I am sure there were a good many clerks who made a lot of extra money in this way.

Another change was the sight of our local Hlinka guards striding around the village in their black uniforms and matching boots. Named after the Catholic priest and nationalist leader, Andrej Hlinka, these were the military wing of the Slovak People's Party. Unfortunately, Hlinka died in 1938 – he had always denounced anti-Semitism and instead called on the Jews to support Slovak nationalism. After his death, party members who hadn't shared their leader's all-encompassing views were free to implement their own brand of nationalism, one that didn't involve those who sported the yellow star on their winter coats. By

1941 the guards – who were, for the most part, made up of unskilled labourers, the poorly educated and the peasants – were being trained in the SS camps in Germany.

Miki had seen these guards in action. It was he who told me what was really going on, from his visits to my mother's sister, Aunt Margo, in Bratislava. Her house was about three hundred yards from the National Theatre and it was here that he watched the guards and party members assemble with their swastika armbands. The crowds would gather to listen to the President – and Catholic priest – Fr Jozef Tiso, rail against the lazy, greedy Jews who were a parasite on the country's economy.

I don't remember my parents making any remarks about Merašice's Hlinka guards. They were men who had grown up with my father, men that my grandparents had known since they were dimpled babies. Even before the real trouble began they were never a very popular group, thanks to their love of alcohol and their explicit need, after several *slivovitzes*, to sing nationalist songs at the tops of their voices. Sunday was their special day, when they put on their black shirts, black caps, trousers and shiny boots to parade about the streets before heading to church for the morning service. Afterwards they retired to the pub, as they had always done, to get a little drunk and loudly hold forth on mundane matters, ranging from the weather to their respective jobs, just as they had always done. Only now there was a new subject to be discussed, at great length and volume. Mariška would arrive at our house to do the chores and have a coffee with my mother, rolling her eyes as she announced: 'That Hlinka crowd are at it again, talking about getting rid of all the Jews. Silly fools!'

Chapter 3
• • • • • •

Uncle Desider Reichental,
the Surgeon

The first of my relatives to be arrested was my gentle and kind-hearted Uncle Desider. Born in 1910, he was the second youngest of the Reichentals, and eight years younger than my father. While his older brother loved to socialise and collected all sorts of friends wherever he went, Desider was much more refined and collected coins. During his college years he joined the scouts, attaining one of the highest ranks within the international Baden-Powell scout movement.

When the anti-Jewish laws were voted into existence he was working at Vsetin hospital, in Moravia. Unlike other

Jewish doctors, who automatically found themselves out of a job as a result of the German invasion, Desider was kept on because he was a surgeon. He was not a man who looked for trouble and his job meant everything to him.

In 1938 Hitler made his first move towards realising his dream of unifying all Germans everywhere under his rule. This was the year that Austria was annexed by Germany and also the year of the Czech Crisis. On 1 October the Czech frontier guards were instructed to leave their posts in order to allow German troops to move in and take over the mainly German-populated Sudetenland – the beginning of the end for the majority of Slovakian Jews. In another six months the Germans would reach Vsetin. Desider's friends urged him to escape, but he wouldn't entertain the idea.

'Why should I leave? I'm a doctor; my job is to help people. I've never harmed a single person in my life so why should anyone want to harm me?'

As it turned out, he was finally sacked by the hospital in May 1939, but, typical of him, he chose to stay on and work unpaid. He was supported by his generous sister, Ibojka, who was married to a Vsetin businessman, Max, with whom she had one daughter, Gita.

The story goes that on 15 March 1939 he was approached by a Doctor Zizlowsky to raise money for a good cause. The doctor, along with a group of Moravian officers and intel-lectuals, were members of a new underground movement,

Obrana Naroda (Defence of the Nation), which was being set up to fight the incoming Germans. Desider was asked to raise funds from the local wealthy Jewish families: 'You Jews owe it to the Czech people!'

I'll never know if he understood the risk he was taking, but, whether he did or didn't, he agreed to help out and began calling on Jewish families in Vsetin to donate money for the cause. It wasn't long before he had amassed a sizeable fortune of 11,000 crown. (At this time a surgeon's monthly wage was approximately 1,300 crown.) Still a fledging organisation, there were just thirteen members, including Desider, when at least eight of them were arrested in January 1940. As it happens, just one was initially arrested, interrogated and tortured until he provided eight other names, including my uncle's. Desider signed a confession accepting total responsibility for the 11,000 crown and the fact that he knew the money was for an illegal organisation. As the only Jew in the group, he had one request for the police: 'Whatever you do, please don't involve my religion. Just treat me the same as everyone else.' Maybe the police and his lawyer believed what they told him: 'There's no need to worry about that. You'll be fine.'

In recent years I was able to find out more about Uncle Desider's arrest. The biggest discovery was three written statements following that first confession; I'm inclined to believe they were written out for him to sign. On 30 May

1940 he wrote that he was asked to collect money for a 'good Czech purpose'. When he inquired of Dr Zizlovsky what the money was for, he was told it was 'for medicine and bandages'. Then a year later, on 6 March, he explained why he got involved in the first place:

I know Doctor Zizlovsky very well because he was my superior and a prominent person in Vsetin hospital. When I was let go, because I was Jewish, in 1939, it was Dr Zizlovsky who let me continue to work on. For this I owed him much gratitude. When he approached me in 1939, with the request to collect monies from the Jews of Vsetin, I could not refuse due to the above reason.

He added that he couldn't afford to contribute money himself and he denied belonging to an illegal organisation.

After being interrogated in Vsetin, he was transferred to a prison in Breslau, Poland, where he spent the next twelve months. Then, in August 1941, he was sent on to a prison in Wolfenbuttel, in North Germany. He wrote several brief letters to the family from here, describing his new career as a maker of paper bags. It seems that all the prisoners were put to work according to their capabilities, and Desider found himself at a disadvantage since he was neither a mechanic nor a carpenter. Censored, these letters were only positive in tone. It seems that he believed he would be free soon.

I Was a Boy in Belsen

My dears, (Wolfenbuttel, 13 December 1941)

What a pleasant surprise. They are distributing writing paper to us much earlier than usual so we can send Christmas greetings to our loved ones. Isn't it thoughtful of them? I'd like to use this opportunity to write a few lines about myself and wish you all a merry Christmas and happy New Year. I have but one wish, that next year should be the last one that we spend apart. ... I am looking forward to Christmas, even more than usual. It's a holy day that spreads its magic everywhere, not only in family circles around the tree or on the skis but, trust me, also between these four walls.

As it turned out, his stay here was temporary, but not because he was being released. Instead, he was sent back to Poland, where, on 24 October 1942, he was informed of his having received the death sentence for the crime of treason. It seems that the harshness of this sentence had *everything* to do with his religion, after all. For one thing, his case was put before the People's Court in Berlin while he languished in jail oblivious to the event, and, for another, the doctor who had asked him to do the fundraising, Zizlovsky, ended up facing just twelve years in jail.

Uncle Desider wrote to the family:

Nothing is hurting me except for one thing, that my sentence will cause you all pain. Do not think about me. Forget me. Thousands and thousands of people are dying everywhere in all kinds of battles.

Human life is very cheap today. Pretend that I fell down in a field somewhere, or that I took my own life. ... I believe that life is eternal and death ... is only a phase. Sooner or later we will all meet up again in another world.

Meanwhile, the family were devastated and utterly powerless to help him, not that they hadn't tried. My Uncle Robert wrote to Mr Geraldini, an old college mate of Desider's, asking for his intervention. Mr Geraldini held a high-ranking position in the Hlinka Guard, but, as it turned out, was rather more committed to his job than to any ties with his past. Instead of offering to help, he merely forwarded Robert's letter to the police headquarters in Bratislava, along with the bald remark: 'I don't help Jews.'

At this point, Desider's only option was to appeal and he wrote several letters asking for clemency, for his death sentence to be commuted to life imprisonment. His last letter, dated 27 January 1943, reminds the authorities, once more, about his vocation and profession as a skilled surgeon and all the good he could do for people. But his words meant nothing and it would seem that he knew there was no hope. This letter also thanked his colleagues at Vsetin hospital for all their help and support:

I am reminiscing about all who were close and dear. Firstly is Consultant Holz, whom I loved like a father ... he, as my teacher, introduced me to our noble medical science. I bid farewell to every-body and everything but to my most beloved profession … I cannot say goodbye … In hopeless times during my solitude it was my faithful companion, again and again I went to my medical books … there I found distraction, calm and forgetfulness …   Three let-ters and one exclamation mark, 'JEW!' persecuted me all my life, everywhere. Consultant Holtz and everybody in Vsetin hospital always dealt with me as an equal… I will remember this till my last moment …

Two months later he was dead. My thirty-two-year-old uncle, who had yet to fall in love, who only wanted to help the sick, who never raised his voice in anger, who thought the world of my father – his big, fearless brother – was guillotined on 29 April 1943. Some years later he was posthumously awarded the Czechoslovakia War Cross of 1939 by President Svoboda, on 23 May 1946.

Chapter 4
• • • • • •

Everything Changes

With Christmas celebrated and the New Year of 1942 welcomed with open arms and best wishes made for a peaceful and prosperous year, Miki and I were rather reluctantly back on the Radošina train. We found it harder to say goodbye this time. Neither of us wanted to return to our sort of 'half-life' in Nitra.

I don't remember much about the following weeks. I assume I went back to learning the alphabet while Jews across Germany, Poland and Hungary were dying in their thousands. Perhaps I do remember hearing whispers about the harassment on the streets that grew more frequent and more terrifying. Jewish men from the nearby Jewish seminary, in Yeshiva, had their beards shorn off by Hlinka guards who were determined to have their fun. I'm sure I only left Aunt Renka's house to go to school because I would have been too afraid to play outside.

Suddenly it was all over. Midway through February I turned up for school one morning to find it closed. And that was that. My mother was summoned to fetch Miki and me back home, much to our delight. As usual, Mr Duraj met the three of us in Kapince station with the horse, carriage and plenty of blankets for the twenty-minute ride in the freezing temperature. Our father looked hugely relieved to have us all together again.

If I thought this was the end of my schooling, I was very much mistaken. Education was the most important thing to my parents and since we weren't allowed into the local school, my father was obliged to search around for a tutor. He found a man in a neighbouring farm, about three kilometres from our house, who had trained and worked as a teacher before giving it all up to farm his land. He wasn't Jewish, and was, therefore, risking everything to tutor the two of us in his sitting room. It was quite a hike of forty-five minutes each way for Miki and me, but we enjoyed it when the weather was good. We had to walk through the village, pass by the cemetery and then turn left onto a dirt road that was suitable only for a horse and cart. As you might imagine, this dirt road turned into a blanket of mud whenever it rained. There was a long driveway to the farmhouse which was almost covered by the tall trees that grew at either side of the road, their branches forming a natural arch, making me feel I was entering a magical tunnel. Beyond the trees were the fields, pregnant with sugar beet, corn, potatoes and wheat, while the air was sweet with the smell of the wild flowers that were just about everywhere.

My brother and I grew very close on these walks. I suppose we had to forge a new kind of friendship since our old football mates would have nothing to do with us now. Well, actually, that's not strictly true – it was we who withdrew from them and in doing so we were following our parents' example, as they didn't want to cause any embarrassment to our neighbours, especially the more vulnerable ones. As far as the Hlinka were concerned, socialising with Jews was a risky past-time if one didn't want to be branded a collaborator. Then one day, 25 March 1942, a month after Miki and I arrived back in Merašice, the deportations began.

The President, Fr Tiso, along with Prime Minister Vojtech Tuka and Alexander Mach, the Minister for the Interior, had met with Hitler for a two-day meeting on 23-24 October 1941. The second day of the meeting centred on ridding Slovakia of the Jews, the beginning of a drive to find a permanent solution.

Since 1939 Slovakia had been recruiting volunteer workers from its own population for Germany to help with the war effort, and initially this proved very attractive to young people with up to a hundred thousand volunteering their services, but then, over the next couple of years, the figures started to dwindle. At the start of 1942 when the Slovaks were asked for twenty thousand extra volunteers the government was obliged to confess that they couldn't provide that amount. It wasn't a situation which suited either country – the Slovaks wanted to remain on the best of terms with their stronger ally. That's when the extreme anti-Semites came up with the perfect alternative: they could send the country's thousands of young Jews. It was a dream come true for the extremists, including a Fr Anton Shalat, who, in 1937, had preached from his pulpit: 'There will come a day when we will wake up and look outside with pleasure because the Jews will have disappeared.'

As soon as the German authorities heard the proposal they summoned their representative in Slovakia, Dieter Wisliceny, to meet with Adolf Eichmann who, tremendously excited at the prospect of 20,000 able-bodied Jews who would work for free, instructed the ambassador to maintain close contact with the Slovaks.

Wisliceny returned to his post and held further negotiations with Tuka and Mach that led to an agreement to send Jews instead of other Slovaks. The only problem was that if the agreement involved only young Jews, the number would fall short of the 20,000 required. Even if the age for recruitment was lowered to sixteen years, that would still only amount to 17,000. Sensing the potential of the situation, Tuka and Mach leant on Wisliceny to consider taking *all* the Jews. However, when the German ambassador consulted Eichmann about this he was told that there wasn't the capacity to absorb a population of that size and so, for the time being, the idea of deporting the entire Jewish community out of Slovakia was shelved.

But on 16 February 1942 the German embassy in Slovakia received a telegram confirming that Germany was ready to receive 20,000 Jews immediately.

They started with the Jews that weren't at all useful to the Slovak economy: the young single Jewish girls and boys from sixteen years upwards, college students, and the newly unemployed, including small shopkeepers and former civil servants. It was at this point that a lot of my cousins in Nitra were summoned by registered letter from the Ministry of the Interior, informing them that they must report on a certain date at a collection point. They were to bring only minimal clothing. The letter described their situation as being called to 'work for the benefit for the nation', which made it sound like a privilege.

It wasn't perceived as unduly bad news because my cousins

believed – all of them having been thrown out of college and their various jobs – that they would at least be given employment once more. Therefore, they didn't consider themselves so much deported as recruited for work. Accordingly, they packed up their suitcases quite cheerfully, glad for an end to their jobless existence.

I remember Martuska, Aunt Renka's daughter. She was a lovely bubbly girl of seventeen years who was always smiling. She visited Merašice many times during the holidays and was one of my favourites from my father's side of the family. I watched her pack her small suitcase and remember her speaking brightly of finding a good job.

The next day we all went with the young people to see them off. Five of my cousins from my father's side, the children of his sisters and brothers, chattered together as they waited for their transport: Gita, Oto, Ferko, Dita and Martuska. Morale was high, such was their desperation to find work and make some money again. They were initially being put up in a work camp in Slovakia. Later on we heard that they had all been sent on to Poland. We never saw any of them again.

Around the end of February 1942, the German representative Wisliceny was summoned once more to Berlin, and he was accompanied on the visit by a Slovakian officials from the Central Office of Economy. There, the delegation was informed by Adolf Eichmann that Heinrich Himmler had agreed to take the entire Jewish population of Slovakia on two conditions: each deportee was to be stripped of their Slovak citizenship before deportation and the Slovak government was to pay Germany 500 marks for every deportee accepted by Germany.

The first condition was an important one as it meant the Slovak government renounced any legal right or responsibility to their Jewish citizens once they crossed over the border.

The second condition, the 'settlement fee', was officially described as a payment towards the upkeep of the deportee until they could support themselves. This, of course, was a blatant lie, as we now know that most of these deportees ended up in the gas chambers soon after their arrival. It was an extraordinary situation. Slovakia wasn't even occupied at the time yet it was prepared to *pay* the Germans to take its Jewish citizens – in fact, Slovakia was the only country in Europe that paid the Germans to take the Jews away. From this point onwards any reference to deportation referred to *all* Jews: male, female, young and old.

My father hurriedly applied for exemption from deportation on the basis that he was a farmer and therefore a useful contributor to the state. His brother, my Uncle Oskar, also applied for exemption because he was a successful architect who was always busy with big government projects. They both succeeded in getting the exemptions, although, as with travel permits, these formal exemptions were only ever valid for a month or two. My father was obliged to make regular visits to the Ministry of the Interior to renew his permit, paying dearly in bribes to keep us all safe. Still, we felt secure, at least for the next couple of months.

Of course, it didn't last. The knock on my grandparents' door came at around 8.00pm on 15 August 1942. It was the height of summer, and was still bright outside. Birds were probably still singing and the bees still buzzing from flower to flower in the evening sun. My parents rushed outside to find my grandfather standing dazed in front of a policeman and a local Hlinka guard, a tall, muscular man, dressed from head to toe in an intimidating black uniform. The guard, well-known to our family, pulled out the order from his chest pocket and began to read aloud as if he was on stage and we were a nameless, faceless audience.

'By orders of the Ministry of Interior, Jew Jecheskel Reichental and wife Katarina, are to go immediately with this defence officer. You are permitted to bring only what is absolutely essential.'

Ludovit Nedelka's voice was harsh and his face set like granite as he looked at my grandparents, his neighbours, without the merest hint of recognition. For years he had stood opposite *Opapa* in the now closed shop, sent on errands by his mother, and then, later on, performing his own errands as a young man, then husband and father.

'Be quick. We are waiting,' he instructed.

There was a stunned silence that my father, looking tense and pale, was the first to break. He addressed his old friend by his first name. 'Ludo, my family and I are exempt from expulsion. As farmers we are essential to the economy. They got the permit.'

'Show it to me.'

My father held out his hands. 'I don't have it on me, but you can check with the office of the Interior Ministry in Bratislava. They're sending it out to us. We're expecting it any day now.'

Nedelka was like a machine. He looked neither right nor left. This was his own show, a rare opportunity to show off in front of the police officer, and he was determined to see, or direct, it right through to the end. 'Those are my orders. Unless you can produce the permit your parents must come with me. When the permit arrives you can ask for their release.'

My father couldn't believe what he was hearing. 'Ludo, please! Don't do this. I tell you the permit is on its way. They're exempt.'

The guard merely shrugged. It wasn't his problem.

'For God's sake, man. We grew up together. We've been

neighbours for – how long – thirty-odd years?' Father continued pleading, refusing to give up.

Tears were running down my mother's face. Finally, it was *Omama*, my gentle, hard-working grandmother, who recognised it was no use. She removed her apron, something she only did at the very end of her working day. Turning away from the men in uniform she addressed her husband. 'We have to go. We should gather our things.'

My mother followed her inside while my father stood his ground, not quite understanding what was happening, not willing to accept it just yet.

Omama took some underwear and a coat from her wardrobe and then went to the tiny kitchen to pack some food. She stood for a minute, gazing upon her things: the pots and pans she had used every day for the past fifty years or so; the table where she had fed all her children, the one we gathered around every Friday night.

Meanwhile, my seventy-five-year-old grandfather was saying his own goodbyes, to his books and his armchair. His spirit had already been broken with the loss of his shop. Back outside, his hands shook as he put on his coat.

'Don't worry, Papa. I'll come for you when we get the permit.' My father was in command of his emotions again. He embraced his mother, who was crying silently. 'It will be fine, Mama. You'll both be back home in a couple of days, I promise.'

My mother hugged her parents-in-law, nodding fiercely as my father told them over and over that it would all be fine, he'd fetch them home as soon as he could.

The two old people didn't believe him for a minute. They walked side by side to the waiting truck, their heads bowed and shoulders sagging, the two men behind them, dwarfing them with their erect posture and confident stride.

And that was the last we saw of them.

The permit arrived two days later. It was dated 31 July 1942, two weeks before my grandparents' arrest. My father sent a request to the Ministry of the Interior, asking that his parents be released and sent home. Nothing happened. In December he received a letter from the headquarters of the Jewish camp in Zilina, where *Opapa* and *Omama* were being held, informing him that: 'Jews Jecheskel and Katarina Reichental were deported on 18 September 1942'. We found out later that they had been taken to Auschwitz.

It was obvious to us that the Hlinka guard, our neighbour, was aware of the permit, but had deliberately delayed its delivery in order to get rid of the old Jews.

My father never forgave himself for not being able to save his parents. But, really, what could he have done?

Chapter 5

• • • • • •

Hunted –
Operation 'Chytačka'

Everything changed after my grandparents were taken away, or so it seemed to me. Their house sat empty and quiet, while I waited impatiently for their return. From time to time I asked Father when they would be coming back; I missed *Omama*'s sweet cakes and her stories. As the weeks passed into months I stopped asking, unwilling to see the pain in my father's eyes. He continued to farm, while Mariška continued to clean the house, and Mother continued to cook our favourite food for our Friday meal, but it wasn't the same as before.

Now we were subject to Operation '*Chytačka*', the hunt

for Jews, when the Hlinka guards would go from village to village, searching for Jews to arrest. Thanks to friendly neighbours, we always received warnings in the nick of time, allowing Mother to grab provisions and lock up the house, and then the four of us would race into hiding. The Hlinka made the mistake of treating the peasants like dirt, which was ironic since they were usually peasants themselves but obviously wanted it known that they, with their fancy uniforms, had moved on to better things and could afford openly to despise their former peers. When they arrived in their lorry-loads to search a village or town for Jews, a surprising amount of people would curl their lips in disgust and band together to thwart them by helping the Jews in their area.

It was usually Mariška who told us when the Hlinka were on the warpath, though Father also had his own informer – but I never knew who it was. Father fashioned several hiding places for us, stocking them with blankets and a bucket for a toilet, while Mother always had food and water standing by in case we had to make a sudden run for it. Perhaps our favourite hiding place was in the barn. We'd climb the ladder to the hayloft where we dried the corn to feed the geese, and after pulling up the ladder, Father would clear a space behind the piles of corn and there we'd sit in complete silence for as long as it took. Not even the farm-hands would know we were up there. Usually we'd come down once it got dark.

If there was time, we'd hide in the corn fields where we'd

be completely hidden by the tall stems. When there was no time at all, we'd hide in the massive haystack that always stood in the back yard, where Father had already dug out a hole for us so as not to delay our escape. This was one of our earliest hiding places.

It was sometime in 1943 when Mariška came running through our door, not stopping until she found my mother. '*Mlada Pani,* hurry, hurry! You have to hide; I've just heard that the Hlinka will be here in thirty minutes, maybe less.'

Mother handed Miki the emergency food bag containing buttered bread, boiled eggs, jam, white cheese and a thermos filled with lemon tea. She also grabbed some sliced meat and boiled potato. Next we ran, one by one, to the haystack, taking care that there was nobody around to see us crawl into it. We lay on our blankets for hours, not daring to talk or check to see if the guards had come or gone. The haystack was a good bit from the house so we couldn't hear a thing. Later on, Mariška brought more food and warned us to stay hidden as the search for us continued. We ended up spending the night inside the haystack, with Mariška arriving early the next morning to tell us it was safe to leave again.

For nightly raids my father's dependable employee, Mr Duraj, would risk his life by putting us up in his shack. This usually meant a night of being bitten by the fleas that didn't seem to bother the farm-hand in the slightest.

It was a tense time, though maybe thanks to my age – seven

– and my family I escaped the brunt of the stress. Hiding from arrest became as normal to me as playing football with Miki or following Father around as he worked. My parents remained good-humoured and calm throughout, determined, I'm sure, to shelter us from their fears and grief. Miki, however, wasn't as lucky. Those four years between us represented a lot more than that when it came to knowing and understanding just how vulnerable the four of us were. It wasn't simply that the Hlinka mob could very literally shatter our existence, it was much worse than that. Anyone could take pot shots at us now.

One late evening, in January 1943, there was a sharp knock on the door. We were all in bed asleep and we all bolted awake instantly. Unexpected visits, day or night, were potentially fatal. My father opened the door to find Ludovit Nedelka in his full Hlinka uniform, accompanied by a police officer. It was a dreadful reminder of the day that *Omama* and *Opapa* had been led away, the only difference perhaps was that Ludo was now Captain Nedelka and more pompous than ever. He brushed passed Father and came face to face with the rest of us in the tiny sitting room. Drawing himself to his full height he pulled a sheet of paper from his jacket pocket, just as he had the previous time, and proceeded to read in an unnecessarily loud voice: 'You have thirty minutes to pack one small suitcase each, with only essential clothing and food. Then you must hand over the keys of this residence and come with us.'

I looked to my father to see what he was going to say, and he did open his mouth – but before he could utter a word there was an explosion from Miki, who stunned us all with his rage. He and I had been sitting side by side on the couch when he suddenly jumped to his feet and unleashed the stark reality of our situation on our neighbour-turned-tormentor: 'How dare you! We are hounded and persecuted and living in constant fear for our lives. It isn't right, we are good people. You are sending us to be killed while your own children sleep in peace every night. How can you do this to us?'

Shocked silence greeted this uncharacteristic outburst. I had never seen a child give out to a grown-up before and certainly, in our house, we were always told to be polite to guests. My mother and father exchanged a bewildered look and before either of the men could react, Father dived in to take charge of the situation. He quickly pulled Nedelka and the officer into the kitchen, allowing Mother to gently push Miki back onto the couch. My brother was trembling and breathing fast, refusing to look at either of us. A couple of minutes later, Nedelka walked out, telling my mother in a much quieter voice: 'We'll be back in an hour. Please be ready.' In his pocket was the money that my father had just given him, to make him and his cohort leave.

As soon as they left we got dressed in warm clothing, packed up food and water, and locked the house behind us. We hid out in the hay loft until the following evening.

Afterwards Father asked his Hlinka informer why he hadn't warned us about the raid and discovered that Nedelka's visit had been made on his own initiative, involving no orders from his bosses. In other words, he had only wanted to frighten us and thereby make some money – simply because he could.

Nedelka had also, unintentionally, no doubt, helped us by making a valid point. We could no longer expect to be left alone or rely on friends to warn us against future knocks on the door. Unpleasant facts had to be faced. Father's exemption papers no longer provided any comfort; time was, quite likely, running out for us. By this point most of my father's extended family had been deported (see Appendix 1) and now my mother's relatives were being picked up for unknown destinations. I think a turning point for Father was that sad day in May when he learnt that his beloved brother, Desider, had been executed the previous month. He and my mother began to makes plans.

(Many years later my brother and I got our hands on Ludovit Nedelka's letters to his superiors. One of them is dated 15 May 1943: '*It's a shame on us and the state that we still haven't expelled the Jews from our village,*' he stated.)

My own personal highlight of 1943 was when my Aunt Margo arrived with my cousin Chava, who was just a year younger than me. By this stage Bratislava was being sub-jected to bombing by British and American planes – albeit infrequent – on their way to Poland and Germany. Clusters of these *Lancaster* or B24 *Liberator* planes, with their noisy four engines, had become a constant sight in the skies over Slova-kia, and even Merašice. You could hear them long before you saw them, thus giving Miki and me plenty of time to run outside and try to count them as they swarmed overhead like giant, shiny bees. Chava was terrified by them, whether they dropped bombs or not, so Margo sent her to us for a few months. It was good timing as our tutor had recently asked Miki and me to stop coming over; somebody must have threatened to report him.

Most evenings we gathered around the radio, a wholly illegal past-time for Jews. My parents were determined to keep up with the goings on of the world; Father had always been interested in politics and current affairs. Other nights we enjoyed a play or an opera, wishing only that we could turn the music up to its full glory, but that was much too risky. I remember well the sound of: 'Dum-de-dum, dum-de-dum: London calling, this is the Slovak BBC broadcast.' We could never relax, however, and would immediately turn off the radio whenever we heard our dogs bark. The downside of listening to local and national news was that we'd hear anti-Semitic propaganda in action. The national-ists were blaming the Jews for anything and everything that was wrong in the country. Extremists called for all exemption papers to be cancelled: why not intern all Jews in work camps, irrespective of their financial contribution, just get rid of them all forever? I listened in amazement to hear us – my parents, grandparents, Miki, me, my cousins, aunts and uncles – reviled as communists, saboteurs and common thieves.

Meanwhile, my parents continued to play cards once or twice a week with Fr Harangozo, the local parish priest. It was a welcome break from bad news and the gnawing anxiety about the future. In the safety of his house the three of them spoke his native Hungarian, now punishable by law in Slovakia. A couple of times he had told my mother that he would be willing to convert them to Christianity, but she didn't take him up on his offer. As it turned out, it wouldn't have made the slightest bit of difference anyway. The other two Jewish families in Merašice had converted, but they too ended up going into hiding after their names appeared on the deportation list. In fact, from 1944 to 1945, they were successfully hidden by the Bircaks, a peasant family who lived in a typically small house – where exactly they hid the Gregushes and the Lowys, I don't know. We were already gone by then and I only heard about this recently from a man who used to work for my father. Apparently it was one of those things that everybody knew (though presumably not Captain Nedelka and his family) but nobody spoke about.

Nevertheless, we did need Fr Harangozo's help.

❋ ❋ ❋

In 1942 most Slovaks, including politicians, believed that the country's Jews were being deported to labour camps in Poland, to be put to work on building roads and railway lines. This was the first wave of deportations, the one that took my father's parents, along with many of his extended family. But then, as early as the autumn of 1942, rumours started to waft around Eastern Europe. Dionys Lenard escaped from Majdanek Concentration Camp, in Poland, reaching Slovakia in July to tell about Jews starving to death in their hundreds. There was no mention of mass murder in Auschwitz just yet, but that would come via the Jewish underground in Poland.

The Jewish leadership in Slovakia embarked on a campaign of bribing government officials to stop the deportations; they even managed to bribe Dieter Wisliceny. Meanwhile, some politicians began to make a fuss. A particular worry was the treatment of those Jews who had converted to Catholicism. The German government had promised that these people would be treated in a suitable Christian manner, but now the whispers suggested otherwise. Pressure was applied by the Vatican via the Chargé d'Affaires, Monsignor Giuseppe Bursio, who asked President Tiso to stop the deportations. At the same time Prime Minister Vojtech Tuka requested permission to send a Slovak commission to Poland to interview captive Slovak Jews there. Wisliceny passed this request back to the German embassy where it was rejected by Adolf Eichmann. Not that Germany didn't try to reassure Slovakia – Fritz Fiala, a pro-Nazi Slovak journalist, was sent to Auschwitz to speak to Slovak Jews to prove that everything was as it should be. He dutifully produced an article which referred to the concentration camp as being a 'rest home' and one in which all the Jews he spoke to, he claimed, were having a fine old time of it. Fortunately, this wasn't good enough for the anti-deportation faction of the Slovakian government and deportations ceased in October 1942.

The extremists were appalled and needed soothing from the government that this was merely a temporary cessation. Sure enough, when the Nazis occupied Slovakia after being asked to help deal with the 1944 uprising, the second wave of deportations began almost immediately. This was when my parents decided it was time to leave Merašice.

Mother and Father decided it was time to make a break for it – that my mother, Miki and I would go into hiding with my mother's mother, *Omama* Rosalia. Her husband, my grandfather Moritz, had died in 1938. She had recently returned from Hungary where she had fled in 1942 to escape the worsening situation in Slovakia. She lived there with her daughter, Adela, son-in-law, Bela Fried, and two granddaughters, Katarina (Kati) and Agnes (Agi), for the next two years, until the Hungarian Jews found themselves being picked off by the new fascist government and their Nazi guests. *Omama* Rosalia elected to be smuggled back over the border in March 1944. It was a wise move. Adela and her family were arrested on 16 June and sent to Auschwitz where they all died. (In fact, we found out quite recently, that Kati could have survived – she had the chance when, on arrival at the extermination camp, she was picked out to be a worker with a friend of hers during the 'selection'. But the sight of her mother and younger sister being led away from the work group proved too much and, ignoring her friend's pleas, Kati ran after them, joining them for the last part of their journey to the gas chamber.)

For the time being, my father would stay behind and look after the farm and the livestock. It had neither been liquidated nor taken away from him, so he was understandably loathe to leave it until it was absolutely necessary. Fr Harangozo's role in our escape was two-fold: he would find us new identities and he would teach Miki and me as much as we needed to know to be able to pass as Roman Catholics. The name Reichental would give us away as Jews so that's why we needed false documents. Fr Harangozo would provide us with identities belonging to long-dead Slovaks. Because my brother and I were fair-skinned and blond, with blue eyes, my parents were confident that we wouldn't attract any suspicion on sight; Jews were typically – or, at least, perceived to be – sallow, with dark hair and large noses, and we looked nothing like this. The priest was a brave man, risking his job and probably his life to help us. When my mother checked with him that he really wanted to be involved with such a dangerous situation, he merely responded 'As a man of God, it is my Christian duty to help you and your family.'

A few days after this conversation, Mother was asked to visit the parochial house. We waited anxiously for her return. She came home with a relieved smile on her face and our new identity in her hands: 'From now on, boys, we are the Vyda family.' Then, in a rather stern voice, she told me: 'Just remember, you are now called Tomas Vyda. When anybody asks you your name you are Vyda, not Reichental. Never *ever* forget this!' This was a huge boost to our confidence as it meant we could travel wherever and whenever we wanted, just like normal citizens of Slovakia. We didn't have to worry about travel permits or anything like that.

Some small village was chosen as our hide-out, where we were going to rent a small house and Miki and I would be enrolled in the local school. Therefore, we'd have more dealings with the population and so a thorough grounding of Catholicism was required. Mother and *Omama* Rosalia need only go outside for shopping. We began our religious training in July and over the next couple of months visited Fr Harangozo for a couple of hours every day, unless he was busy. I wondered what my orthodox *Opapa* would have said had he seen his grandsons bless themselves, or merrily recite the Lord's Prayer or the Rosary or responses to Sunday mass, and talk about the blessed angels and saints as if they were our dearest friends!

Just like every other Jew who had yet to make a run for it, our 'D-Day' was the aftermath of the uprising in Banská Bystrica, when the German army entered Slovakia to help stamp out the insurrectionists. At that point the Slovak Jewry, or what was left of it, was doomed. The extremists got what they wanted: all exemptions were cancelled, and, that September, Jews were rounded up for deportations once more. Many went into hiding, sheltered by gentiles looking for money or, the more fortunate, by gentiles who only wanted to help.

It was time for us to leave our village, as the Hlinka would be much more efficient now that they were being accompanied by the Gestapo on their Jews hunts. Of course, by now, we all knew what was happening, that mass murder was taking place in the gas chambers of Auschwitz. For the first time I saw lines of worry and fear on the faces of my parents. Father was confident that he would evade capture because he had so many friends in the area, but neither he nor my mother was especially confident that we'd ever be under the same roof again together. Once again my age shielded me from the worst of it, although it was still horrible to me that we'd be leaving my father behind.

And so it was, one morning in the middle of September that my mother began to pack our cases. The atmosphere in the house was one of desperate sadness and resignation. I had never seen my parents cry, but now they sobbed freely as we clung to one another in those last moments on that day. Mariška, the only neighbour who knew we were leaving, arrived to say goodbye to us, also in tears.

As always, the ever-faithful Mr Duraj was taking us to the station. Father instructed him to have plenty of blankets in the carriage for the two-and-a-half-hour ride to Leopoldov, from where we were catching the train to Bratislava. We wrapped ourselves up, Miki and me on either side of our mother, and then Father stood down to watch and wave us off. I could hardly see him through my tears. Mr Duraj prodded the horses and away we went, my father growing smaller and smaller until he finally disappeared from sight.

There wasn't much traffic on the road and we mostly had it to ourselves; the only sound was the clip-clopping of the horses and their sudden, violent snorts. There were plenty of opportunities to think about what we were leaving behind, particularly when we passed the deserted synagogue and the houses of Jewish friends that we had lost contact with. I remembered visiting them in happier times. After a while, as the sun began to descend, our route took us through a forest, the massive green trees on either side of the narrow road reminding me of the tunnel of greenery that I used to walk through to reach our tutor's farmhouse. The scenery was so beautiful that I felt blessed in spite of everything.

We reached the top of the hill which was also the end of the forest. Below us, in the distance, we could make out the lights of the town of Hlohovec, and beyond that was Leopoldov. The horses started to descend, keeping to a brisk trot. We had just reached the entrance to the town when, all of a sudden, we heard shouts from the darkness: 'Stop! Stop!' Mr Duraj reined in the horses, bringing the carriage to a standstill. The railway track ran through the town and was guarded by the army. Two soldiers appeared at either side of Mr Duraj, guns at the ready: 'We need to see your ID.' Mr Duraj behaved as if he was exasperated in an attempt to hide his fear: 'But we're in a hurry to catch the Bratislava train,' he said. It was then that the soldiers spotted the three of us. Somehow, in spite of Miki's and my blond hair, they guessed our true identities. One of them got quite excited and shouted, '*To su Židi!*' (These are Jews). With that, Mr Duraj whipped the horses, roaring at them to go on. The animals jumped, sending us slamming against the back of the carriage, our feet lifting in the air for just a second. We took off, Mr Duraj flailing like a madman as the soldiers screamed after us in rage. It was a miracle they didn't open fire – in fact, it's a bit of a mystery that they didn't. We reached the station in Leopoldov in the next few minutes, Mr Duraj urging us to get out as fast as possible and grabbing our suitcases while pushing us on in front of him: 'Hurry! Hurry!' There was barely enough time for him to wish us luck or for Mother to thank him for literally saving our lives. There was never enough time to thank anyone for doing something like that. Besides, this was only the first stage of our journey.

When we walked into the station we found ourselves standing in the midst of a crowd of passengers – Hlinka guards, German soldiers and the dreaded Gestapo. This was the new taskforce that was formed to round up Jews and other people – like gypsies and homosexuals – whom they wanted to get rid of too. Free from any kind of restriction by the civil authorities, the taskforce could do whatever they wanted, with no repercussions, and, consequently, they were renowned for their brutality and torture techniques. They were easy to recognise in their long leather coats with a swastika adorning a red armband, as they checked the ID cards of the people who were boarding the train. We joined the queue – Mother praying, I'm sure, that our false papers were perfect. I wanted to hold her hand, but she was fishing our papers out of her bag, doing her best to be calm and confident. I couldn't take my eyes off the man as he took the cards, peered hard at the small black-and-white photograph and then back at my mother's face. It took maybe three or four seconds, but felt longer, until he handed the cards back, waved us through and gestured to the people behind us to move forward. There was no need for him to say a word, this stranger from another country, he directed us all with absolute authority. We got on the train and took three seats in a carriage which quickly filled up. Fr Harangozo's handiwork had passed the first test.

The journey to Bratislava took about two hours and a very quiet time it was. Nobody spoke. It was too dangerous to strike up conversations with strangers. Tensions were high, thanks to the brooding presence of Gestapo agents and Hlinka guards, who kept up a constant patrol, checking and re-checking passengers' documents. I would imagine that nobody felt particularly safe or comfortable in this atmosphere, no matter who they were. Our papers passed a second inspection, this time by the Hlinka guard who entered our carriage. How I longed to see the bright lights of Bratislava, although my mother was surely wondering how many more people would check our cards before we could exit the station. As it happened, it was just once more, immediately on disembarking from the train. Finally we were free to board the tram that took us to the Carlton hotel. From there it was a few steps to a house beside the Reduta cinema. That was where Aunt Margo and her family used to live, and where Margo, thanks to the reliable housekeeper, had found us a tiny, furnished, one-bedroomed flat in the backyard. We could rest here for a couple of weeks, before meeting up with *Omama* Rosalia for the final phase of the plan. The stress of the past few hours had exhausted us and Margo, within minutes of greeting us, was obliged to leave us alone to sleep.

We kept a low profile. Since Miki and I should have been at school, like other 'normal' Slovakian children, we couldn't ever leave the flat until late afternoon. Mother went out first thing in the morning to buy our food, and then she stayed indoors for the rest of the day. On our first morning we received two short visits from relatives we hadn't heard from in a long time, including Mother's brother, Gejza, who turned up with his elegant Swiss girlfriend, Hella.

Aside from the worry of being caught, there were also the daily bombing raids to be dealt with. When the sirens screamed out their warnings, everyone ran to the shelters that had been built specifically for public use – everyone, that is, except us. We were confined to the small, filthy coal bunker that was set into a wall that stood just inside the yard, as part of our constant goal not to draw attention to ourselves. Here we sat in silence, our clothes covered in black dust. Fortunately, no bombs exploded nearby or we would surely have been buried alive. When a bomb fell on the cinema next door, it didn't explode. We heard that the Hlinka guards made two young Jewish men go into the cinema to retrieve the device.

We had been in Bratislava for seven days when we received

the horrific news that my father had been arrested. It was a terrible shock, even though it was such commonplace news at the time. We were really sad and everyone felt depressed. We thought we would never see him again. The next few days were a bit of a timeless, shapeless blur until we received a postcard with the wonderful words: '*I'm alive – don't worry*', in Father's handwriting. Our spirits soared, though we wondered where he could possibly be.

A few mornings later, the three of us were sitting quietly in the little sitting room when there was a loud knock on the door. It was a frightening sound, considering that barely five people in the whole world knew we lived there. When Mother opened the door two men pushed their way inside. Just one of them spoke: 'Police! Can we see your ID?' They were the Slovak secret service. Somebody must have reported us; it's the only reason they could be standing in our flat. Miki and I watched our mother calmly retrieve her bag from the table and fetch out the cards which had already proven so successful both with the Hlinka and the Gestapo.

'You are Jews.' The man barely glanced at the card, so sure was he of our real identity.

My mother held his gaze and coolly replied: 'What are you talking about? Of course we're not Jews.'

Just then there was another knock on the door. Miki went to answer it but the other policeman beat him to it. I was so glad to see Uncle Gejza and Hella standing there and had to fight the urge to run into their arms. For a moment it had felt like nobody else existed outside our sitting room. They were immediately asked for their IDs. Gejza said he had left his at home, while Hella, taking stock of the situation, politely asked the two men to follow her into the next room. This they did without any further discussion. As usual, she was impeccably dressed, carrying herself with that air of assurance that more than suggested comfortable living. Negotiations took place involving large amounts of money, and a few minutes later the two men were happy enough to leave. Perhaps Hella kept large sums of cash on her for this very purpose.

As soon as the men left, my mother turned to thank Hella; our lives had been saved once more, but, once again, there was no time to dwell on the fact. Hella spoke quickly: 'They know you are Jews so they'll be back again. You must find somewhere else to live, as soon as you can.'

This my mother did, the very next morning, telling us to pack the cases in her absence. She found a house on the outskirts of the city belonging to an elderly couple who asked no questions but, nevertheless, told Mother, 'There are no uniformed men living here', meaning presumably the Hlinka guards. In other words, we didn't have to worry about them betraying us. We moved in immediately and, because of the other tenants, had to adapt to a whole new timetable. We all left the flat each morning. Miki and I pretending we were going to school, while Mother pretended to go to work. My brother and I had approximately six hours to kill each day and we couldn't be seen out on the streets. Luckily there was a forest not far from where we lived so we headed over there, following a dirt path that led deep into the midst of the trees and foliage. We sat there quietly for hours since we couldn't play any games in case anyone heard us. Mother gave us food to bring with us so it was like being on a very long picnic, though nowhere near as fun. The weather, of course, could play havoc with our day. When it rained we got soaked through to the skin.

Meanwhile, Aunt Margo and her family – her husband Dula, son Laco and daughter Chava – had gone into hiding too. They had been lucky. The house beside the cinema, which had been their home, had been given, as was the new law, to an Aryan from the Sudetenland called Anni Skoda. Fortunately for the Mayers, Anni had no intention of disrupting their lives or causing trouble. Instead, she opted for them staying on in the house while she took just one room, sharing the kitchen and bathroom with them. It was an amicable arrangement that only ended when the Germans arrived in Bratislava. But Anni wasn't finished with helping them. She arranged for the family to move into her brother's empty villa, which stood on the outskirts of the city. Since the house had to continue looking empty, they were obliged to live in silence and, once the sun went down, in darkness, not so much as twitching a curtain. Three more relatives moved in with them: Margo's brother Osy, his wife Erzi and her sister-in-law Emma.

Miki's and my forest sojourns came to an end some time in the middle of October 1944, when Uncle Gejza brought *Omama* Rosalia, who was dressed to look like a poor peasant, into a shop near the cinema to wait for our mother. That morning our mother took our suitcases to the train station and put them away in a locker. Next she led Miki and me to a shop that stood across the road from the National Opera House where we were told to wait for her to return with our grandmother. The shop sold photographic equipment, so we had something to look at while we waited. I don't remember how, but there was some connection with Anni Skoda which allowed us to hang around the showroom. We wouldn't have too long to wait, anyway, since *Omama* was only a few hundred metres away. Mother had told us to be ready, saying: 'I'll be back in a few minutes.'

A few minutes went by, and then some more, and more after that. There was no sign of her. Neither of us would have dreamt of leaving the shop, so we just sat there and waited. It's impossible to guess now how much time passed – we didn't have watches – before the door was pushed open. Miki and I looked up eagerly at the two figures entering the shop, absolutely expecting to see our mother and grandmother, but it wasn't them. It was two men – tall, blond, and wearing long leather coats with a swastika sitting in the centre of a red armband.

They approached us immediately, one of them addressing Miki: 'You are Jewish?' Miki shook his head. 'No, my name is Miki Vyda. I'm not Jewish.' We firmly believed that this name would save us so it was a bit of a shock when the man persisted: 'But you *are* Jewish.' Again my brother denied it. Without warning, the man slapped Miki across the face. 'Tell me the truth. We have your mother.' However, Miki refused to give in, obedient to his parents only, even after he was slapped again. The man turned to me then: 'You are Jewish, aren't you?' Following my brother's lead, I said my new name: 'No, my name is Tomas Vyda. I'm not J—' Before I finished my sentence the man had given me a blow in the face, almost knocking me off my feet. I was very small for my age. Miki jumped in horror, instinctively protecting me by blurting out: 'No, don't beat him! Yes, yes, we are Jewish.' The man smiled in satisfaction: 'You could've just said this in the beginning and saved yourself a beating.'

We were under arrest, escorted between the two Gestapo agents to the shop where we were re-united with our mother and grandmother, along with Uncle Gejza and Mr Figenbaum, who was related to our Aunt Erzi. *Omama*'s face was bruised and swollen, where she had been repeatedly punched to reveal her Jewishness and the names of her family. Someone had betrayed her. When Mother entered the shop they asked to see her ID card. Fr Harangozo had thought it unnecessary to change my mother's birth name, Scheimovitz, because it wasn't necessarily a Jewish name. Therefore, as soon as my grandmother said she was Jewish, with Scheimovitz on her own ID card, my mother was immediately identified as Jewish too. A taxi was sent to the station to retrieve the suitcases. When they were opened to reveal children's clothing it was only a matter of time before Miki and I were picked up.

While we stood with Mother, one of the men said to her, 'You know, your kids don't look Jewish.'

'Let them go then,' was her swift reply. He declined, of course.

Meanwhile, the occupants of the 'empty' villa were undergoing the same experience. There had been a knock on the door accompanied by shouts of 'Aufmachen!' (Open up!). A group of Gestapo agents stood on the threshold, all clad in the leather coats with the red armbands. Uncle Dula tried to push Chava into the bathroom, but she wouldn't let go of him. They didn't even look for ID papers, only wanting to know their names. It was later disclosed that Anni Skoda's brother had been brought in for interrogation and had cracked, thus informing on the seven Jews sheltering in his holiday home.

There was a second family re-union at the Gestapo headquarters at 6 Edlova Street. Margo and the others joined us about an hour after we arrived as we sat there waiting to have our details registered.

And so, in just one afternoon, thirteen members of our family were arrested. After all our near brushes with capture since leaving Merašice, our luck had finally run out.

Chapter 6

• • • • • •

Detention and Deportation

The Gestapo HQ was crowded, but strangely quiet. Each new arrival was another Jew, like us, whose time had finally run out. Nobody had the energy to make conversation; there was too much anxiety in the air for that. Likewise, Miki and I were struck dumb, only good for clinging to our mother, lest anyone should think of taking her away from us.

We were sitting in the basement of what had previously been the Jewish Central Office of Slovakia, the organisation that looked after the affairs of the whole community. Margo's husband, my Uncle Dula, had worked here in the office, along with my mother's brother, Osy. Almost a hundred years earlier, the building had been a comfortable home to Chatam Sofer, a famous rabbi and scholar, and then, following his death, in 1839, to his family and later descendants. The neighbourhood surrounding the house had always been known as the Jewish quarter of Bratislava, and was one of the city's more affluent areas — or, at least, had always been up to now. When the Germans moved in to occupy Slovakia on 28 August 1944, the office staff, knowing exactly what this meant for the remaining Jewry, fled into hiding. The building that had always sheltered Jews, in one way or another, was promptly claimed by those men who answered to the highest ranking Jew hunter of them all, one of Heydrich's most trusted colleagues, Adolf Eichmann. Thus Chatam Sofer's home became the headquarters of the Gestapo, his walls adorned with Nazi slogans and swastikas, while the Nazi flag flapped obscenely over his front door. There was also an added bonus for the new occupants: because the office staff had left in such a hurry there was no time to destroy any paperwork, so the Germans feasted on addresses and details of the remaining Jews still at large.

The corridor where we sat in a row was dimly lit, with only a couple of well-spaced bare bulbs shedding any light. I had no idea what we were waiting for. My mother slowly reached for her bag and took out our ID cards. I watched her glance quickly around before reaching down to slide the documents under the thin carpet that ran the length of the basement. By this stage I didn't have to ask any foolish questions. She was hiding our cards to protect Fr Harangozo, and probably saved his life by doing so. I don't know how easily he would have been traced through the cards, but it wasn't something that Mother was about to take chances with.

More and more families continued to arrive. Mostly these were the well-established Jews who had been exempted from earlier deportations through their connections or careers. Everyone around me looked swamped by hopelessness. It was over. We had all been successfully trapped by the hunters. I tried to catch my cousin Chava's eye, but she hardly raised her head from her father's arm. We spent the night in that gloomy corridor; none of us got much sleep.

By the following morning the place was completely over-crowded. At last we were told we were going to be moved elsewhere. A number of trucks arrived in the afternoon and we queued in single file to board them. A two-hour journey brought us 55km east of Bratislava, to the former work-camp of Sered, now serving as a detention camp for Jews.

The Jewish Central Office had supported the Minister of the Interior, Alexander Mach, when he decided to set up the labour camp in 1941, believing that this was a practical alternative to deporting Jews to the camps in Germany and Poland. Instead they could offer their services in Sered and Novaky, and thereby remain alive and safe in their native country. Jewish craftsmen, including carpenters and tailors, thrived in the workshops. All sorts of items were churned out, from wooden clogs and toys to hats and silver jewellery. The idea was to show how Jews could contribute to the nation. Tailors worked away on uniforms for the Slovak army, while a graphics department, full of experienced staff, produced propaganda material for the state. Indeed, the Jewish Centre believed that this was the way to save the Jews and was the perfect solution to everyone's problem. It didn't last. In the summer of 1942, something like 4,500 hard-working inmates of Sered were dispatched to Auschwitz and similar places in Poland. Then, however, things improved once more with the cessation of the first wave of deportations. The work camp was eagerly expanded, with cultural activities laid on for the adults and classes for the children. There was even a Jewish Council permitted, chaired by Alexander Pressburger, who worked with the Hlinka Guard camp commandant, but, of course, everything changed again with the uprising in August 1944, when the camp disintegrated, with most of the inmates running off to join the Resistance, along with members of the Slovak police force who hated Fr Tiso's fascist, Nazi-friendly regime.

We arrived in the late afternoon, disembarking from the trucks in silence, focusing only on remaining as close as possible to each other. Fear of separation was growing all the time – I suppose it was a consequence of our feeling utterly powerless about our immediate future. The urge to be surrounded by relatives was a fierce one. Familiar faces were keeping us relatively calm. All I could see was large wooden huts, rows and rows of them. After our details were registered, we were handed out the essentials – one blanket, one metal bowl and a spoon. The camp was being run, for the Germans, by the inmates themselves; it was Jews who registered us and led us to our hut. The camp's commander was Eichmann's second-in-command, SS–Hauptsturmführer Alois Brunner. After the war Brunner was one of the most sought-after war criminals, being responsible for sending thousands of Jews to their deaths in the gas chambers. Germany put a price on his head in 1995. He was known to be living in Syria and the *Jerusalem Post* reported that he lost an eye and three fingers in bombs sent to him there. He is probably no longer alive as he would be ninety-eight years old at the time of writing.

The huts were divided up into sections to house different families and groups, and the only furniture was wooden bunk beds. They must have been new as I distinctly remember the fresh smell of the wood. Within the sections, people hung up blankets for some sort of privacy, which was minimal, thanks to the flimsiness of the wooden partitions. I don't know how many people we shared the hut with, but the noise was tremendous and a welcome break from the gloom of the previous twenty-four hours. The thirteen of us were rooming together. While our mothers sorted out the beds, Miki, Chava and I took off to explore, searching for the toilets and seeing whatever else was on offer. Our walk was short-lived, however, as wandering around the camp was against the rules. We were told to return to our hut and stay there.

There wasn't much sleep to be had that night thanks to a frightened old woman who constantly cried out for her family and her sons to come and save her. She was all alone and ignored the entreaties of those around her, who tried to be kind, pleading with her, in vain, to consider the children whom she was frightening with her shrill hysterics. Her mind was gone, probably due to shock at her situation. She sobbed all night and well into the next day until she was eventually removed. We never saw her again.

The food was actually quite good, both in quality and quantity. I don't remember what we ate, other than we had three adequate meals a day and nobody went hungry. Surrounded by barbed wire and towering walls, the biggest loss we had experienced so far was our freedom. The camp was patrolled by both Hlinka guardsmen and German soldiers, and we were never allowed to forget that our very existence was a most fragile one. All inmates lived in fear of the dreaded announcement from the camp's sound system: '*Achtung*! *Achtung*! (Attention! Attention!)' that usually signalled a transport was about to take place – that about a thousand people were going to be sent off to somewhere like Auschwitz. New inmates arrived almost every day, ensuring that the camp was always bursting at its seams. The tension would build, and just as it seemed that there was no more room, a roll-call would summon, by the number of their hut, the ones who had been chosen to fill the next train going to Germany, Poland or wherever. In fact, the grown-ups knew a lot more than they pretended to.

The ominous roll-call was made by Camp Commander Brunner and it was he who carried out the 'selection'. This one word came to mean absolutely everything to a Jewish person. It was this process that ultimately allowed the selector to play God, when the ones who were leaving the camp would be split into two groups, decided by Brunner:'Women over the age of 60, mothers with children under the age of 13, stand to the left; everyone else – men and women from the age of 13 upwards to 60 – to the right-hand side.' At the time I didn't know that this meant that everyone on the right-hand side was being sent off to work while those on the left, the scared-looking women with their children clinging to them like leeches, were more than likely heading for the gas chambers.

Two weeks after we arrived in Sered, the speaker called everyone to attention, spat out the hut numbers and this time ours was on the list. We gathered our belongings in silence and followed the other clusters of families to the open ground. It was a glorious morning; the sun warmed our faces as we were instructed to stand in line with our suitcases at our feet. Facing us was a long table at which a handful of Hlinka guards and German soldiers were seated at either side of the scowling Camp Commander. Miki and I had a firm grip on our mother as the Commander addressed us in a loud, angry tone: 'I know you Jews. You are a sneaky lot, capable of smuggling illegally held money and valuables in the hope that they will somehow save your life. Keep in your lines and as you pass by this table I want all money, all jewels and any other valuables to be placed here. And I warn you, if I find anybody trying to hide something I will shoot them dead on the spot!'

At this, the first line of people began to remove rings, watches and their wallets. They were watched closely by Brunner and the others as they passed by the table. Every so often the SS guards would roughly frisk someone to make sure their pockets were really empty. The thirteen of us waited our turn and then joined the end of the last queue, to walk nervously in front of the stern-faced soldiers. Uncle Osy led the way, followed by Gejza and then *Omama* Rosalia. Next was Miki, our mother and me. We had nothing to offer, nothing to hide and walked on without stopping. Behind us was the Mayer family – Uncle Dula, Laco, Chava and Aunt Margo, who was carrying a green jacket across her arm. Just as she passed Brunner, however, he roared at her, 'HALT!' and tore the jacket from her hand. Our entire group froze, expecting the very worst. Brunner held the jacket aloft and grinned meanly at his companions: '*Da ist die Smugglerin!*'

(Here is a smuggler!) He proceeded to pull a bit of paper out of the pocket. It was an old shrivelled up tram ticket that was twisted around a 10 crown coin, no more than a few cents, change after buying the ticket. We stared at him in confused horror. Margo's face was white with fear. Would he really shoot her for this? Looking as if he was thoroughly enjoying himself, Brunner took note of the terror that was clearly visible on all our faces. Then, as if satisfied that we were scared enough, he began to laugh. He threw the jacket back at Margo, and shouted at us to keep moving.

When everyone had handed over their valuables, Brunner announced the next event of the morning: the selection. The cattle carts were waiting at the camp's platform; it was just a matter of sorting who was going in which carriages. Instructions were issued through the loudspeaker: all women over the age of 60, with mothers and children up to the age of 13 were to move to the left, while all single women (including married women who had no children) up to the age of 60 were to form a line on the right-hand side. There wasn't enough time for Uncle Dula to say a proper goodbye to his wife or sisters, or for Uncle Osy to bid his wife an emotional farewell. The young women were quickly led away to their particular section of the train. It was very upsetting to see families all around us being torn apart. Next, the men were being led away, including my three uncles, my fifteen-year-old cousin Laco, and a friend, Mr Figenbaum.

Unbeknownst to me, my mother was caught up in a huge dilemma. Miki, my brother, was twelve years old, but he was tall for his age and could pass for thirteen. She knew that the first cattle trucks on the train were ferrying away the ones who had been chosen to work. Should she release her son to join his uncles or keep him with her probably to die beside her? Meanwhile, an SS guard came over to the three of us and pointed at Miki, asking Mother: 'How old is he?' She was forced to make an instant decision: 'He's only twelve.' So Miki stayed with us. Perhaps it would have been different if my father had been with us. She would surely have let Miki go then. I suppose she thought that, in Father's absence, my brother and I were her responsibility and, therefore, she wasn't prepared to let either of us out of her sight. In other words, whether we were going to survive or otherwise, the most important thing was that we had to stick together.

And so we stood in the sun along with the rest of the mothers, children and elderly women for just a few seconds more, until we were told to move towards the cattle trucks. The guards shouted at us, '*Schnell! Schnell!*' (Hurry! Hurry!). When we reached the platform the Hlinka guards began splitting us up into groups of about fifty or sixty. Nobody cried or created any fuss. Even the babies were quiet. The air was just heavy with sadness as we obeyed all orders. Just as we passed by the carriage that held my uncles and cousin, Uncle Dula shouted out to his wife, Margo: 'Take care of yourself and don't worry about us. We'll be fine.' Somehow he had managed to conceal his wristwatch during the inspection and now he flung it out to Margo: 'Here, take this.' Miraculously, none of the guards noticed.

In the intervening years since then, what strikes me over and over again is how dignified we were. There was no pushing and no signs of exasperation or panic. The thousand of us could have been first-class passengers in any grand city of the world, such was our immaculate behaviour. Of course, on that sunny morning, I had no idea of the dreadful possibilities awaiting us. I shudder to think what my mother must have been going through.

It was a box on wheels, the cattle carriage that we were pressed into, along with up to fifty others. All the time we were being harassed to 'hurry, hurry' by the guards. It wasn't easy to board the train because there were no steps, so mothers had to pull their young children up after first clambering on board with the suitcases. Miki, Mother and I had to push and shove *Omama* Rosalia on board; we were the last ones in. Making sure we were together, along with Margo and Chava, we squashed into the right-hand corner of the carriage, beside the door. The carriage stank, not surprisingly, of animals – its normal cargo. There was straw on the floor and a large barrel in the centre, along with a couple of buckets.

This was our toilet. Once we found a spot to stand on, it was impossible to move, we were so tightly packed in together. These cattle trucks also went by the slang name of '40–8', which alluded to the fact that they were made to hold either 40 men or eight horses. There were maybe sixty of us, with almost the same amount of suitcases.

The closing of the door behind us signified the end of our civilised life. It was dark, only the merest hint of light wafting almost accidentally through the tiny openings in the four corners of the roof. Outside, we could hear all the doors being padlocked by the Hlinka guards, who assured the railway employees that each 'consignment' had been secured. We were no longer citizens, no longer human beings. Inside, nobody spoke. I think everyone was too full of fear about where we were going. The adults all knew about the gas chambers and worried that we might be heading there. They were also desperately worried about their husbands, fathers, brothers, sons, wondering if they would ever see them again.

The train whistled and pushed off, slowly at first then gathering speed. The noise of the steam engine was so fierce that it made conversation impossible anyway. Hours passed by, just listening to the monotonous chug-chug. It wasn't until the late evening that people began to be brave – or desperate – enough to relieve themselves in the buckets. When one of us needed to go, the rest would do their best to stand around the person and hide them from the other passengers. At least, this was the case for the first day or two. After that, nobody really cared. It was the same with the stench of urine and faeces. It was nauseating that first night, but we soon got used to it, because we had to.

We were in that carriage for seven days. Our bodies became cramped from holding the same position for hours on end. At night, it was freezing cold, obliging us all to huddle together for warmth. There were various stops along the way, when the door would be slid open so that the stinking barrel could be emptied. How we gulped in the fresh air – it was almost as good as having a proper meal. The first stop took place two days after we left Sered, when we were given water and bread, our first food on the journey. Water was precious and for consumption only, so for a week we didn't wash. At that first stop we noticed that there seemed to be only Germans on the platform. Did this mean we weren't going to Poland, to the gas chambers in Auschwitz? Of course, it was just the adults who worried about this. I am sure all of the children were as ignorant as I was about the goings on at Auschwitz. Rumours were rife regarding our destination. It was the only topic of conversation, when anyone did bother to voice an opinion over the noise of the train. Also, at each stop, there was a lot of manoeuvring, the train moving slightly forwards and slightly back again, with sounds of carriages being disconnected and connected. Had they taken away the carriage of men and single, childless women? Where were they going? Where were we going?

For me the most upsetting thing on the journey was when one of two elderly sisters died in front of me. She had got sick almost immediately after we boarded, probably with the shock, and without medication or even mediocre sanitary conditions, she deteriorated quickly. Powerless, her sibling could only hold her and plead with her to get better. When she died, the sister became hysterical, sobbing with grief and bewilderment. The worst thing was that there was no alternative but to leave the dead woman where she lay. It was my first time seeing someone die. I tried my best not to look at the corpse, but I couldn't forget for a second that it was right there, inches from my feet, day and night.

It rained on the last day of our journey. I remember this because the water seeped through the gaps in the sliding doors, soaking us for hours on end. It was 9 November 1944 and we were approaching our final destination, though we didn't know that. We also didn't know how lucky we were, if that's not too inappropriate a word to use. Just two days earlier the Germans had blown up the last gas chamber in Auschwitz to hide their evil doings from the approaching Russian army. Had we been part of the previous week's consignment from Sered, you would not be reading this particular survivor's account of the Holocaust.

But, of course, we knew nothing of this. The train slowed down on the evening of the 9th, before coming to a halt, with a final hiss of steam. While we wondered if this was just another brief stop the padlocks were unlocked and the doors flung open. A chaotic chorus of German voices began to scream at us, all at the same time, over and over again, making us frantic: '*HERAUS! HERAUS! SCHNELL! SCHNELL!*' (OUT! OUT! HURRY! HURRY!) There was also a relentless barking that just wouldn't stop. Bright light flooded the carriage, stunning us after the hours spent sitting in a false dusk. Desperately frightened, I grabbed my mother's hand as everyone moved, as one, towards the entrance.

'Stay in line, you Jewish bitches!' I had never heard such language before, had never heard women addressed so vulgarly. It was like an outlandish nightmare where there were no obvious rules and thus no security. Everything was upside down; my mother's hand was the only sure thing and I gripped it, determined never to let it go. As we moved out together, a soldier roared '*HERAUS!*' at the grief-stricken woman who remained by her dead sibling's side, holding her in a pathetic embrace. She replied '*Tot*' (dead), pointing to her sister. At this, the soldier seized hold of Miki and shouted, '*Komm hier du Hurensohn!*' (Come here, you son of a bitch!) Terrified, I watched the man shove my brother back towards the corpse, gesturing that he was to help carry the body over to a waiting truck. We lost sight of him for a few minutes, which caused us some panic, but my mother called and called his name until he found us again.

We were being thumped and shoved to get into rows of four. Surrounded by enraged SS soldiers, with manic Alsatian dogs and huge guns trained on us, we stumbled around, blinded by the searchlights, trying to find the right place to stand. It was raining heavily; the soldiers were wearing their long, waterproof raincoats, and helmets and boots, while we shivered from the cold and fright. There were about a hundred and thirty people in our group. *Omama* Rosalia walked between Margo and Mother, while Miki, Chava and I followed closely behind. They began to herd us off as if we were cattle. Soldiers stood either side of us, pointing their guns at our heads, shouting non-stop: '*Schnell! Schnell!*' It was pitch dark once we moved away from the platform and the ground was muddy and gooey thanks to the weather. Within minutes we were being directed through a forest, where the mud pulled down greedily on our shoes, making it difficult to keep up the required pace. We walked for something like two hours. Margo and Mother held onto my grandmother, who had begun to stumble in her tiredness. The soldiers never dropped their weapons and the big dogs never stopped barking at us. At one stage we could smell something burning – and, sure enough, in the distance we could make out flames leaping out of a chimney.

Eventually we came to the end of the forest and found ourselves standing on a road. Facing us was a barbed-wire fence. A searchlight from the nearby watchtower picked us out from the shadows of the trees. We were marched forward as a ramp opened up, allowing us to walk inside the fence. There we found ourselves surrounded by more barbed wire and more watchtowers, from which I could make out soldiers focusing large guns, which were actually machine-guns, on the new arrivals. Just like Sered, all I could see were rows of huts. The ground was well illuminated by lamps. There was no sign of life in the buildings because it was the middle of the night. We were marched another few hundred metres before we took a sharp left and were ordered to enter the large hut standing there. Inside, it was quite dark, but we could see that the entire hut was filled with bunk beds. The wooden ceiling was low, which meant that the light thrown out by the few dim bulbs was mostly obscured by the bunk beds. We took the first three available, simply dropping our suitcases beside us and lying down. Exhausted and drenched, nobody had any interest in or energy for anything else and, to be honest, it was a blessed relief after being cramped up in the cattle cart to be able to stretch out and lie down properly.

And so, that first night we slept the sleep of the dead.

Chapter 7

• • • • • •

Arnold Reichental, the Farmer: My Father

A few days after we left, my father decided to visit his fields to check their progress since their recent ploughing. It was a beautiful day, the sun high in the cloudless sky, perfect for a walk. Had it been raining he would have taken the horse and cart as some of the fields stretched all the way out the other side of Merašice. Stopping only to take up his walking stick and whistle for the dogs to join him, he started out. As far as he knew, we were safe and, ever the optimist, he probably believed that everything was going to work out just as he and Mother had planned. I think I must have learned to appreciate the wonder of the world around me from Father. Before all the madness he had been a supremely content man who loved where he lived, and, therefore, where he came from, and loved what he did for a living, taking pleasure from the sight of the summer breeze, perfumed with wildflowers or, depending on where he stood, the sweetness of just-cut grass, gently lifting and then dropping the leaves of the trees and the crops, *his* crops, in a dance of sheer jubilance. Perhaps in the days immediately following his wife and sons' departure, he had worked from morning to night, to keep himself from missing us, and that morning, because the sun had beckoned, he suddenly felt that it was going to be okay, and that a walk was well deserved after the stress of the past few weeks.

As he reached the edge of the village he saw a small truck in the distance. It was coming in the direction he was taking, but he was more interested in watching the dogs chase one another, turning tail to run at the cheeky crows that squawked in demanding tones for attention. In those precious dwindling minutes of freedom, as the vehicle neared him, he simply must have forgotten that he was despised and hunted for his very being.

'*To je Žid!*' (That's a Jew!)

The voice belonged to Captain Ludovit Nedelka, the man who had led my grandparents away, possibly delaying their exemption papers in order to do so, and the man who had frightened us needlessly, in the hope of receiving a pocketful of bribe coins. Now he had finally got himself the biggest prize of all, his former school friend, the ever popular and infinitely more successful Arnold Reichental.

Father was taken away immediately, not even allowed to return home for the usual single suitcase of essentials – no doubt, Nedelka didn't care to be seen actively betraying a friend in front of their neighbours. He spent the next two days in a detention camp, eventually being picked, along with approximately a thousand other Jews, to board the cattle cart, they assumed for Auschwitz. It was typical for this sort of 'cargo' to be transported in the late evening, out of sight – and, hence, minds – of the general population; ignorance was certainly bliss, as well as a very particular luxury, in those days. His carriage contained about fifty other men and the door was secured with a heavy chain. At some point in the journey, when the train was at full speed, one of the 'passengers', a Hungarian, made an announcement: 'Listen, I'm going to make a break for it. Anybody who wants to save himself can jump after me.' Nobody made a comment as the man hugged his briefcase to himself – there was so little space – in order to slide out a small blade from its handle. Resignation clouded the air, dampening, for a time, even fear itself.

Just a few, including my father, had a clear view of the man sawing away at the heavy chain. Perhaps the men at the back had no idea what was happening until the chain dropped heavily to the floor and the Hungarian pulled open the door, allowing a sudden gush of night air inside the carriage. It was pitch black outside and the train was hurtling along. To be sure, it was an imperfect and thoroughly risky opportunity, as far as opportunities go, but there it was, the only alternative on hand to arriving on time at the gas chamber. The Hungarian addressed the others once more: 'Jump, if you want to save yourselves', and then he was gone, disappearing, as it were, before their very eyes. My father followed him approximately two seconds later. He had been standing right in front of the door, so maybe it was easier for him to jump through that gaping black hole than for someone who needed to push their way through ten or fifteen others, giving themselves too much time to think about it. As it happened, Father was slammed against a telegraph pole, dislocating his left shoulder, before falling onto the cold, hard railway track.

He was in agony, but he was alive. Looking around, he discovered he was just a few yards from a main road, while, on the other side of the track, was a forest. He needed to reach the forest before he was spotted by a passing car, but as he tried to lift himself the pain was so bad that he feared he might lose consciousness. Knowing, however, that he had to bear it if he wanted to stay free, he struggled in vain to get to his feet. He was determined that jumping from a speeding train shouldn't be for nothing, so he was not about to give up here – wherever that was – yet he found it impossible to lift his shoulder from the ground. What he needed was another pair of hands.

He heard a voice: 'I'm Martin. Quickly now, we need to get to the other side of the track. Here, lean on me.'

The man had jumped after my father and, having seen him writhing helplessly on the ground, was unable to leave him behind. Father asked about the Hungarian.

Martin chuckled: 'Oh, don't worry about him. He's an old hand at this. Every time they catch him he goes and escapes again. You see, his career provided him with the perfect training for this kind of life.'

In between gasping from the pain, my father was intrigued. 'What do you mean? Was he a policeman?'

'No,' replied Martin. 'He was a safe-cracker, a first class crook. With nerves of steel, I'm sure.'

They reached the forest and kept going for the next two hours before deciding they were too deep to be found and lay down to sleep. The Germans disliked forests for two reasons: they couldn't drive armoured vehicles into them and they possibly contained refugee partisans who could easily ambush unprotected foot soldiers.

The following morning the two continued walking through the forest until they came across a dirt road, indicating that there must be someone living in the surrounding area. Hunger drove them to search it out and they found a small shack belonging to a husband and wife. The couple didn't appear surprised at the sight of visitors and immediately gave them food. However, they couldn't offer shelter because they had been called on, a few times, by German army patrols. So Martin and Father did the next best thing. They found a large hollowed-out tree trunk, at some distance from the house, and moved into it for the next few weeks, only stepping out in the dead of night to get food from their benefactors.

Eventually they met up with some partisans and their Russian officer. When it was discovered that Father could speak fluent German, the officer asked him to join them as an interpreter for the German soldiers they had captured and wanted to interrogate. My father readily agreed.

Chapter 8

• • • • • •

Uncle Oskar Reichental, the Architect

My high-achieving Uncle Oskar was born in Merašice on 4 May 1905. After the 1914–1918 war he served in the air force and was one of the country's first pilots. Next he studied architecture and graduated top of his class and, consequently, was never short of work. His many projects include the train station in Brezno nad Hronom and the extension to Bratislava's main train station.

In 1942, when all unmarried Jewish boys and girls were ordered to report for deportation, Oskar was exempted thanks to his professional standing with the state. Then one fine Thursday in June that same year, he was strolling down a street in Bratislava when he bumped into my Uncle Dula, who was married to my mother's sister, Margo. They talked for a few minutes until Dula asked Oskar if he could show him something. Oskar agreed and they immediately took a taxi to a house in Riska Street.

At the door Dula pressed the bell twice, indicating that it was a friendly caller and not the Hlinka Guard. A woman let them in. Intrigued, Oskar followed Dula into a room that was full of anxious-looking people. The woman nodded at Dula and said she'd be right back, and so she was, a few seconds later, with a very pretty young girl. Dula didn't waste any more time. He turned to Oskar, looking him straight in the eye, and asked: 'Will you marry this girl – yes or no?'

Edith was twenty-one years old. On receiving her deportation order, she had run away from the tiny village she grew up in and made her way to the capital, to hide amongst the bigger population. But single girls were very vulnerable and it was essential that she be married in order to save herself. Her Jewish friends had decided to try to find a partner for her.

To be sure, Oskar was shocked, to say the least. However, there was no doubting the girl's beauty or the wisdom that shone in her eyes, plus this was a time when really big decisions would be made in a heartbeat.

'Yes,' he answered.

Everybody, including the girl, smiled in relief. Dula shook

Oskar's hand in congratulations. 'Come to my house on Monday, the rabbi is booked for two o'clock.'

Five minutes later Oskar was back on the street, running late for a business meeting.

The following Monday he bumped into my parents in Leopoldov train station.

'Hello, where are you two off to?' he asked.

My father laughed. 'Where do you think, silly – to your wedding, of course!'

They all took a train and then a taxi from the station to Margo and Dula's house where some relatives had already gathered. The rabbi was late and rather distressed when he eventually arrived. A typical occurrence by now, he had been held up by Hlinka guards who had abused him and cut his beard. Nevertheless, he managed to gather himself enough to conduct the short ceremony. Aunt Margo served up goulash for the wedding meal and as soon as everyone cleared their plate they headed home. Oskar decided to come to Merašice because he wanted Edith to meet his parents, and so they got the train back with my parents.

I remember their arrival, positioning myself outside so that I would see them before anyone else. I was seven years old and very excited about meeting my new aunt. As soon as I saw her I fell in love, and blurted out: 'Oh, Uncle Oskar, your new wife is really, really beautiful!' Everybody laughed as Edith rewarded me with a hug.

It was a day for celebration, a rarity in the midst of all the tension and worries. Less than two months before my grandparents' arrest, this was probably one of the last good days we all had together. *Omama* and *Opapa* took to Edith immediately and were delighted that their clever, handsome son had made such a wonderful match. They blessed the happy couple and gave Oskar a special silver coin as a symbol of their good wishes for their future.

The next day the couple headed back to Bratislava. For the next two years they travelled around, thanks to Oskar's job, although he had to have his permit renewed every month and could never leave it behind. Being stopped on the street without the permit would mean instant arrest. It was a stressful time, but they both knew they had it better than most.

But that all changed in September 1944. Oskar was working on a job at the airport in Trencin when he saw two German planes land. The doors opened and eighty heavily armed German soldiers disembarked. Tiso, the Slovak president, had requested help from the Nazis to put down the recent rebellion in Banská Bystrica against his own pro-Nazi regime. My uncle recognised trouble when he saw it and hurried home to consult with Edith. They packed two suitcases to be ready to flee, and Oskar went back to work, where one of his colleagues offered to hide him and Edith in his weekend house, a cottage in the forest, should they need to run.

It was only a matter of days before the deportations widened their net. Oskar felt it was time to go and approached the man who had offered them shelter. He agreed to take the couple to the cottage immediately, promising to return with their suitcases. Leaving them to finish the journey by themselves, he waved goodbye, saying he'd be back the following day. It was the last they saw of him and their luggage. Meanwhile, when they reached the house they found it was already occupied. In fact, it was full of Jews who refused the newcomers entry on account of there being no room. Edith pleaded with them in vain, and the couple were obliged to continue on into the forest. There was no going back now. They later heard that the cottage was raided by German soldiers. Oskar's colleague had obviously received a tidy sum of money for his betrayal. They had had a lucky escape.

That night they slept under a tree. All they had was the clothes they were wearing and the remains of Oskar's last wages. They decided to make their way to Banská Bystrica and join the rebellion. Along the way they met a group of Jews who gave them some food, blankets and the necessary directions. Their destination was over a hundred kilometres away, but they met plenty of Jewish refugees throughout the journey, who kindly gave them food.

When they reached Banská Bystrica the uprising was in its final days. Having run out of money, Oskar decided to try his luck at finding work. He went to the train station and offered his services, having worked there previously on a job that had never been finished. All it took was a brief word with the building contractor and he had a job again. He was also drafted into the Resistance, and he inspected train passengers to make sure there were no spies or Germans amongst them. Typically, he did well enough to receive a promotion.

However, it was only a matter of time before their position became precarious. The German army was advancing quickly so the rebels gave the order for a full retreat into the forest. Edith and Oskar were back where they started. For a while they were simply stranded, until they met up with a Resistance group who gave them a hand-gun, a hatchet, blankets and some food. A Resistance sergeant and soldier decided to go with Oskar and Edith, and the four of them spent the next few days hiking deep into the forest. At one point they had a terrible scare when they accidentally happened upon some German soldiers. There was a stand-off as the Germans cocked their weapons, as did Oskar's tiny group. Then the sergeant took control, hissing at his three colleagues: 'Hold your fire. Just follow my lead.' Very slowly he began to step backwards, inching his way from a potentially fatal confrontation. Miraculously, it worked. The Germans obliged by copying them, backing away in the direction they had come from – only God knows why.

The stragglers continued on their way, the sergeant leading them to an isolated village which he knew would be a safe place for a few days' rest at least. It was an arduous trek as the forest floor was covered with snow, while at night the temperatures plummeted. Food was rationed, with everyone surviving on a daily diet of two slices of dry bread and some dried meat. The snow provided water, so that was something. One day they were lucky enough to come across a dead cow and they cut off some flesh and cooked it on a fire. The foursome finally reached the village ahead of the Germans, where the sergeant knew a farmer who put them up in his barn. They ate a good dinner, washed themselves and lay down to sleep for a solid twenty-four hours.

It was only ever going to be a brief respite. No more than two days went by before the farmer told them the Germans were in the vicinity and they would have to leave. The group split up and, for the third time, Oskar and Edith found themselves back in the forest. Not far from the village they found a cave and quickly moved in. A few days later they got a fright when they heard footsteps nearby, but it was only the farmer. He had brought them food, but advised them to keep moving as the Germans were everywhere now. Oskar decided they should go to Brezno nad Hronom where he knew a clerk who would help them. The farmer pointed them in the right direction and wished them luck. They had to stay in the thick of the forest because the Germans were patrolling all the roads. It was a nerve-racking time, their only consolation being the little hand-gun. Oskar assured his wife: 'If we're caught, I'll shoot you first and then myself.'

Just like the previous time, they met plenty of other Jews who gave them bits of food. The snow was still thick on the ground and nights were spent huddled together in an effort to keep warm. They arrived at the clerk's front door, exhausted, hungry and filthy, but it was worth it. Oskar's friend took them in, fed them and put them up in his spare room. It was too risky to leave the house, so they spent the next few days inside, enjoying the chance to relax in a proper house and sleep in an actual bed. Then the clerk's father paid a visit. For some reason he opened the door of the spare room and was instantly terrified at his discovery: 'God help me! My son is hiding Jews! He'll have us all killed.' With that, the embarrassed clerk admitted that the Germans were putting up notices to warn that anyone hiding Jews would be shot. Oskar and Edith immediately took their leave, thanking the young man for his bravery.

But where were they to go this time? They both vetoed a return to the forest. A sort of resignation set in and they decided to return to Oskar's room in Trencin, the site of his previous airport job. They also decided that they'd use the main road; their exhaustion was beginning to curtail their desire to survive. When they heard approaching traffic they would duly jump off the road and hide, but otherwise they didn't much care anymore. At a crossroads, which was manned by a German soldier, they briefly hesitated before deciding to take their chances. When they reached the young soldier he waved them through, obviously assuming, by their shabby attire, that they were local peasants.

In Trencin they were welcomed by Oskar's landlady. As usual, they had only a few days to relax before the woman told them that the Germans were threatening to execute anyone found harbouring Jews. It was time to move on again. However, she suggested that they make their way to her sister-in-law's house in Tri Dubi. As it happened, Oskar knew the place well, having served there in his days working as a pilot. At this point they decided to make their way separately to the village – neither of them had any paperwork and they would only attract more attention as a couple. The courageous landlady managed to get some false papers for Edith and there was an emotional farewell between husband and wife before the landlady took Edith to the train station.

Oskar stayed on in Trencin for several days. The Germans were everywhere now and it would have required some amount of courage to go outside, knowing that all it would take was for one soldier to ask to see his non-existent papers. But, of course, he did leave the house eventually. What other choice had he? He sneaked into the train station and headed straight to the manager's office – he knew him from when he worked there. The manager agreed to help him board the train, and put him into the first carriage behind the driver.

A dangerous situation became even more so when Germans boarded at the next big station and began checking the passengers' identification papers.

Oskar had to think fast and act even faster. He made his way to the driver's cabin where he told the driver and his assistant that he had a gun which he would use, if necessary. 'I am a soldier in the Resistance Army and you have to help me.' After their initial shock, the men helped Oskar squeeze into a small service box, where there was just enough room for him to spend the remainder of the journey. When the train pulled into Tri Dubi station the driver asked Oskar where he wanted to go.

'Take me to your house and I'll decide my next step.'

And the driver did. He introduced him to his family, fed him and put him up for the night. In fact, my uncle ended up staying for a few weeks as it was much too dangerous for him to walk the streets.

Eventually, though, his impatience to see his wife overcame any qualms of being caught. At great risk he made his way to the landlady's sister-in-law's house and was absolutely horrified to find it had been destroyed by a bomb. He stood there in shock, feeling, possibly for the first time, desperately afraid. Was Edith dead? How would he even go about finding out? Not wanting to attract attention, he walked around for a bit, at a loss to know what to do. Suddenly he was approached by a young man. 'Are you Oskar?' the man asked.

My uncle nodded and the youth handed him a letter from Edith. 'I've been coming here every day since the house was bombed,' the youth explained. 'Edith knew you'd turn up here looking for her.'

Almost dizzy with relief he followed the young man back to where Edith was living. During their weeks of separation she had, thanks to her false papers, got a job as a maid in the local doctor's house. The doctor frequently received visits from German soldiers who flirted with her and happily drank the bottles of beer she served them. She was staying with the youth's family and it was decided that Oskar needed a different hiding place. Strangers stood out in villages where new arrivals were quickly suspected of being Jews on the run. In a nearby house he was hidden in a tiny store room. There was barely enough room for a single bed and the doorway was covered by a wardrobe. He was forced to spend several weeks there, listening to the numerous bombing raids that were growing in intensity as the Germans began to lose the war. His wife visited him whenever she could. When the Slovak government called for all men between the age of sixteen and sixty to make themselves available for work, Edith had her doctor write a sick note for him and she also managed to get him false papers with a new identity.

One day there was no shooting to be heard, no sound of aeroplanes dropping bombs, and Oskar just had to look out the window where he saw the most thrilling sight: hundreds of Russian soldiers marching victoriously down the street.

It was over.

On 25 April 1946 Edith gave birth to their son, Juraj. Three years later the family emigrated to Israel where, in 1952, their daughter Shosana was born. The marriage, born out of a split-second decision, was a tremendously happy one, ending only when Edith lost her battle with cancer in 1979. Oskar lived for another eleven years, passing away on 3 March 1990. He was eighty-five years old.

Chapter 9
● ● ● ● ● ●

Uncle Artur Scheimovitz, the Lawyer

U ncle Artur was my mother's older brother. A successful lawyer, he lived in a rather nice house in Piešťany, in western Slovakia, with his wife, Klara, and their two sons, Bandy and Juraj, who were a few years older than me. Thanks to his profession they were one of the first families in the area to receive the dreaded letter telling them to make preparations for deportation to a Jewish camp. It was 1942, the year that the concentration camp in Auschwitz became an extermination camp. This summons wasn't their first experience with the 'New Order'; in fact, it came on the back of quite a lot of harassment. Artur had a lot of enemies due to his successful prosecutions, and these included members of the Hlinka guards.

Long before the arrival of the deportation letter, the family had been subjected to frequent surprise raids from the state police, who would inform Artur that they believed him to be hiding illegal weapons in his home. Thus they would go from room to room, searching and ransacking the family's belongings, even helping themselves to Klara's jewellery or any other trinkets that were lying around. The raiders were invariably accompanied by Mr Reis, the chairman of the National Socialist German Party in Piešťany. He used to be a small shopkeeper, but now, thanks to his fashionable sympathies, could seek to get rid of Artur, Klara and the two boys primarily because he fancied having their house as his office. So, there it was: the Hlinka guards wanted revenge, while Reis wanted their house. The family didn't stand a chance.

Klara packed four rucksacks for herself, her husband and her children, being careful only to pack what was allowed, according to the letter, and then they counted the days until their deportation. On the morning that they were to be picked up, however, Artur and Klara, after an anxious, sleepless night, decided to attempt an escape. They took the boys to stay in the attic of another local Jewish family who hadn't been put on this first deportation list. A few hours later their host told them that the police were searching every house in the neighbourhood just for them. The family decided to split up: Artur went to his brother and Klara took Juraj to a friend of hers, while Bandy went to stay with a classmate. They agreed to meet up later.

Using one of his many contacts, Artur hired a man, for a hefty sum, to collect the family that same evening, and drive them to Merašice, where they surprised us with their early-morning visit. I remember it very clearly, the sound of a motor car getting louder and louder as I reluctantly left sleep behind. Who on earth could that be? Leaving my parents' bed to investigate, I was stunned, and then delighted, to hear the voices of my cousins, Bandy and Juraj. Before the 'New Order' they had been frequent visitors to our house, especially during the summer months.

I think this is what caused me the most upset at that time, the fact that our relatives didn't see us anymore. I couldn't understand why my cousins couldn't continue on squeezing into the tea house, like previous summers, to giddily consume bowls of my mother's homemade ice-cream.

Not stopping to put on slippers, I ran outside in my pyjamas, bellowing an ecstatic welcome at the two boys. I felt the anxiety in the air, but happily ignored it. The adults looked grave and stern, though my uncle and aunt did their best to smile at me. Mother ushered everyone into the house, telling me to get dressed quickly: 'You and Miki, take your cousins off to play,' she instructed us. I remember the date, 29 April 1942, because it was Juraj's birthday, his eleventh. Mother was resolute: 'This is an important day for Juraj, yes? So we must celebrate with the best birthday cake I can make.'

For me it was a typical visit, for the most part. The four of us went to our usual spots: to gawk at the machinery in the main barn and then on to climbing and sliding down the towering haystack, with plenty of hoots and laughter. Lastly, just before we were called to lunch, we went to the stables to greet all the cows and horses. My mother's cake was ready at lunchtime, so we enjoyed a brief party. I was disappointed to learn that our visitors were only staying for one day and the rest of the day passed too quickly. My cousins were instructed to go to bed after lunch as they had a long journey ahead of them and were already yawning from their early-morning start.

Meanwhile, Klara's brother was organising their next step. He contacted relatives in Budapest who immediately offered to put the family up – the persecution of Hungarian Jews was still in the future. The following day they were taken by the same driver to a small village near the Hungarian border where he handed them over to their hired guide, an unsmiling youth. They trekked about two kilometres in soft mud when the guide called halt. Pointing ahead of them, he said: 'The border is there in front of us. That small light to the right is the checkpoint, so avoid that. You've another five kilometres to walk before you reach Vrbov, in Hungary, but this is as far as I go. So you should pay me now.'

Artur paid up another hefty sum, which only made the

youth pout and ask: 'Haven't you anything else?' Their life was in his hands; all he had to do was shout to attract the guards at the checkpoint. Without a word of reproach, Artur quickly removed his gold ring, along with his wristwatch, and handed them over. Fortunately, it was enough. Their guide wished them good luck and farewell.

The family walked until they reached the graveyard of Vrbov, the first town over the border. Crossing illegally without the required documentation meant certain arrest if they were caught by the Hungarian police. Artur bade his wife and children to remain hidden while he went off in search of a friend, a fellow lawyer. It was an anxious wait, but well worth it as his friend provided him with the time of the next train to Budapest, along with a large sum of money. They went straight to the station and a few hours later stepped off into the arms of their frantic relatives. But it was only a short stay because it was much too risky without proper identity cards. The relatives decided to send the family to a small village south of Budapest where a sympathetic friend provided a tiny, damp room for shelter. It wasn't an ideal solution since a small isolated village was no place for four illegal immigrants on the run – all it would take was for one blabbermouth to start asking questions. Two weeks later the relatives managed to obtain false ID cards for the family, which brought them some relief from the constant worry about being caught. Also, it

My paternal grandparents, Katarina and Jecheskel Reichental – *Omama* and *Opapa*. They lived in another part of our house and owned the village shop in Merašice – here they are standing outside the door of their shop. The shop was taken from them and closed in May 1941, and in August 1942 they were arrested and taken to Auschwitz, from where they never returned.

Below: My father as a child with some of his siblings. *Left to right*: Renka, Dezko (Desider; guillotined in 1943), Robert, Misko, Oskar, my father Arnold.

Left: My beloved maternal grandmother, Rosalia Scheimovitz. *Omama* Rosalia was taken with us to Bergen-Belsen and died there. I saw her body being taken away to be thrown onto the heap of dead bodies, an image I will never forget.

Above: My mother's family. *Standing, left to right*: my uncles Gejza (died in Buchenwald), Osy (died in Buchenwald), Dusi, Artur, Aunt Adela (died in Auschwitz), my mother. *Seated*: Aunt Margo, *Omama* Rosalia (died in Bergen-Belsen), grandfather Moritz.

Right: My parents, Judith and Arnold, on their honeymoon in Venice in 1930.

Left: A family group in Merašice in 1940. On the right is my mother, and on the left Aunt Klara; *the children, top to bottom*: my cousin Bandy, my brother Miki, my cousin Juraj, myself.

Below: The Scheimovitz family and spouses pictured around 1934. Top row, left to right: Dula (Margo's husband; died in Buchenwald), Bela (Adela's husband, died in Auschwitz), Gejza (died in Buchenwald), Osy (died in Buchenwald), Dusi, Arnold Reichental (my father), Artur. Second row: Margo, Adela holding her daughter Kati (both died in Auschwitz), Grandmother Rosalia (died in Bergen–Belsen) holding Juraj, Grandfather Moritz, Judith (my mother), with my brother Miki on the bike, Klara (Artur's wife). Two children in front: Laco and Bandy.

Right: A group of cousins in the snow at our farm in Merašice. Back, left to right: Laco, Bandy, Miki, Juraj, Kati (died in Auschwitz). Front: Chava, myself, Tikva.

Left: Laco, Miki and myself

Left: My mother with her brother Osy. He was arrested with us, but was separated from us and sent to Buchenwald. We never saw him again.

Right: Laco, baby Chava, Margo and her husband Dula.

Left: Aunt Margo's husband, Dula, and son, Laco. During our time in Bergen-Belsen she had no idea whether they were alive or dead; Laco survived, but Dula died.

Left: Our family in 1942: myself, Mother and Miki. This is the photo that my father carried with him during 1944–1945, not knowing if his family was alive or dead.

Right: This is my Uncle Osy in 1937 with (left to right) Laco and Chava, and my brother Miki. Osy was arrested with us, and at Sered camp was separated out with the other men in the family and sent to Buchenwald where he died.

Left: My wonderful Aunt Margo in later years. Her strength and ingenuity helped keep us alive in the dreadful time spent in Bergen-Belsen.

Left: Fr Ladislav Harangozo, the Catholic priest in our village who was a friend of my parents. At great risk to himself he got false papers for my mother and us boys when we had to flee the village and he taught Miki and me how to bless ourselves and a little Catholic doctrine in order to disguise our Jewishness in case we should be questioned.

Right: Grandmother Rosalia on the day of our arrest 1944.

was agreed that it was too dangerous to remain where they were, so they were sent on to Szodliget, just outside Budapest, a popular spot for tourists, where the locals were used to seeing strangers about the place. They rented a house and Artur pretended to their new neighbours that he worked as a clerk in Budapest. However, actions speak louder than words: every morning, Monday to Friday, he took the train to Budapest where he was obliged to spend the day in the library or the galleries – anywhere that didn't involve spending money. Money was understandably tight since there was no wage coming in. They were being supported by their Budapest relatives, who were compensated, in turn, by the Slovakian relatives.

In fact, it was an expensive existence. Due to food shortages the Hungarian government introduced a ration system. Families received points, depending on their number, that permitted them to buy allocated rations of sugar, meat, flour, butter and so forth. No points meant no shopping. Naturally, since Artur and his family were illegal, they weren't eligible for any points, so they had to buy everything on the black market. But at least they were safe ... for now.

Then, in April 1944, the government was overthrown by the fascist party, with the help of the German army. As Germany started losing battles, Hitler grew twitchy, wanting only his ardent fanatics ruling the countries around him. Inevitably, as soon as the Nazis entered Hungary, the persecution of

Hungarian Jews began almost immediately.

Suddenly, my relatives found themselves unexpectedly living next door to the enemy when German soldiers moved in, parking their armoured vehicles in the street outside. The situation took a sort of comical turn when the soldiers befriended Bandy and Juraj because they could speak German. One day they invited the boys for a drive, telling them they were going to get petrol. They were lucky to survive as, on the way to the fuel depot, the sky filled with American planes that began emptying their bombs on the town. The Germans stopped short of the depot just as it exploded in front of their eyes. Day instantly turned to night as clouds of black smoke expanded thick and fast, cutting off the sunlight. It was only the first of many raids to come.

Still, the Hungarian fascists, spurred on by the Nazis, increased their efforts to rid the county of its Jews. Deportations were enforced with train-loads of Jewish men, women and children being driven to Auschwitz. When this proved too slow a system for the impatient authorities, they simply shot their prey on the shores of the Danube, taking the time only to fling the bodies into the water.

Artur and Klara grew nervous, convinced that their Hungarian neighbours had begun to suspect their true identities. They were right. One morning in November 1944, there was a knock on their door. Two policemen stood outside, demanding to see their ID cards. As soon as Artur handed them over, the officers wanted more proof: 'This isn't enough. We'll need to see your birth certificates and your citizenship papers too.' Thinking fast, Artur explained that he had left the papers in his office in Budapest. The men replied that he had three hours to fetch the documents; meanwhile they would remain outside his house, thereby holding his family hostage until his return. My uncle thanked the men for their patience and went into the kitchen to tell his wife and children where he was going: 'Okay, this is it. It's the only thing I can think to do. I'll go to Budapest and you must try to escape and meet me there, at the station. If you don't turn up within three hours I'll assume you've been arrested and will give myself up to make sure we're not separated.'

Klara kissed him goodbye, knowing that it was all down to her now – her family's freedom and ultimate survival. As quickly and quietly as possible, she got the boys to put on as many layers of clothing as they could while she packed a few things for herself and Artur into one of their rucksacks. Next they headed out the back door and down to the end of their garden where she ripped out a piece of the flimsy fencing, allowing the three of them to squeeze through into the neighbours', who luckily weren't at home. Two minutes later they were on the street behind their house, the police still standing at their front door. They could have walked to the station, but Klara felt there wasn't time for that. She was convinced that once they were discovered to be missing, the officers would immediately know they had gone to get the train after Artur. Therefore, they needed to move faster than on foot.

Glancing at her watch she saw that the only bus that passed by the train station was due in the next couple of minutes. 'Come on, boys, as fast as you can to the bus stop,' she said. This involved a wild sprint to the other end of the town, but they got there just as the bus trundled into sight. Klara felt helpless, though, when she saw how packed the bus was. It only made this journey once a day so it was in great demand, and when it was full the driver would merely shrug a half-hearted apology as he kept his foot down on the accelerator. She stuck out her hand, sending a little prayer heavenwards. My aunt always proclaimed what happened next to be 'God's good miracle'. Slowly, the bus pulled in by the stop while she and boys pressed close together, torn between not wanting to look behind them to see if they had been followed and not wanting to appear as if this bus could actually save their lives. When the old bus eventually braked in front of them, the door cranked open and not one, not two, but *three* individuals disembarked, thus allowing three more to get on in their place – Klara, Bandy and Juraj.

And so they made it to the station, got the train to Budapest and met up with Artur before the three hours were up. But now what? Unwilling to hang around the capital now that the police were after them, they decided to return to Piešťany in search of help there. After all, it was their real home. They took the next train to Vrbov and waited until it was dark to make the journey back over the Hungarian border, this time without a greedy guide to lead the way. They certainly had God on their side because not only did they remember their way, but they also got safely onto a train once they reached Slovakia. It seemed too risky for the four of them to go to Piešťany, there were so many people who knew them there; and so they decided that Artur and the boys would get out at a smaller station en route and that Klara would continue on alone, in search of her brother, Imro. It was another nerve-racking journey for her as she hadn't heard from Imro in a long time and had no idea whether he was still in Piešťany or not – and if he was, would he be able to help them? Once more, the safety of the family weighed heavily upon her.

As it turned out, Imro had managed to avoid deportation thanks mainly to the kindly gentile who had taken over his shop. Also, he had bribed a few important officials to destroy his paperwork. Klara was overjoyed to see him; they hadn't set eyes on one another for two years. Typical of her brother, he was determined to help her out in any way he could – and it wasn't as if he hadn't already had his hands full. Both his mother, Gisela, and his wife, Marta, had just been listed for deportation and he had been making enquiries about safe houses for them. He told Klara to fetch Artur and the children; he would put them up in his own house until he found them a place.

Fortunately for all involved, he made contact with the Vavrov family who lived in the town and had made it known that they would help them out. This brave family were actually going to dig a bunker under one of their bedrooms. What with the constant Jew hunts and houses being searched, it was the only practical solution. Work began immediately. The room was cleared of furniture, then the floorboards were carefully lifted up, one by one, and then the digging began, in silence. Every bucket of earth was taken outside at night and flattened into the ground so that the neighbours wouldn't wonder at the sight of dark soil where there had previously been none.

It wasn't a big hole, just three by four metres, for eight people. When it was finished, lathes of wood were placed around the wall with support beams, and a tube, for air, was fed to the outside of the house. The floorboards were laid back down and the furniture returned to its rightful place, and the tiny building site was a normal bedroom once more. To access the bunker you had to squeeze through a small, square opening behind the kitchen cabinet. Inside, there were just two sets of bunk beds, side by side, with a bucket behind a curtain for a bathroom. That was all there was room for. Light was provided by one solitary light bulb.

The four Scheimovitzes, as well as Imro, Marta and Grandmother (*Omama*) Gisela moved in overnight. There was also a girl, Dusi, a twenty-year-old cousin of Klara and Imro, who had been discovered hiding under her bed by a neighbour. A Hlinka guard had arrived one afternoon for her parents. Luckily they didn't bother searching the house or she would surely have been found. For the next few days she lived on the food in the pantry and was extremely lucky for a second time that the person who saw some movement through a window was a genuine friend.

Klara's mother proved a little too wide for the small entrance, but they managed to shove her through. It meant, however, that while the others could sneak out for a few minutes at night to breathe in some fresh air, she was to be stuck in that pit for the next five months. As you might imagine, it was an extremely confined existence. Reading and knitting were the only occupations. The women would knit the same garment, over and over again, unravelling it as soon as they had finished, recasting their stitches anew. There was no room to walk around, you either sat on one of the two bottom bunks or you lay down, it was as simple as that.

Every meal was cooked by Mrs Vavrov. This was no mean feat as it meant she had to buy food for extra mouths without causing any suspicion. Using several shops, she bought the same ingredients over and over in small amounts. Not content with hiding eight Jews beneath their house, this family went a giant step further and built a second bunker beneath their stables, where they hid another ten people. It was an incredible and courageous act. I honestly don't know how Mrs Vavrov managed to shop for more than twenty people in secret.

However, the family didn't escape suspicion for too long. When the 1944 rebellion took place, that is, when Slovaks – Jews and Gentiles – began to fight back, the Vavrovs helped the partisans in any way they could ... and it was noticed. A few months later, on a winter's evening, a fierce group made up of Hlinka guards and German soldiers arrived to search the house. They had dogs with them too, and I can only imagine that the sight of those animals must have been a particularly horrific one for the Vavrovs. As the men walked the dogs into *that* bedroom, Mrs Vavrov and her farmer husband and two sons must have expected the worst – only it never came; there was no excited barking, no scratching at the treacherous floorboards and no triumphant cry at finding Imro and the others. Yet the Vavrovs did suffer in the end. The disappointed guards, finding no evidence to support whatever they had suspected, decided to make a point, at any rate, by taking away the two sons. Just one of them made it home after the war, for a brief visit. He was dangerously emaciated and died shortly after liberation – a heavy price to pay, for any family.

The Jews remained in their bunker until the morning of

4 April 1945, when Mr Vavrov wrenched open the entrance behind the kitchen cabinet and yelled to the bewildered occupants: 'Come out! Come out! The Russians are here. You're free. It's all over!'

After the war, the Vavrovs were awarded a medal for their bravery by the Slovak president, and a few years ago their names were added to those listed as Righteous Amongst Nations, as compiled by the Yad Vashem Holocaust museum: this is the not terribly long list of people who, in a period of great fear, somehow found the strength to risk everything to save Jewish friends, neighbours and even strangers.

PART II
BERGEN-BELSEN

Bergen-Belsen is situated in the middle of a thick forest in Lower Saxony, approximately 60km north of Hanover, Germany. Huts were built here in 1936 to house three thousand German construction workers who were employed on a nearby site. Three years later, in 1939, these workers were replaced with prisoners of war (POWs), the first batch of six hundred or so made up of French and Belgian soldiers. Sometime in 1941 about twenty thousand Soviet prisoners arrived, instantly stretching the meagre facilities to breaking point. Thanks to freezing temperatures, starvation rations and the spread of disease, eighteen thousand inmates died within twelve months, under the command of SS officer, Adolf Haas.

In 1943, on the order of Heinrich Himmler, Bergen-Belsen was turned into a concentration camp and over the next few months thousands of Jewish men, women and children found themselves interned here, along with Roma gypsies, homosexuals and anti-Nazi Christians. The camp was divided into sections: the men's camp, the women's camp, Hungarian camp, Star camp, Special Camp for Jews (the meaning behind this name is unknown) and the neutral camp. The Star Camp was so named as its residents, mainly Dutch Jews, had to wear their Yellow Star. They received better treatment because of their hostage status – these were the prisoners that the Germans exchanged for their own imprisoned compatriots in other countries.

A few witnesses claimed that the camp had its own gas chamber, but no evidence has been found to support this. There was a crematorium, built in 1943, which burnt corpses, two at a time, twenty-four hours a day, in an effort to hide from outsiders the huge numbers that were dying here. Though it wasn't an extermination camp, it is estimated that over seventy thousand prisoners lost their lives here, mostly due to the lack of nourishment, the extreme temperatures of the ferocious German winter and the inevitable rampage of diseases like typhoid that thrived in circumstances such as these.

The camp was finally liberated by British soldiers on 15 April 1945, and they subsequently burnt it to the ground to prevent the spread of disease.

Chapter 10

• • • • • •

Life in Bergen-Belsen

Screams woke us up a few minutes after we closed our eyes, or that's what it seemed like. A whistle was shrieking at us, along with the female SS Guards: '*Aufstehen, schnell, heraus auf Appell*' (Hurry up and get out for rollcall!). It was 7.00am and getting bright outside. We were slow to move, despite the rudeness of the guards, all of us still exhausted from the previous day's and, indeed, week's events. The dormitory smelt of damp clothes and unwashed bodies. We struggled to shove our wet feet back into our muddy, tattered shoes. Meanwhile, losing patience with us, the guards started to hound us with what was becoming a familiar refrain: 'Get out, you dirty Jews!'

My mother helped me with my shoes and, when we were

all ready, we followed the others outside. We were instructed to form lines at the back of our block under the suspicious eye of a male SS officer, who was flanked by his female colleagues. He stood watching us, his legs apart and a leather strap dangling from his hands which were clasped behind his back. Two other guards were in the watch tower, idly following the proceedings, their fingers curled around their guns, ready to shoot. What did they think we were going to do? I looked around and could only see a bedraggled group of mothers, children and grandmothers. My breath caught in my chest. I had never known fear like this before.

There was a lot of stumbling around; none of us knew what we were meant to be doing. Suddenly I heard one voice above the rest, giving us all instructions. It was Margo. She was taking charge, arranging us into neat lines. This was typical of my mother's sister. When she spoke, people listened. Back in 1922 she had done something that was completely out of the ordinary, for Slovak women at least: armed with her qualifications as a dentist – or perhaps I should say dental technician as dentistry was not the same as it is today – she opened up her own practice. Later, after she was married, she had her own laundry and dry cleaning business. Margo was very enterprising. Miki and I were very fond of her. In fact, I would go so far as to say that she was my favourite aunt. She was very like our mother – dark brown hair, neat figure, always dressed in stylish clothes and wearing make-up, plus she shared Mother's outgoing personality and ability to make friends. The biggest difference between them was that Margo always had a cigarette in her hand, whereas our mother didn't smoke. Her natural bossiness sometimes annoyed my father, but overall they had a good relationship based on mutual respect – which was a good thing, since, back in the carefree days, she was a frequent visitor to our house. But she certainly wasn't a push-over. I remember her locking me into the bedroom when I didn't do my home-work – education was very important to her and she had little patience for slackers.

Her efforts were noticed. The SS officer pointed to her and asked her if she spoke German: '*Sprichst du Deutsch*?' The man had such a hard, mean face that I became very scared for my aunt. Everyone stopped what they were doing, wonder-ing what was going to happen next. Margo calmly replied in German: '*Ja*' (Yes). He called her over and said in a voice loud, and harsh enough to be heard by the whole crowd: '*Du wirdst die Blockälteste sein*' (You will be the hut leader). It wasn't a question. He ordered her to continue getting us all into four lines, one behind the other. When we were in position she had to go and stand beside him while he addressed us.

It wasn't a welcoming speech, nor did he provide us with any information beyond the fact that we were in Belsen camp, in Germany. Gesturing to Margo, he told us: 'You are not permitted to bother any of the staff. Any questions or problems should be brought to your block leader, this woman here. You should also know that trouble-makers will not be tolerated.'

Next he turned to Margo, leaving her in no doubt as to the serious nature of her new job: 'You are in charge of everyone standing here. You will organise roll-call twice a day, first thing in the morning and then in the evening. You will make sure that the block is always spotless and my officers will be making regular inspections to see that everything is exactly how it should be. You must collect the food from the kitchen, so you will need to choose four women to help you, and it's also up to you to share it out. It is your job to pass on all orders and I hold you personally responsible for their upkeep. If anything goes wrong or rules are broken without your preventing it, you will pay with your life.'

I don't think that there would have been any volunteers for such a precarious position.

Margo was told it was breakfast time, prompting her to choose four women to accompany her to the kitchen. While she was doing this, everyone else took the opportunity to settle in and exchange their wet clothes for whatever they had in their suitcases. We had been wearing the same clothes for eight days now, so it was a relief to put on clean underwear and socks.

I didn't eat the breakfast. It was some sort of watery black coffee with two thin slices of bread. There was no canteen or dining area; we just had our meals sitting on our beds. My mother begged me to eat, but I refused to touch the ugly-looking bread, a far cry from the wonderful pastries that she and my grandmother used to bake. It was to become a typical conversation between us because I had always been a finicky eater. Margo warned against drinking the water from the taps in the washroom because it was contaminated and sure to give us typhus or diarrhoea, and she advised us to stretch out our coffee ration since it was the only liquid available.

It wasn't that I wasn't hungry – I'm sure I was – but I was much too scared to deal with the strange bread and horrible coffee. Why did everything have to be so different? I had hardly spoken a word over the past few days. I suppose I must have gone into some sort of shock. Chava was the only one of our family who looked as terrified as I felt. The angry guards, the big guns, the barbed wire – we really didn't understand what was going on. Why couldn't we just go home, back to our own bedrooms with their clean blankets and soft pillows? Why did we have to take that awful train journey to end up in this dreadful place? I longed to see my father, wherever he was. I pictured him ploughing the fields in Merašice, even though I knew he was no longer there; but I didn't know how else to picture him. Miki did his best to hide his own fears, no doubt feeling he had to lead by example and be brave for his younger brother and cousin.

Seeing me refuse the miserable breakfast, *Omama* Rosalia quietly called her three grandchildren to sit beside her, on her bed. From her suitcase she took out a roll of salami. I couldn't believe my eyes. The smell of it was so familiar – and downright comforting – that I felt my heart tug with nostalgia. 'Now, my dears,' she said, 'we must make this last. So we'll just have a small slice each, enough to make the bread more agreeable.' We sat beside her every morning until the salami was gone.

Later in the day we managed to have a quick, unpleasant wash. The washroom was outside the block and completely open to the elements. Very basic, it was just a row of taps over a long sink beneath a battered sheet of corrugated metal. There were no walls and since it was November, the temperatures were freezing. We also discovered the 'toilets' – latrines, really – as they were no more than a filthy trench dug into the ground. The stench almost knocked me off my feet, making me determined to use them as little as possible.

Margo had to assemble us again when the German soldiers arrived to take our details. The children merely stood by silently while their mothers reeled off their information: name, date of birth and country of origin. All the inmates then received a square piece of cloth on which was our own individual number. Our mothers were instructed to sew them onto the left-hand side of our coats. And so we no longer had names, only numbers.

Lunch was a thin soup consisting of beet, which was normally fed to pigs, and some small potatoes boiled in hot water. It smelt bad. I took no more than a few mouthfuls. By the time everyone had been registered, it was supper time. This meal was just a second breakfast – a small cup of watery coffee and two slices of bread. Immediately after we ate, we lay down to sleep. There was nothing else to do and we were still very tired after the train journey. And so ended our first day in Belsen concentration camp.

The next morning we were already outside, ready and waiting for the roll-call at 7.00am. I realise now that Margo's life depended on efficiency in this sort of thing: she couldn't afford for any of us to dawdle or be sloppy. We were, however, completely at the mercy of the bitter-faced female guards. Obviously they knew we were standing in the cold weather – it was winter after all – which was probably why they made us wait for them, sometimes thirty minutes, sometimes two hours. It was all about reminding us that we were their inferiors and they were our masters. These women never had a hair out of place. They were always perfectly groomed, with painted nails and lips, dressed in their trim uniforms and polished boots. This was all part of the ploy to show us up: in comparison to their perfection, we were dirty Jews. They each carried a leather whip and were given to lashing out at inmates who didn't immediately stand to attention when they passed by.

On that second day we took more notice of our surroundings. Our block backed up against a wire fence, behind which was a watchtower. When I look at maps from 1944 now I can say for sure that we were in what was then called the 'special camp for Jews', a very strange and inexplicable name. We couldn't see much of the rest of the camp from here as our view was blocked by other huts; only at night when lights were on did we have some sense of the huge size of Bergen-Belsen. Except for brief visits to the washroom and latrine, we spent the day in our hut.

The constant smell of burning was something that followed us around until we just stopped noticing it. It was coming from the crematorium, the chimney of leaping flames I had seen from the edge of the forest. I don't think I was aware of what it really was, only that the smell was bad. Another detail that I managed to ignore, as a frightened young boy, was the mortuary, which was only about one hundred metres away. Over the next couple of weeks we would become very used to the sight of dead bodies being collected every day to be brought to the mortuary to await their turn for the crematorium. Thankfully, I was completely ignorant of the magnitude of all of this activity, despite the fact it was being carried out in front of my eyes. None of us children seemed to notice anything beyond what we needed to know to get through our day – that's the beauty of childhood, when ignorance is sometimes bliss. On the other hand,

I'm sure the mothers and grandmothers were considerably burdened by what they saw and knew. It was they who had to worry about dying every single day while we, the ignorant children, just dealt with our situation from moment to moment. I certainly had no idea that things could get any worse than they already were. The SS guards and soldiers never spoke to us or laid a finger on us children. We were completely ignored.

But I remember one day in particular when we, the children, were forced to deal with the realities that our adults were living with. We had been at the camp for maybe ten days or so when we followed Margo out for the morning roll-call. As usual, we were kept waiting, this time for an hour, for the SS women. By this stage we were used to this. However, what was unusual about that morning was the fact that they were accompanied by several soldiers who were fully armed. All around me there was feverish whispering: 'Something is wrong. Why all these soldiers?'

We all had to answer '*Ja*', when our number was called. But after the roll-call on this morning we were instructed to return to our hut to fetch blankets and towels because we were being taken elsewhere for a hot shower. Now, this was unexpected. I was glad to hear that the water would be hot and very much relieved that I wouldn't have to face the freezing washroom. Margo led us back to our huts and there was a bit of a scramble for towels. I saw some of the women exchange strange looks while one leaned in to whisper to her neighbour: 'What do you think? Do you believe them?' The friend just shrugged in reply, her eyes full of tears. I wanted to ask my mother what was going on but she was busy helping *Omama* and Chava find towels. Margo stood at the door, urging us to be quick; the guards were outside waiting impatiently. We rushed back out and were put in rows of three before being marched along the perimeter of the camp with soldiers on either side of us. It was very cold and eerily quiet. I felt more scared than usual, but wasn't sure why, although it did bother me that none of the adults would meet my eye.

Just in front of me I saw a woman remove her wedding ring and fling it into the dirt, muttering to her companions: 'Those bastards aren't getting their hands on my gold!' I couldn't understand why everyone looked so petrified. Why were they so worried about having a shower? I had heard plenty of women wishing they could have a decent wash in hot water. What was the problem? Of course, the adults knew about the gas chambers at Auschwitz, we children did not. I can only imagine now what those women went through, wondering was that where we were heading.

It felt like we walked miles but maybe it was only for thirty minutes or so. They stopped us in front of a large concrete building which had a tall chimney protruding from its roof. There were several gasps at the sight of it. One woman even cried out: 'Oh my God!' Miki and Chava looked as puzzled as I felt.

'*Schnell, schnell*!' The guards began to hurry us inside. It was like a long hall and there was a strong chemical smell that stung the back of my throat. There were many wooden benches and steel trolleys with a long bar on top, where we were told to hang up our coats and clothes. Margo passed on the order to undress and leave everything, including our blankets, on the trolleys. The soldiers stood around and stared at the naked mothers and grandmothers, cracking jokes about them and making rude faces. I was ashamed and shamed at the same time. At nine years of age I couldn't have articulated my feelings, but I did feel tainted in some way. Needless to say, I had never seen a naked woman before. It was shocking to see the garishly white, wrinkled, pathetic bodies of the older women, not to mention my own grandmother's; they seemed so sad and defenceless. The leering soldiers added to the horrible tension. There was a particularly uncomfortable moment when one of the soldiers, who looked much younger than the rest, approached us, his gaze firmly on the naked Chava. Just like Miki and me, my eight-year-old cousin didn't look typically Jewish. Her hair was blond and very fine, and fell well past her shoulders. Margo stepped in front of her daughter and coolly met the soldier's eye. Haughtily he asked her: 'What is this little Aryan girl doing here?' My aunt's reply was brief and purposely loud enough to be heard by the SS women: 'Go away!' Fortunately he did what he was told, without another word.

Despite the constant cries to hurry up, everyone seemed to move in slow motion. As soon as we were undressed, we were each given a bar of soap and pushed through a metal door, into a large room which had a concrete floor and pipes, with shower heads, criss-crossing the entire ceiling. Then it went silent.

The soldiers stopped shouting and hung back from us, as the door was slammed behind us. All the women stared at the ceiling, and some of them began to cry quietly. My mother grabbed me and Miki into her body which was icy cold to touch. Her heart was beating very fast and her breathing sounded forced, as if she was gulping for air. I was too confused and terrified to say anything; in fact, nobody spoke a single word. I don't know how long we stood there, perhaps it was a few minutes or perhaps it was only seconds before we heard a rumbling in the pipes. All around the room, women embraced their children, never taking their eyes off the ceiling. Suddenly warm water spurted out of the shower heads – which, of course, was just what I and the other children had expected. I waited for my mother to release me so that I could wash myself with the soap. Once again I was mystified by the women's reactions. Some of them sobbed and laughed at the same time as they reached up to touch the water. Others hugged each other, smiling in delight, and using words like 'blessing' and 'miracle'. Children were kissed and even splashed playfully by their mothers. I hadn't seen such smiles nor heard such laughter in a long time.

When the doors opened again we were told to put our clothes back on. It was a wonderfully pleasant surprise to find that they were warm to the touch. Margo was told that all clothes, blankets and towels had been deloused while we showered. Some women found that their leather belts were completely shrivelled up with the heat, but no one was complaining. For the first time in weeks we were clean and warm. Fortunately, we couldn't have known that it would be many, many months before we'd have a shower again – in fact, we would have to wait until after liberation.

One very cold morning we had to stand waiting for roll call for well over an hour, but the guards never came. Finally we were sent back to our block and told that we would be registered later. For now, we were to collect our belongings because we were being moved to another part of the camp. Typically, we had only minutes to do this and assemble ourselves once more in orderly fashion. An SS officer led the way, with Margo in step just behind him, while on either side of us were armed guards as we trudged off. It was our first opportunity to see more of the camp. When we came out on to the main street of the camp we suddenly saw lots of huts with hundreds and hundreds of prisoners wearing the official uniform of what looked to be grubby pyjamas

– loose-fitting jackets and trousers, with long, dull stripes running from neck to ankle. There were even stripes on the caps that the men wore. I couldn't believe how big the place was. It looked much bigger than Merašice and far, far busier.

We passed by the women's camp, which was on our right, and next to that was the men's camp. Each part of the camp was separated by a high wall of barbed wire and then there was a second fence between the camp and the main thoroughfare that we were on. After walking for a few minutes, we took a left turn into the northern part of Bergen-Belsen.

The scenery changed as we followed a narrow path. There were trees to our left and in between these clumps of trees were more wooden huts. We passed what I guessed to be a kitchen from the big aluminium pots and containers that sat outside its door. The path led us off again to our left and this time there were trees on either side of us. I remember thinking how quiet the whole place was; I never heard a single bird sing from all those trees. There were more inmates here, but they were very different from the ones we had passed before. I have to say that it is my adult self rather than the child I was then that shudders at the memory of them – at the time I was too distracted to dwell upon what I saw in front of me. Their heads were shaven and their 'pyjamas' hung from them, making it impossible to tell if they were men or women. Their faces were pale and expressionless, their eyes sunken into their skulls. Occasionally one of these feeble beings would slowly raise an arm at the sight of us, possibly wanting to greet the young children. I do remember a woman – for some reason I am sure of her gender – do her best to wave, but then give up, letting her arm fall down gently back into her lap.

A last turning in the path brought us to the right where we found a hut with the number 207 over the entrance. We had reached our destination. Margo was informed that since she was the *Blockälteste*, she could take the little room inside the door, to the right, with the rest of her family. The whole building was approximately 45 metres long and 9 metres wide, with one bulb in the centre of the ceiling. Down the centre of the hut was a long corridor – on one side was a large dormitory, with our room separated off, and on the other side was the maternity hospital of the camp, where we never went. The dormitory was occupied by about one hundred and thirty Slovak mothers, children and old women. There was another door leading to the maternity hospital across the corridor from our door, but I wouldn't discover what that was for until later.

Chapter 11

· · · · · ·

Settling In

There were two perks to Margo's job. The first one was having our own family room. Any kind of privacy was an absolute luxury, even one that involved sharing a small, bare room with five others. We even had our own lone electric light bulb. That was the only other piece of furniture aside from the beds. Actually, I found it hugely comforting to escape the prying, not to mention eternally worried, eyes of the strangers in the big dormitory outside and certainly my mother, grandmother and aunt looked very relieved with the sleeping arrangements. Our room was approximately 6 metres by 4 metres, ensuring that there was just enough space for the six narrow beds, under which we shoved our suitcases. There was no room to walk around. Our beds came to mean everything to us; we stretched out on them, sat on them to talk or day-dream and also ate on them. As far as I remember, there were some hooks on the wall to hang our coats up – should it ever get warm enough to take them off. Those hooks, apart from the one little window, were the only decoration.

It was quite an ugly, depressing scene on the other side of the window, a world away from the colourful pictures through the windows at home. Merašice seemed as far away as were the perfect, sunny, blue-sky days of summer. To the left we had a great view of the stinking latrine and some trees behind it, and beyond them was a high, wire fence, dotted throughout with hundreds and hundreds of barbed knots. If you turned your head to the right, there was the bit of waste ground where the roll-call was held, more trees and then our nextdoor neighbours' hut, Number 206.

The second perk of Margo's job involved the food, dinner in particular. The three daily meals were sparse and satisfied nobody. I was always hungry and if my small, skinny frame wasn't filled by the meagre portions you can imagine how much worse it was for a grown woman. It appears that we in the children's and mothers' hut were relatively lucky, since the other sections in Belsen received even less to eat.

When the container of watery soup arrived in our hut, our fellow residents would form a queue and, naturally, most of them raced to be first in line, or as near to the front as they could, in their eagerness to eat. Our family group, however, did the exact opposite. Margo told us to wait until the end when any substance in the liquid – the bigger potatoes and cubes of beet, and sometimes even actual pieces of gristle – would be sitting at the bottom of the container, the lighter stuff having floated to the top.

I cried a lot during those first couple of months, mostly at night-time so as not to upset my mother. Miki and I had talked about the fact that since there was nothing Mother could do, and since she was suffering just as much as the two of us, there was no point in adding to her woes with our miseries. It wouldn't be fair. I often thought about my father too, though I wouldn't say that I dwelled on how much I actually missed him. I don't even remembering worrying about him much, more wondering, really, about what had happened to him and where he was now. Isn't that the best and worst thing about human beings, that we can get used to pretty much anything? Sometimes Margo and Mother would whisper together, wondering how the rest of our family was doing. Margo must have been a very strong woman; both her son and husband were gone from her, but if she was ever pained with jealousy at the sight of all the mothers with their children around them, she never let on. Of course, *Omama* Rosalia had lost plenty of her children by now, or, at least, she could only assume she had.

It was the practical things that upset me the most. The weather was absolutely dire that winter and I was cold all the time. My mother would remonstrate with me when I refused to use the wash-room: 'You have to wash yourself. It's important to be clean and, besides, I want to wash the clothes you're wearing.' The taunt of 'dirty Jews' was, undoubtedly, still ringing in her ears, but I didn't care. Instead I would cry: 'No, I can't. I'm freezing! It's too cold and the water stings my skin.' Usually my grandmother would intervene at this point, putting her arm around my shoulders, offering to accompany me so that she could dry me off in no time at all: 'Come on, pet, I promise you that you'll feel a lot better afterwards.'

I recognise now that it was also something to *do*, attending the awful wash-room to lather up in sub-zero temperatures. A certain amount of routine can probably help to retain one's sanity in times of undue stress. The women, including those in my family, only ever left their huts to wash themselves, do their laundry or use the latrine. Having said that, during those first few months, *Omama* sometimes had me walk with her behind the hut for some semblance of exercise. It was a very short walk indeed, but it was something we could *choose* to do, marching a few paces one way and then repeating it again in reverse. It felt like a sort of freedom. Every night my grandmother, just before lights-out at 9.00pm, would let down her long, silvery grey hair and plait it for bed. Then, the next morning, after her breakfast, which included her medication – a revolting green powder that she stirred into her coffee – she would slowly unravel her hair and carefully comb it out before twisting it up again into a bun. Over the coming months an extraordinary amount of time was given over to performing very small, ordinary tasks like these.

The other practicality that caused me much distress was going to the toilet. I've already described the place as an open, stinking trench, but the actual reality was horrible. It was open, which meant you had to get used to crapping in public, sitting alongside other people who were doing the very same thing, forced to listen to the creaks and squeaks that escaped from people's stomachs and bowels, trying not to hold your nose in utter disgust, especially with the older women. And then there was the 'seat' itself, a narrow plank of wood covered in urine, shit and even blood. I noticed how some of the women hovered over the plank, but I was much too small to attempt this. In the early days I had *Omama* or my mother accompany me so that they could hold me over the plank. But after a few weeks they no longer had the strength to lift me up. Therefore I had to sit on the mess, my feet dangling, as I desperately tried not to think about the obvious. In fact, this was easier than you might think. For instance, in the early days I used to wonder about the 'dolls' in the latrines, their naked, glazed limbs and empty staring eyes. I was bewildered by such wanton carelessness. How I wished I had some of my toys with me, but Mother had said there was no room in any of our suitcases, and anyway wasn't I big boy now? But if I had brought my favourite teddy bear or wooden soldier I certainly wouldn't be throwing them out – and what a place to dump them! If these dolls weren't wanted by their owners, then surely they could have been passed on to some other little girl who might appreciate them more.

And then I realised I was mistaken: they weren't dolls at all. Our family room wasn't the only room off the main dormitory in our hut. Earlier I mentioned another door, through which I had discovered another room full of metal beds, one where no children were allowed to enter. The women who worked here always chased us children away, which only served to make us more curious about what went on. One day I heard the most horrific screams coming from behind the door and the strange thing was that none of the women gave it the slightest bit of attention – they just went on with whatever they were doing, continued on with their conversations, as if they couldn't hear a thing. Perhaps it was their nonchalance that encouraged me to investigate – presumably, whatever it was it couldn't be that bad. As soon as it was safe, I gently pushed open the door, just a little, but enough to see a woman lying on the bed, her ridiculously skinny legs up in the air, with two of the workers peering into her naked bottom, from where a bloody mess was protruding.

She was in terrible pain. I couldn't understand the words that she roared, in between ferocious grunts, as she was probably Dutch or Polish.

Needless to say, as the son of a farmer I had seen plenty of births in my short life, but this was the first time I had watched the birth of an actual human being. It was a hundred times more violent than watching a cow bring a calf into the world. There was no sense of order here. The rudeness of the metal bed, the woman's freakishly loud convulsions, the splattering of blood and other liquids, along with the stern, stony expressions on the faces of the nurses, who didn't seem to know how to talk to their patient, provided a blunt education about a world I had, quite rightly, known nothing about. As soon as one of the nurses spotted me I was chased off. But I went back, time and time again. I suppose it was something to do, to watch these dreadful births. God knows how many there were. I'd purposely wait until the screams were at their fiercest, before attempting to push open the door, knowing it must be time for the baby to come out.

None of these newborns survived. Their malnourished mothers had no milk for them, so invariably they didn't last beyond a day or two, whereupon their tiny corpses ended up in the latrine.

The atmosphere in our hut was badly affected by the death of a young girl soon after we arrived. Her name was Miri Reichsfield. An only child, her mother absolutely doted on her. I hope I don't sound too ungenerous when I say that I remember her as being rather spoilt. Aged about thirteen, she had obviously lived a very nice, very easy life before ending up in the camp – as we all had, I suppose, relatively speaking. She didn't try to talk to the other children or anyone else. Her mother was her only companion. During those first days, like most of us, she went into severe shock. Unlike the rest of us, however, she never came out of it. I have already described the horror of the train journey; to have survived that was something in itself, but then to realise that the horror was continuing indefinitely was a hard fact to accept. She didn't have any siblings to distract her from her own thoughts and, I suppose, she was old enough to know more than she wanted to. Very quickly she succumbed to full depression, and would neither talk nor eat, and it took all her mother's strength to get her up for the roll-call. I think Margo may have had to help out with this. The other mothers fretted that their own children would be influenced and scared by seeing someone so young give up.

The speed of her physical deterioration was frightening. When I think about it now it was as if Miri quite simply made the decision not to live anymore – her mind simply shut down, and so, following a week or maybe two, so too did her body. It must have been perceived as a dreadful omen for the other mothers, including my own mother and my aunt. This young girl's death was a blatant reminder of what could so easily happen to their own children. Life in a concentration camp meant – surely – death, sooner or later.

Only one thing, perhaps, continued on as normal inside Belsen. Each night I enjoyed a typically deep, unbroken sleep. Lights had to be out by 9.00pm but I was usually asleep long before that. We couldn't eat enough, go to the toilet in privacy, wash in warm water, go where we want, be re-united with our banished relatives or live in our own homes because 'they' had taken everything away from us. In other words, sleep was the only bodily function that remained ungoverned by the Jew-haters. It remained our one luxury, the one thing we still possessed.

Chapter 12

• • • • • •

Evil Women in
Red Lipstick

One morning in December the six of us were huddled together in our room. Allotted two thin blankets each, we sat in groups of three under six thin blankets, still shivering anyhow, in the freezing temperature. Outside there was a thin, hard layer of snow on the ground. We had had to stand on it for a couple of hours while we waited for the SS women to bother to turn up for the roll-call. I could hardly take my eyes off their heavy coats and thick boots. They looked so warm and comfortable compared to us. Because my family and I had been arrested during the summer months, we had no heavy clothes with us. Our coats and boots, along with hats and scarves, were back in the tiny flat in Bratislava, or maybe they were in Merašice? I couldn't be sure. Our suitcases were small and for all anybody knew then we would be back home well before Christmas.

That morning the guards had inflicted on us a particular favourite of theirs. It wasn't enough that we had had to stand in our flimsy clothes and broken shoes for hours on end. Perhaps one of them picked up on the weary relief we felt, but tried our best to hide, at their eventual arrival, and this provoked them to torture us even further. Every day, from the very moment that we assembled outside, usually well before the 7.00am deadline for Margo's sake, all we thought about was getting the performance over with as fast as possible so that we could head indoors, back to the cheerless comfort of our narrow beds. And, of course, this was especially true on a winter's morning. And, *of course*, anything that we dirty, no-good Jews wanted, anything that might give us some sort of relief, however temporary, or hope for an improvement, however minor, in our day-to-day routine was utterly abhorrent to these glamorous girls, some of whom were only seven or eight years older than my brother.

So, this is how they would proceed: We had to answer '*Ja*' when we heard our number called out. There were 130 of us and it could take a while, particularly when the SS women put their minds to delaying it. Just because they were finally standing in front of us did not mean that we were close to returning to our beds. It always seemed to be the coldest, wettest mornings that somehow they would reach 127 or 128 and then, just as the group dared to become restless at the thought that we were almost there, almost free to escape inside, the woman in charge of the drill would suddenly exclaim to her already smirking friends: 'Oops, I've made a mistake. Now, how did I manage that? Oh well, we'll just have to start all over again.'

There were new huts under construction a couple of hundred metres away from where we stood each morning. Some token pieces of wood jutted out of the snow while all was quiet on the building site. I didn't think anything about them until Miki whispered to me, as we sat under the flimsy blankets: 'That wood. Did you notice it when we were outside?' I nodded, not knowing what he meant. 'Well, couldn't we grab some to burn in the stove?' What a brilliant idea. How clever my brother was to think of it. There was an old, disused stove in the communal room, where the rest of our block slept. I sat up straight: 'Yes, of course!' The two of us headed off before our mother or Margo could stop us. In fact, I was glad to see that the wood wasn't too far from the door of our hut. We ran over and, as quickly as we could, chose only the small, seemingly insignificant pieces before turning 'homewards'.

It was a horrible shock to suddenly hear, in the distance, angry shouts of '*Halt! Halt!*' Neither of us stopped nor turned to see who had caught us thieving; instead we sprinted, much like the rabbits in the fields at Merašice when they'd been surprised eating the crops, back through the door of the hut and into the room, making the others gasp in fright. There was no time to explain. I copied Miki, throwing the precious wood, now thoroughly unwanted by the both of us, under the bed nearest the door, and then pulling the blankets over the side to hide it from sight.

It was only a matter of seconds before we heard one of the SS women shouting: 'Where is the *Blockälteste*?' Margo, instantly pale and grave, hurried outside. This was her job, after all. Whenever there was trouble of any sort she had to accompany the commanding officer until the whole business had reached its end. A couple of days earlier she had had to stand by and solemnly watch a woman beaten almost to death with a leather strap for not jumping to attention for a passing SS guard. Actually, we were all made to watch. The beating took place in the area where we stood for the roll-call. All through it the officer screamed abuse: '*Du verfluchte Jüdin!*' (You damned Jewess!) I couldn't look away. None of us did. The SS women were never nice or warm or friendly, I knew that much, but I would never, ever have believed that a woman with pretty hair and fiery red lipstick, that reminded me of my mother dressing up for cards at the priest's house, would be capable of such violence. The inmate was thin and already broken, the complete opposite of her attacker, who was plump and vibrant as she dropped blow after blow down upon the woman's head and shoulders. The blood that flowed was as bright as the lipstick.

So, you see, this was deadly serious. I was so scared I couldn't even cry; the tears were frozen somewhere in the back of my head, which was pounding with every beat of my heart, while Miki, who never showed his fear, was actually trembling. Again we heard the voice of the enraged guard: 'Two people were seen running with stolen property. Therefore this block is going to be searched until the culprits and the illegal goods are found.' I imagined my aunt barely nodding her head in agreement, eyes to the ground, trying not to appear unduly worried and then I imagined her being beaten up for our thieving, just like the other unfortunate woman. Or, worse still – for hadn't the SS man told her that she would be held responsible for any wrongdoing in the camp – that she would pay with her life? Or maybe our mother would be murdered instead, since it was her children who had committed the crime? I looked over at my brother who appeared to be having the very same thoughts as me. What had we risked?

The door to our room was flung open. The inspection would begin with us. Miki, Chava, *Omama* Rosalia, Mother and I stood up straight, each beside our own bed, staring dead ahead. We were as practised as any army when it came to discipline. Margo's white face peered in at us from behind the broad shoulders of the SS guard. It wasn't the one who had beaten up the inmate – not that this was of any comfort, since they were all as mean as each other. She was fairly small and had dark brown hair that matched the colour of her eyes. Flashing us all a look of disgust, she marched over to the first bed and yanked up the covers to check under the bed. To this day I cannot be sure that I continued to breathe as she made her way from bed to bed. How long did it take her to reach the bed under which we had thrown the wood? Five seconds – one for each bed she checked?

It was the strangest thing. Perhaps she reasoned, during those few seconds, that none of us in this luxurious family room would dare to be so stupid as to steal camp property since we had more to lose than the others in the main dormitory and, furthermore, that Margo, who had proved herself to be an efficient and intelligent leader, would never allow her actual life to be jeopardised like this. Or perhaps it was an act of God. Whatever it was, she straightened herself up after the fifth bed and strode by the sixth, declaring to us: '*Da ist nichts!*' (There is nothing here!)

Margo followed her out to the main room where we listened to her scream and shout abuse at the other mothers and grandmothers for the next twenty minutes or so. Only when she had given up on her mission and left our block did we dare to speak. Miki and I promised our mother that we would never again do anything like that. When Margo finally returned, it was to breathe the huge sigh of relief that she had been holding in. Before she could give us a piece of her mind, Mother rushed to tell her sister of our fervent promise never to steal wood or anything else again. The six of us returned to our previous positions, two groups of three under the paper-thin blankets and together we discussed the miracle of the sixth bed, and the dreadful possibilities that might have befallen us had the SS guard not cut short her search.

If I had to remember what the camp sounded like, what noise would make me remember living there every day, I would have to say it was the sound of enraged SS women screaming foul-mouthed abuse at the tops of their voices. It was pretty much a daily occurrence. Within our camp the screaming usually started at some point during the daily inspection. Perhaps some bed was dishevelled or a dirty plate had been left out. The perpetrator of this domestic outrage would be slapped and/or told they wouldn't be allowed a meal until the following day.

In fact, this was relatively easy-going when compared to the punishments meted out in the women's camp next door to us. They tended to be a lot more fierce. I remember a constant barrage of beatings and punishments inflicted on the inmates there. The two camps were separated by a tall wall of barbed wire, but we could see in. This was a typical sight: some poor emaciated woman standing barefoot on a wooden box, her head shaven to the skull, her flimsy dress utterly pointless in the freezing weather, bearing around her neck a sign of shame. More often than not the sign told of the heinous crime: 'I stole a potato', for example. Some of these women would fall down after a couple of hours, never to be seen again. That was probably the point of the exercise, forcing desperately starving women to stand for hours on end in sub-zero temperatures – a cruel, slow death.

Irma Grese, the renowned 'Beautiful Beast', arrived in Belsen in March 1945. Her fierce reputation, which was developed and nurtured during her time in Ravensbruck and Aus-chwitz concentration camps, preceded her. She was indeed beautiful, one of Hitler's finest, with her bright blue eyes and blond hair. Born in 1923, she had trained to be a nurse after leaving school. I wonder what might have become of her had the war not intervened because, of course, she didn't go on to care for people, to dote upon children or to look after the sick – in fact, she did the very opposite. This is why I want to mention her because, for me, she represents, with her behav-iour, the personification of the horror that sprang from the Nazis' hatred for the Jews.

When she was just twenty years old she ran the selection

process at Auschwitz with her mentor, Joseph Mengele — that is, she actually chose who was to live as well as the thousands who were to die. She walked about in heavy boots and carried both a pistol and a whip, and all three items — boots, pistol and whip — were wilfully inflicted on human beings who crossed her in some little way. She shot men, women and children in cold blood, whipped inmates until they were bloody and torn and on the ground, when she would kick them about the head until they lost consciousness or died, whichever happened first. We heard about her penchant for setting her half-starved dogs on prisoners, whom she had tied up in some way and made completely unable to defend themselves.

I was very lucky in that as a child I remained ignorant of the barbarity she was capable of. She visited our block just once. It was a sunny morning in March and we had just finished the roll-call. What I remember is how her blond hair shone in the sunlight and how young she looked. All we received from her was a brief, cursory glance, and nothing more. I remember her whip, her polished nails and her heavy boots.

Tried by the British military court a few months after the war ended, Irma Grese was sentenced to death. Rumour has it that she spent her last night singing German national ballads in her cell, proud and haughty to the very end. Her last words to the hangman, as he put the rope around her neck, were an order: '*Schnell! Schnell!*' (Hurry! Hurry!) She died on 13 December 1945, just twenty-two years of age.

Perhaps one of the most dreadful aspects of the whole camp was the fact that the SS women and armed soldiers were not the worst of our tormentors. No, that position was held by the prisoners themselves – that is, the ones who cosied up to our captors by walking over the backs of their fellow inmates. They were known as the 'Capos' and were invaluable in the running of such a big camp. In order to become one, you had to earn the trust of the SS and, as you may well imagine, that meant performing feats of stoic cruelty upon the other prisoners while displaying an ardour for full cooperation with the Nazis by betraying everyone around you. Success meant life-affirming privileges, from warm clothing to sufficient edible food. They also had their own residence, a reserved section away from the other inmates' huts. Their responsibilities ranged from running the labour squads to supervising the distribution of food, to managing entire blocks, and the camp authorities encouraged them to whip and punish their unfortunate companions for the most minor breaches of discipline. In their enthusiasm to impress their superiors they frequently proved far more brutal than the SS themselves.

One of these lethal hypocrites was a Jewess from Slovakia. Her name, Zuza Gross, had been on the first list of deportations, sending her on a train to Auschwitz in 1942. Two years later, in December 1944, this Jewish prisoner arrived in Belsen with the fancy title of '*Lagerälteste*' (camp leader), which meant she was in charge of all the Capos. They reported to her and she told them what to do. But what had she done to earn this promotion? God only knows. She was a good-looking girl in her twenties and though she didn't wear the SS uniform there were certain similarities with those women, most notably the vibrant lipstick and pretty hair. Rumours spiralled that she had slept her way into management. Unfortunately, I can't verify them, although there was a story involving a German soldier falling in love with a Jewess in Auschwitz and promising to save her if she married him – but this, I don't think, was Zuza.

When she heard about the mother and children's block – our block – she made it her business to come and visit us. It was the first of maybe three visits in all. She was actually quite pleasant unless there were Germans nearby, and then she would compete with them to see who could scream the loudest over a dirty dish or an unmade bed. One day, Margo, after some deliberation with my mother, decided to go and see Zuza in her office and ask her if she could help get more food for the children. My aunt obviously felt she could make this request to a fellow Slovakian who had chatted with her on previous visits. However, Zuza exploded in anger and actually pushed Margo down the steps outside her door, shouting for all to hear: 'How dare you come to me like this!' But a couple of days later our rations improved ever so slightly.

Today I'm a little unsure about what I think of Zuza and her ilk. In one way, I think it's a revolting feature of the Holocaust that these people were forced to collaborate in their own destruction. After the war, many of the Capos were put on trial and some were sentenced to death for their beastly behaviour. I suppose they were just trying to survive like the rest of us – they had found a way to improve their lot and were desperate enough to ignore any ethical foibles that might have occurred to them. Regarding Zuza, I never actually saw her whip or physically abuse anyone (aside from pushing Margo), but she certainly enforced rigorous punishments, like food deprivation or solitary confinement, especially if she caught one of the women trying to talk to a male prisoner in the next block.

Zuza was one of those arrested after the war. She was put on trial, back home in Czechoslovakia, for crimes committed in Auschwitz. The reason I know what happened to her is that she wrote to Margo, begging her to come to her defence. Her letter caused quite a stir in our family and Margo, confused about her own feelings, consulted her lawyer brother, Artur. In the end, she decided to ignore Zuza's request. The woman had obviously caused pain to a lot of prisoners to earn such a sparkling career under the Nazis. We never learned the outcome of the trial and Margo never heard from her again.

Chapter 13

· · · · · ·

'The Beast of Belsen'

In trying to remember my time in Belsen I frequently experience frustration at the lack of detail that would distinguish a certain week from the previous one, or even one month from another. The truth is that most of the time we did nothing at all. One day was like any other: we were afraid, we were constantly hungry and we shivered from the cold, all the while just waiting for the world to right itself again.

Yet there were, I'm glad to say, some highlights that shine out like the comforting beam of a lighthouse on a dark night. Miki's birthday was on 18 December and this year in Belsen was no ordinary birthday because it was his Bar Mitzvah year. He was turning thirteen, the age of significance in the Jewish religion, whereby the child was now an adult and wholly responsible for how he conducted himself in the practice and rituals of his faith. As a man, he now had to take responsibility for his actions and determine to live his life according to the Ten Commandments; in fact, the term 'Bar Mitzvah' means 'Son of Commandment'. It also meant that he was allowed to participate in all areas of Jewish community life.

If we had been back in Merašice there would have been a grand celebration, with the whole family and all our Jewish friends, beginning with a ceremony at the Galanova synagogue where Miki would have read to us, in Hebrew, a passage from the Torah scroll. After that, there probably would have been a party in either our house or our grandparents'. No doubt, our mother and *Omama* Katarina would have baked all the wonderful cakes and pastries that I loved. Maybe we'd dance to music on the gramophone and my father and his brothers would have pulled my ear and teased me about my being the only child in the house now that Miki was one of them. Mr Goldberger, his cheeks tinted after some glasses of wine, would tell me again to set myself up as a glazier and hire a partner to break all the windows in the next village. My mother would be wearing her best dress and my father standing proudly by in his one good suit, his own parents beaming at him in pride. All those good people gone somewhere else now, characters from a play that I had seen too long ago, memories of an existence that was but a lovely dream.

In spite of everything, despite the hatred for us and our religion, despite the horrendous situation we were in, we did manage to celebrate Miki's coming of age in that awful place, that hell on earth where ordinary people were dying every day from hunger or disease. And it was largely down to one person.

I remember Judith Marosi as an attractive girl, slim and well-developed, with a permanent smile on her pretty face. She was fifteen years old, but seemed so much more mature and courageous than her age would suggest. Her father had spent some time in Palestine (now Israel) in the thirties and possibly because of that Judith was, like her parents, a committed Zionist. They were nationalists, believing it necessary to set up a Jewish homeland in the land of Israel, the historical birthplace of the Jewish people. As it happened, her whole family was now in Belsen. Judith's eleven-year-old sister, Naomi, played with us children, and adored Judith, just like the rest of us. Their father was held in the men's camp and the thrilling thing for Blanka, their mother, was that he collected the food for his section. As a result, Blanka always volunteered to accompany Margo to collect our food, hoping and praying that she might bump into her husband – and, miraculously, every so often they did get to snatch a few sentences with each other. It was extraordinarily good luck for the little family. But, of course, nothing good ever lasted in Belsen.

For some time now, Judith had been begging her mother to take her along to fetch the food. Naturally, she was desperate to see her father for herself. However, it took a while for Blanka to agree to this request. When I think about it today, I'm sure Blanka was worried that her daughter might get too excited at the sight of her father and inadvertently draw attention to the clandestine meetings by crying out or rushing to embrace him. Another reason perhaps was that her husband's physical appearance might prove too shocking for Judith, because, when Blanka finally relented, it was too late. Judith was overjoyed at the prospect of finally being allowed to go and see her father, but when Margo and her volunteers arrived at the kitchen on the appointed day, the mother and daughter made the bitter discovery that the poor man had died the previous day.

Judith was like a big sister to me and the other kids in the camp. She taught us songs in Hebrew and organised games to keep us busy and cheerful. And she certainly was resourceful when it came to making something out of nothing. Some old woollen jumper, unwanted and sadly misshapen, was picked apart by Judith so that she could make little figures out of the wool, which she would then hide around the hut for us to find, teasing us with her shouts of: 'No, you're nowhere near it. You're freezing cold,' to the more encouraging: 'You're boiling hot! There, you've found it. Well done!' Crumpled pieces of paper were transformed into little boys and girls with names and exciting lives imagined for them by Judith, for our pleasure.

On the morning of Miki's birthday, an extremely cold December morning, after roll-call was finally done, Judith called us into the communal room where the little stove was actually lit. We children did our best to squirm as near as possible to the modest heat, enjoying the aroma that wafted about our heads – a few potatoes that had been cut in half were baking on top of the stove! This was a lovely surprise. To this day, I've no idea who was responsible for those small, mouldy potatoes, but I can still remember how wonderful they smelt. And then there was an even bigger surprise when one of the women appeared carrying a 'cake' to mark the special day. At first glance it looked like a cream cake, but closer inspection revealed it to be much more precious than that. It was actually three layers of bread slices with margarine and sprinkled with sugar. The woman, whose name I have shamefully forgotten, had crowned her achievement with a single candle, that flared brightly that day, represented a burning hope that was still alive in that most desolate of places. To make the cake, our friend had saved her own bread rations for a few days – in other words, she went hungry to give Miki a treat. We wished Miki '*Mazal tov!*' (Good luck!) on his birthday. Both the potatoes and the cake were cut into the smallest bits to allow everyone to enjoy some. It was an emotional party. Of course, we wished it was taking place elsewhere and that our fathers, uncles and grandfathers were present. Yet still, here we were, celebrating a traditional Jewish event in Belsen concentration camp, still smiling and still singing. That was the most important present to us all.

Another source of light in that dark place was a young wife and mother by the name of Lydia Kucerova. She and her six-year-old son, Palo, had ended up in Sered with her husband, and like so many others, the husband had then been separated from them during the selection and sent to Buchenwald, where he later perished. Mrs Kucerova found herself very popular with us children after we discovered that she had brought a children's book with her. The story *Cin Cin* (Tweet Tweet), by Slovak writer L'udmila Podjavorinská, was about a little bird called Cimcara and it followed his life from the time he cracked out of the egg beneath his mother's breast until he found himself, as a fully grown bird, with a wife with whom he would live happily ever after. Lydia managed to stretch out the little book by reading just a few sentences a day and asking us lots of questions about it, forcing us to use our imaginations and escape into Cimcara's world for an hour or so. It was a much-needed break from our drab surroundings.

One day Lydia received exciting news from a friend of hers that her beloved brother, Karol, had been spotted collecting food in the kitchen. The first thing she did was ask Margo if she could accompany her to collect our three meals. Margo agreed, of course. It took a few visits, but eventually the timing was perfect and she got to see Karol, who was equally overjoyed to find his sister. They had only a couple of minutes to catch up and had to be extremely careful. Female prisoners were not allowed under any circumstances to talk to the male prisoners and punishment for this particular transgression could be most severe. In those two minutes, however, they decided that they would keep in touch by leaving notes for one another under a large rock which permanently sat in the corner of the kitchen. It was an immense risk, but proved to be worth it, especially when Palo fell dangerously ill and Lydia was able to ask her brother for his help in obtaining medicine on the camp's black market. You could get lots of things on the black market as long as you didn't mind going hungry as, not surprisingly, the currency was slices of bread. When the opportunity arose, Margo starved herself in order to buy herself a cigarette, her taste for nicotine overcoming her need for the camp's black bread. Acquiring any kind of luxury in the camp was all about taking a huge risk. I wouldn't like to consider the consequences had my aunt ever been caught smoking her illegal cigarettes.

As it turned out, Lydia and Karol traded notes safely right up to liberation. Some of the originals were given to the Bergen–Belsen collection, as part of their resource materials.

Recently the notes were published together in a book and presented to Lydia's son, Palo.

Some time in December our mothers and grandmothers were told that we — the children — would be paid a visit by the Red Cross. Of course, we were expected to play a prominent role in the sham of a play put on by the SS guards. The day before the visit saw tremendous preparations taking place throughout the camp, under the ever-watchful eyes and hysterical screaming of the guards. The noise was ferocious and the atmosphere was charged with near panic as there was so much to do to transform the filthy place into something approaching decency. Hundreds of inmates were put to work, scrubbing buildings, windows and clearing the whole place of waste. The horrible trench toilet was also subjected to a thorough cleaning; I pitied the women whose job it was to make it presentable. Paths were swept clean, while any child that looked hideously starved and malnourished was locked away out of sight, along with the adult inmates of our camp. Only the relatively healthy-looking children would be paraded in front of the Swiss officials to show that all was well in Belsen. Orders were issued that we were to be dressed in clean clothes, so a lot of frantic laundering also took place within the twenty-four hours before the visit. I am quite sure that many of us were forced to wear damp clothes as there was too little time, and no heat, to allow for drying our shorts and shirts.

The following morning was a cold but sunny one. All was quiet outside our block since everyone else was locked inside their own blocks. At 10.00am we received the call to assemble outside for roll-call, just the children. The SS female guards lined us up quickly to check us over to see that we were clean and healthy. I remember one or two children being told to return inside. The rest of us were told to be silent – or else! About an hour later the Red Cross officials arrived, men and women, along with four SS officers and two SS women. We stood to attention and calmly met the gaze of these friendly-looking civilians. Obviously, we didn't understand how much power we held at that moment, not that anyone actually spoke to us or asked us any questions. The usually scowling SS guards beamed at us in the most jovial way as they pointed us out to the officials, presumably saying something like: Don't you see how happy they are? Surely, now, you will believe us when we tell you we do not harm Jewish children? After a couple of minutes of judging us to be satisfactory, one of the officials, a smiling, middle-aged woman, approached us with a box of chocolates, moving down the line until we had all received one bar each. And then they were gone, swiftly escorted onto block 209 to briefly gaze upon the scrubbed faces of the 'happy' Dutch children. No doubt they were as thrilled with their chocolate as we were. It certainly didn't have time to melt in our hands as most of us had swallowed our bars in one or two hungry bites.

Christmas 1944 was certainly a far from typical one. I suppose the only reassuring familiarity was the snow on the ground, a couple of centimetres deep, and it was freezing cold all day. Judith Marosi was determined to celebrate the day using the scant materials around us. She collected a few small branches from a fir tree and managed to stick them together so that they looked like – or something like – a small Christmas tree. Next she decorated it with scraps of coloured paper; all of this was about impressing the SS female guard who arrived for the daily inspection of the hut. Gathering the kids around her, and her tree, she had us serenade the uniformed woman with a shaky rendition of '*Stille Nacht*' (Silent Night). We would have done anything Judith asked of us. Of course, strictly speaking, Christmas wasn't an important day for us; my parents had celebrated it because they didn't want us to feel left out in the village where every other child received gifts and revelled in the excitement of the day. However, it was important to the German staff. I don't know how she did it, but Judith also managed to find a small gift for the guard, which was duly wrapped up in a bit of paper. I can't even imagine what it was, but presumably Judith must have asked someone to donate something worthy of the occasion. It was quite a show that she orchestrated, all about asking the visiting guard to be nice to us. Which guard it was on duty that day, I couldn't say, but I don't remember any shouting or beating, so Judith's preparations paid off and 25 December 1944 was a – relatively – good day.

The situation in Bergen–Belsen took a definite turn for the worse when we received a new commander in the form of *Hauptsturmführer* (Captain) Josef Kramer. In 1932 Kramer was an unemployed electrician casting around for something interesting to do with his life. He found it in the SS, which he joined that year, moving quickly up the ranks thanks to his unquestioning loyalty and natural ability to follow through on orders, no matter what. His reputation, as a callous sadist, was developed in Auschwitz–Birkenau, where he was in charge of the gas chambers.

His arrival was signified by a sudden decrease in food – our three meals were reduced to two. We were permitted our breakfast of watery coffee with two small slices of bread, and then our mid-day bowl of watery soup. And that was it. If we had been hungry before, we now experienced actual starvation every day, though I dare say we were still much better off than plenty of inmates in the other sections of the camp. A bureaucrat and harsh disciplinarian, Kramer put the hated capos in charge of the huts and gave them free rein to exact whatever punishments they dreamt up for real or imagined transgressions. He was obsessed with discipline, so punishments grew more severe and a lot more frequent. The roll-calls in the freezing winter temperature took longer and longer; sometimes it felt that they would never end.

From time to time we heard gunshots, and rumours circulated that it was the camp commander practising his shooting skills on inmates he saw rummaging around for scraps of food. The corpses were left where they fell, as a warning to the rest of us. Somewhere along the line he acquired his infamous nickname 'Beast of Belsen'. He was executed by the British.

As soon as the British army entered the camp in 1945 a group of British investigators began to take evidence about the neglect in the camp from the inmates to establish the guilt and reponsibility of those in charge. Josef Kramer and Dr Fritz Klein had headed up the camp, and on 16 November they were tried at Lüneburg, not far from Bergen-Belsen. A number of other SS officers and some of the capos also ended up in the dock. Kramer, Klein and Irma Grese were sentenced to death by hanging, along with eight others. The sentences were carried out on 13 December 1945. Many SS guards claimed they had only carried out orders and never stood trial.

Chapter 14

• • • • • •

'Death Marches'
to Belsen

One item I have mentioned but not dwelt upon is the camp's crematorium. It burned for twenty-four hours every day, seven days a week. The smell of burning flesh was incredible in the beginning, when we first arrived, but after a few days we all became immune to it. Only the dead were burnt, the objective being to hide the number of deaths from the likes of the Red Cross. This generally worked well, as a system, until the number of deaths escalated into impossible numbers – and that's when everything fell apart.

At the beginning of January 1945 the population of the camp was somewhere between fifteen and twenty thousand inmates, spread over ninety huts, with maybe 250 inmates to each hut. Midway through that month, however, the population doubled after a sudden influx of prisoners from Auschwitz. The Red Army was advancing from the east and so that camp was evacuated because the Nazis were, at long last, on the retreat. Since the railway lines were mostly destroyed from Allied bombing, the prisoners, already weak and starving, had to walk to the nearest functioning train station and from there they were transported to various camps in Germany, including Bergen-Belsen. These arduous 'walks' became known as 'death marches', due to the number of inmates who died along the way. Thousands fell by the roadside, succumbing to cold, exhaustion and starvation. In one group, numbering about sixty-five thousand prisoners when they set out, over fifteen thousand died before they reached the train station.

Throughout the period from January to March forty thousand people arrived into a concentration camp where conditions were already sparse and severe. The consequences of this were immense and immediate: there were too many people, too little food and absolutely no hygiene facilities to speak of.

But there was a small bit of good news: the adults now knew, from the newcomers, that Germany was actually losing the war. Of course, there was also the worry that we all might die anyway, that the Nazis would do their best to liquidate us all before help arrived. After all, we were damning evidence of their cruel treatment — every last one of us, with our sunken cheeks and malnourished frames.

One day, towards the end of January, a woman with a shaved head knocked on our small window. She was obviously an Auschwitz prisoner. She kept knocking to get our attention, but we just ignored her. Maybe she was looking for food, but we didn't have any. However, instead of moving away, her knocks became more insistent. What on earth did she want? Margo was about to rouse herself to go out and chase her off. Nobody recognised her until she began to call my mother by her name, shouting: 'It's me, Jolanka!' My mother jumped off her bed: 'Goodness! Is that really you?' Turning to the rest of us, she said: 'It's Jolanka Schlesinger.' I stared at the woman in confusion. She was completely unrecognisable to us. The last time I had seen her was when we visited her house in Galanova, a village just outside Merašice. Her house was the scene of much hilarity and pleasure, and our family were frequent visitors to impromptu tea parties there. Back then she was impeccable in her appearance, always neatly dressed, with her dark brown hair tied nicely into a bun. Her years of starvation and hard work had definitely left its mark; she was very skinny and looked a great deal older than she should have. But she had managed to survive and that was something rather spectacular. She wasn't alone either; her two sons, Roby and Palo, had been with her in Auschwitz and had survived the infamous Doctor Mengele.

We followed my mother who ran outside to greet her friend properly, throwing her arms around her. 'Jolanka, how wonderful to see you. How did you know we were here?'

Jolanka smiled in spite of her exhaustion: 'Oh, I was hoping to see someone I knew when I heard this was the Slovak Jews section. I feel very fortunate to have found such good friends. Tell me, how are you keeping?'

My mother shrugged: 'As well as can be expected. But, what about you?'

Jolanka, not wanting to upset us children, merely pulled at her murky clothes, showing, presumably, how little was left of her. Mother nodded quickly.

'Well, I am still here anyway, so I can't complain,' Jolanka said. 'And you do know that the Germans are starting to retreat, don't you? That's why we're here. The Russians are advancing fast, putting the Germans to flight.'

'Yes, we've heard,' my mother replied. 'Maybe our prayers are answered at last.'

The adults huddled in closer together; I heard words like 'terror' and 'murder' and didn't wish to hear anymore. But then their hushed chat was suddenly interrupted when my aunt's name was called. Another shaven-headed woman was approaching us.

'Margo! Margo! It's me, Relly Bineter!'

Once again, there was a gasp of disbelief at the appearance

of another skinny, beaten-looking woman. It was Margo's turn to hug her old friend. 'My dear, sweet Relly. What a miracle it is to find you, safe and sound.' The woman's face twitched slightly at the words 'safe and sound'. 'Come and meet my sister, my mother and my two nephews. And, of course, you remember Chava.'

'Ah, little Chava. How much you have grown!'

Margo filled us in on their background. 'Relly's two boys went to school with Laco.'

At this, Relly looked up sharply. 'Is he here, your Laco?'

Margo took a few seconds to answer: 'No. No, he's not. We were all in Sered together, but then the men and teenage boys were taken elsewhere while the women and children ended up here.'

Relly looked over at Miki and me, saying very quietly to us, 'You were the lucky ones, then.'

There was a pause before Margo placed a hand on her friend's arm. She didn't have to ask the question because Relly answered her gesture with: 'My boys are gone. Gassed in the chambers at Auschwitz. I didn't even get to hug them goodbye.' With that she smiled tightly, bitterly: 'But at least I know where they are. Right?' The women nodded dully, obviously not knowing how else to react.

Grandmother Rosalia spoke: 'Yet their brave mother survived and that counts for something. They won't be forgotten.'

Relly thanked her for the kind words. She told us that she

had escaped sharing her sons' fate because the Nazis discovered she was fluent in several languages, including French and English, and put her to work for them. Now, just like Jolanka and the forty thousand newcomers to our camp, she was trying to find some food for herself. Margo managed somehow to get her hands on a couple of slices of black bread for the starving women.

At that time, neither Miki nor I might have considered ourselves to be very 'lucky', as Relly had described us. But in one way we were: our mother did her best to shield us from the horrors that she would have heard about from the Auschwitz survivors. The worst we had had to deal with was the relentless cold and the gnawing hunger that was never satisfied with our meagre rations. We never saw our mother falter or give in to fear. Nearly every day she told us the same thing, 'Don't worry, we will be all right', and we believed her.

A few days after my mother and Margo had been reunited with their friends a young Hungarian girl came to our hut and told one of the younger children to tell the rest of us to make our way, that evening, to another hut nearby where we would be given some food. Only the youngest of the children were invited and fortunately I was one of them. We were told to wait until it was dark. Apart from the guards in the watchtowers, there really weren't any other Germans around at night, so it was relatively safe to walk from our hut to theirs, which was a bit of a distance from the perimeter and, therefore, a bit of a walk from the nearest watchtower. As it happened, the girl returned to collect us and led the way back to her hut. Not a word was uttered by any of us on the short journey, though our guide, at intervals, would look back to give us a friendly smile. When we reached her hut, she held the door open and we filed past her, one by one, expecting goodness knows what. Two things struck me about the Hungarian hut: the first being that the light was very dim indeed, and secondly, the place was absolutely packed with busy-looking women. We were instantly surrounded by a group of young girls in their mid-teens, who seemed to choose a child each from our group, to especially fuss over. 'Hello, precious, what's your name?' 'How old are you?' My parents had often spoken Hungarian in the house so I was well able to hold my own in conversation.

The entire hut was filled with beds, which were set in tight rows of three, blocking off the light, one beneath the other. I couldn't get over the amount of movement. There seemed to be a constant stream of women and girls, either leaving or returning to the hut. The reason they had food to give us was that they all worked in the camp kitchens and had obviously become very efficient in helping themselves to the supplies. They worked in different shifts, which explained the endless traffic.

They were angels, these girls, as far as we were concerned. Each of us ten children was brought to sit on a bed, in place of a table and chair, where we were given sumptuous meals of bread with margarine *and* jam, soup and black coffee. There were even some drops of milk to be had. While we gobbled down the treats they made us laugh by tickling us and pulling comical faces, just as if it was a birthday party or some other kind of celebration, but only involving us kids. It was marvellous to be treated as children again and properly doted upon like this. While we giggled and scoffed the food, we completely forgot, for the duration of our hour-long visit, the daily misery that accompanied living in the concentration camp.

We went back every evening after that for the next few weeks, always collected by the same girl, and every evening it was the same routine. Like little mother hens they would each pick their 'chick' to pamper and spoil. And then it stopped, just as suddenly as it had begun, without a word of warning. One evening our friendly guide didn't show up to fetch us and we never heard from them again. Perhaps a capo had discovered what was going on. I would have to assume that, for whatever reason, it had simply become too dangerous for them to continue feeding us.

I had forgotten about these girls for many, many years until 17 February 1989. It was a Saturday night and I was watching television with my wife. We were enjoying one of our favourite programmes, the popular Irish chat show *The Late*

Late Show on RTÉ (Radio Telefís Éireann, the national station), when the host, Gay Byrne, announced his next guest as a survivor of Auschwitz. Her name was Isabella Leitner and she spoke in great detail about her horrific experiences, including seeing her mother and sister led away to death in the gas chambers. However, she then mentioned another sister who had died from typhus in Belsen, where she was transported in January 1945. Ms Leitner told how her sister had been in the company of a group of young Hungarian girls. I bolted out of my chair, frightening my wife, who asked me what was wrong. 'I have to phone RTÉ immediately!' My wife was bewildered as I had never discussed my time in Bergen-Belsen and naturally she had no idea what I was talking about. I raced to the phonebook and began to look for the station's phone number, but I couldn't find it. My hands shook violently and tears prevented me from reading the small print. I never placed the call.

One of the most immediate consequences of the sudden influx of the death marches from Auschwitz was the voracious onslaught of typhus. According to my dictionary, the main symptoms of the disease, which is transmitted to humans via lice carried by rodents, are: fever, severe headache, a reddish-purple rash and delirium. Typhus is most prevalent in overcrowded and unsanitary living conditions. And that's when the inmates of Belsen started to die in their *thousands*.

Chapter 15

· · · · · · ·

'Muselmann'

February was another icy cold month and it was also a very wet one. We hardly left the hut. Apart from everything else, our clothes and shoes were in tatters. Our mother did her best to repair what she could, but there was little to be done with wet shoes that had started to come apart at the seams. It rained a lot, so nobody was eager to trudge through the mud that always ensued, dragging it back inside, making a mess and causing more worry for Margo as, first and foremost, the hut had to be spotless for the daily inspections – or else.

The atmosphere in our family room was rather subdued. All eyes were on our grandmother, *Omama* Rosalia, who began to look very frail indeed. She still continued to comb out her hair each morning, but now she needed Chava to plait it and tie it up. Her physical strength was deteriorating from the relentless cold and hunger and her interminable sadness at the horrors outside our door. She never joined in the conversations with her daughters anymore, instead she just sat by quietly, on her bed, never complaining or causing any fuss. By this stage, her medication was long gone, as was her desire to exercise or even just stretch her legs. Not that she was alone in this. Apart from roll-call, none of us went outside anymore. Some days I imagined that we were all just sitting around in a miserable waiting room, counting the minutes as they dragged by.

The thing about being hungry is that it's extremely hard to ignore the emptiness and the gnawing pain in your stomach, day after day after day. Margo and my mother fell to passing the dreary afternoon hours discussing their favourite recipes and how to make them. Sometimes they got into quite a heated debate over the best way to cook a dish, the correct temperature, the correct quantities, or where to buy the best coffee and so on. Food – it was all we could think about. I didn't take part in these conversations, I didn't have to. My dreams harboured my deepest desires at that time. Forgetting about freedom or my perfect childhood before all the hatred set in, I merely dreamed of such tantalising sights as rice pudding smothered in jam, the thickest, most generous of cream slices, slabs of *Omama* Reichental's apple strudel and buckets of rock sweets from my grandfather's shop. Despite my yawning hunger, my mother had to push me every day to eat the two meals. 'Please, Tominko, don't look at it, just close your eyes and swallow. If you won't eat you won't survive.' I was heartily sick and tired of the black bread that tasted of nothing in particular, to say nothing of the smelly, watery soup. My ragged clothes were hanging off me, my ribs could easily be counted beneath my shirt. My grandmother looked at me as if we were in different worlds. Where once she would have helped cajole me into eating, she no longer had anything left to offer.

However, there was one good thing about the cold that we all agreed upon. When it was freezing, the air didn't stink quite so badly from the rotting corpses that were strewn about the entire camp. We weren't overcome by nausea with every breath. Is it really possible for me to convey what that was like? Probably not.

Today I can look back upon those first two or three months of 1945 and appreciate how it was a period of calm, the quiet before the storm of liberation. We were on the edge of the forest, but no birds could be heard singing or cooing to one another. The camp was bursting at the seams, but a blind man would not have known this – for noise required energy and that was at an all-time low. People had no energy to waste on chatter and unnecessary exercise like washing or even caring much about anything in particular. A veil of apathy slid out over the stricken population. The distinction between the living and the dead lessened with each passing hour as hunger and disease knocked men and women to their knees. Even the distinction between men and women began to evaporate as physical attributes slowly faded. Men no longer stood strong, no long had wider necks and shoulders or thicker limbs, while women no longer had breasts or hips that might bear children. After all, when one sees a skeleton it takes an expert, an anthropologist or a doctor, to determine its sex.

'*Muselmann*': I'm not entirely sure when this term came into existence but this was how the inmates of Auschwitz and then Belsen came to be described. There is no specific translation; it means a number of different words that all paint the same picture: apathy, physical weakness, starving, exhaustion and lack of responsiveness to one's surroundings. People moved very slowly, if at all, and lost the usual harried, fearful look in their eyes. Being constantly afraid was another waste of energy. This might sound strange, but the mental apathy and the all-pervading physical weakness resulted in an atmosphere that was peaceful and sound. Life was lived only from one minute to the next; we didn't bother looking back and had lost our natural curiosity about what might occur the following moment, hour or day. In short, we had no worries.

The human body is a force to be reckoned with and that is something I can never forget. What I mean by this is that it took some time for a person to die, whether of hunger or typhus. It began with diarrhoea, which brought dehydration in its wake, which in turn made a person weak – too weak, in fact, to eat – and then this was followed, at some stage, by death.

I cannot remember when it began to escalate. I cannot pinpoint when the crematorium could no longer cope. It hardly seems likely that one day there were only a few bodies to be seen and the very next they were everywhere. Up to that point there had been a system in place, and there had to be because there had always been people dying in the camp. Each morning the *Sonderkommandos* (Special Commando) – inmates from the men's camp, this was their full-time job – went from hut to hut looking for the dead from the previous night. I am sure that their visits were never unnecessary. There were no niceties involved. Upon being told about a body, one of them took the corpse by the hands while the other grabbed the legs and they would trudge outside to fling it clumsily onto their two-wheeled wooden cart. Then, when the cart was filled to capacity, they would push it together to the crematorium.

But this exercise was rendered ridiculous when the daily number of corpses began to climb into the hundreds. There simply was no point in collecting them anymore since there was already a pile outside the crematorium, a hill composed of twig-like arms, legs, sunken chests and dead-white, expressionless faces that stared and stared. So the bodies were just carried outside the huts and left to rot there in peace. Though that wasn't always exactly true: sometimes you could imagine that a body was still living and breathing – you would see a movement out of the corner of your eye, but it was only rats tearing at a corpse.

Many inmates fought a losing battle with swarms of lice; they were responsible for the spread of the disease and could be clearly seen marching all over a person, as efficient and bloody-minded as any army. This was a big factor in my mother hounding me and Miki to wash every day, although we didn't appreciate her motivation at the time. If you didn't at least try to stay relatively clean, then you were simply giving up. However, merely washing in ice-cold water is not going to prohibit bugs and fleas in any way. We used to sit around like monkeys, picking the lice out of one another's heads. Our clothes were crawling with infestation and scratching became a full-time occupation. It became difficult to sleep or rest properly as you permanently felt your skin and bed to be crawling with activity.

As with everything else, we got used to the sight of dead people lying about the place as far as we could see. Very quickly they became part of the monotonous landscape and I gave them no more thought or attention than I did the guard's watchtower or the sky above me. Towards the end of February there were some days when the tentative spring sun warmed the air for the first time in months, encouraging a few of the children – and me – outside for a while to play for short bouts of activity before we felt too tired to continue chasing one another. One of our favourite games involved splitting into two groups; one group was the evil Nazis while the second one was the brave Jews who would fight the battle for the greater good. As you can imagine, we all wanted to be in the latter group, and 'our' Nazis were usually very similar to the real thing, in that they were angry, sulky and loud in their disapproval of the brave Jews. Once the battle commenced, we used our pointed fingers as guns and ran about ducking and diving from the rain of imaginary bullets, all the while trying to find the winning shot that would take down the enemy. It used to be that we hid behind the hut; there wasn't much else to shield ourselves from the imaginary artillery, but from February onwards we had plenty of obstacles to hide behind – the bodies of real Jews became our silent playmates; we pretended they were walls of buildings or the exteriors of secret passageways.

You might ask, quite naturally, how we did this. How we huddled up close behind the decrepit remains of a man or woman. Were we not repelled by the smell or by the dull skin that resembled candle wax or just by the simple fact that here was a dead person? It is a hard thing to explain. The only answer I have today is that we just got used to them, along with the smell of decomposition. After a while, if truth be told, we sort of didn't see them anymore. There were just so many. Furthermore, one body looked no different from another and, of course, it helped that they were complete strangers to us.

However, if we thought things were as bad as they could be in February, they were about to get far, far worse in March.

Chapter 16

• • • • • •

Typhus

It is reckoned that five hundred inmates died in Bergen-Belsen every day through March 1945. We still received our meagre portions, but Margo now had to carry a stick to beat off the starving women who would try to snatch our food as Margo and her assistants brought it from the kitchen to our hut. It wasn't something that she was proud of. I overheard her make a pitiful confession to her mother and sister: 'I hate doing it, belting them away as if they're dogs, though I've yet to see a dog so hungry or desperate.' My mother, however, was quick to tell her that she was doing a necessary job: 'If you didn't protect the food, we'd all go hungry and die. I know it's horrible, but that's just the way it is.'

Chaos was starting to build as everything else in the camp

started to crumble. Of course, this was not a coincidence. It seemed that the SS guardsmen and women had finally met something that they were more scared of than failing to perform their duties to their *Führer* – and that was the typhus. It was rampant. There were two types in Belsen, but the end results were the same. Either a person developed a raging fever, where it literally felt like their blood was boiling, or else they were afflicted with acute diarrhoea. In both cases, the sufferer was left physically incapacitated, with severe dehydration that eventually killed them.

All I knew was that we no longer had to stand in the cold and rain for hours listening for our names to be called. Thanks to the epidemic, the camp authorities were too afraid to come near us so that meant no more roll-calls, no more hut inspections and no more angry guards shouting abuse at the tops of their voices. But that's not to say that there were no guards at all, that we were now free to go. We were still under observation from the men in the watchtowers, only they weren't the usual haughty Nazi soldiers. Elderly men wearing assorted uniforms of various colours manned the towers now. I later found out they were Hungarian prisoners of war.

I remember one of them. One morning I was playing quietly with a couple of others not far from the perimeter fence. There were maybe three of us – the faces and names of my companions escape me – when we heard an insistent voice from above us, 'Come! Come!' Looking up, we were bewildered to discover that the owner of the voice was the soldier in the watchtower. This had never happened before. He was beckoning us over to him, 'Come, now!' I remember not knowing what to do, being absolutely stumped. It was the first time that children had been addressed by anyone in uniform. Resisting approaching his tower because we were afraid, we quickly realised we were also too afraid to run away in case he shot us in the back with the big machine-gun. So we waited nervously until he showed us that he meant no harm. He looked very old to me, but that could have been down to the starvation rations. In any case, his age didn't matter. What did matter was his heart. We peered at him. There was something in his hand and he seemed to be offering it to us. With a collective gasp we suddenly under-stood his intention. He was holding up a crust of bread. Well, that gave us the courage we needed. As soon as we took a couple of steps forward he flung the crust down to us. We pounced on it and tore it unevenly into three small bites. No, that's not right. The three of us fought viciously over the crust and perhaps we all managed to win a piece. With one gulp it was gone and we looked up expectantly for more. The man smiled down, gesturing to us that he was eating a second slice of bread and would share the crust as before. I'm sure we looked like three eager pups, with wagging tails and lolling tongues. In any case, he didn't let us down. As soon as he finished his favourite part he threw down the crust again and again we set upon one another until we had a piece – a shred – of the bread.

This continued over several days. It was a wonderful secret between the three of us and our benefactor. The thought of the extra food would make me giddy with excitement. Yes, it was only a few crusts and I had to battle my two mates for it, but it was so much nicer than the awful black bread we got for our breakfast. It also smelled exactly like bread should and was so soft that I could almost swallow it whole. The black bread, on the other hand, was so hard that some days I imagined this must be what it would be like to try and bite into a brick. Unfortunately, some of the other children spied on us and our secret was no more. After that, the battle for the crusts was much too hard and I preferred to go without.

One morning sticks out in my memory. It was 7 March, a Wednesday, and I woke to the sound of weeping. To my bewilderment the sound was coming from Aunt Margo and my mother. I had never seen my mother cry before; she was always so strong and determined in her belief that we would all survive this particular experience. But I suppose it would have been too much of a miracle that we would *all* survive.

'Mother, what's wrong? Why are you crying?'

Chava and Miki looked at the floor while my mother wiped her eyes and whispered, '*Omama* Rosalia is dying.'

She had been very ill for the past few weeks and her skeletal frame couldn't take anymore. Her eyes were closed and her breathing short and wretched, yet she managed to utter the words, 'Please, open the window.' They were her last. With one, maybe two more gasping breaths, she shuddered slightly and everything stopped in that moment.

I remember the silence in the room and the two women staring at their mother, who was no more. For Miki and me, it was our first experience of the death of someone we knew. By that stage we actually had plenty of other dead relatives, but we would be spared that information for another couple of months yet; and we hadn't actually known the woman who had died in front of us on the train. But this was *Omama* Rosalia, our own beloved grandmother, who had died right there in front of us.

After a while, her grief-stricken daughters got up to prepare her for the callous removal. Her body was stripped of clothes, as instructed, so Margo carefully covered her with her blanket. I don't remember what became of her clothes; I presume Margo or Mother hung on to them as a last poignant souvenir since everything else she owned in the world was gone. There was nothing to say. If prayers were recited they were said in private.

Goodness knows how long we sat there awaiting the *Sonderkommandos* to take her body outside to be put on the heap. The tears had stopped flowing because, if you can understand, there was no point. Death was all around us, and my grandmother had merely succumbed to what thousands had before her. In the last week or so she had contracted dysentery that, in the absence of medicine or nutritious food, literally dried her out. She had slowly dwindled away physically and mentally, so her death seemed only natural. Another way of putting it was that in a situation where approximately five hundred men and women were dying every single day, my elderly grandmother's death was absolutely inevitable. Crying or raging against the circumstances of her demise seemed like a luxury for the very foolish or the blissfully ignorant.

Eventually we heard the two men whose job it was to take out the bodies. One of them entered the main dormitory, making his usual query: 'Any dead here?' Someone must have pointed silently to our door because it suddenly opened and in they came. Completely ignoring us, neither looking left nor right, they threw off Margo's blanket. One of them took *Omama*'s hands while the other grabbed her feet. In fact, one of them could have carried her out by himself since she wouldn't have weighed more than a few stone. Their cart was already straining under the weight of other dead inmates, so my grandmother was thrown on top of these. It is an image I will never forget. The men then wheeled the cart some distance away before stopping to empty it. The bodies were flung into a pile as if they were firewood – or, this is what we assumed to have happened. None of us followed the men out to be sure. Why would we? We had all seen many, many other corpses treated in the exact way I have described; there was no desire to see our own flesh and blood being discarded as if she was rubbish.

Later I went to see if I could find her among the piles, but I couldn't, which was probably for the best. My gentle grandmother's resting place was as part of a pile-up; she was buried not by the earth but by the bodies of other inmates. It was barbaric.

At the height of the crisis in Bergen–Belsen, suicide became a popular alternative to dying slowly from starvation or disease. And it didn't take much organisation either. All someone had to do was make a run for the perimeter fences as if they truly believed they could actually scale the barbed wire and make good their escape. Success meant a bullet in the head or chest from the guard in the watchtower. I wonder if the guards knew they were often performing an act of charity when they gunned down another desperate would-be 'escapee'. At night we would hear the shots ring out and know that when we got up the following morning there would be at least one woman hanging from the wire as a dire warning to the rest of us. But it proved no deterrent to starving colleagues; if anything, it might be truer to say that those bullet-ridden corpses served only to inspire.

Towards the middle of March there were between three and five bodies on that fence every morning in our section alone.

Incredibly, throughout that miserable month, prisoners continued to arrive in their thousands. Afterwards I realised how much worse it could have been for us. Other huts were inundated with hundreds of arrivals. Luckily for us, we didn't have to make room for any new inmates. I don't know why: maybe there were no mothers with young children left in Auschwitz? We heard tales of four sleeping to a bed in other huts. Is it any wonder that disease was widespread? Some huts, which were the same size as ours, were now home to seven hundred people, some even rumoured to be holding up to a thousand. The smell of faeces was overpowering as people became too weak to make their way to the latrine, barely making it outside the door of their hut to relieve themselves. The whole camp was turning into one big latrine, with the smell of faeces filling the dank air around us.

Unbeknownst to us, our Camp Commander, Josef Kramer, was desperately trying to get food for us (see Appendix 2). He wrote urgent letters to his superiors in which he detailed the dreadful state of the camp, even going as far as to organise trucks to drive around the surrounding villages to collect food for his starving thousands. Does this mean he was a good man? Certainly there were plenty afterwards who believed he was an honourable man who did his best under atrocious circumstances. Furthermore, there are some who completely disagree with his nickname, 'Beast of Belsen', preferring instead to call him the 'Scapegoat of Belsen'. You may want to know what I think about him today. Well, I have read the documents, his pleading letters, but I cannot forget that by the time he wrote them he surely would have guessed that Germany was losing the war. In other words, he knew that all was going to change very shortly and maybe he thought about preparing to absolve himself of any potential charges. But we will never know for sure, one way or the other.

Meanwhile, the sounds of war were getting nearer and nearer, and perhaps this was what kept the rest of us going. Did we know at the time how near we were to the city of Hanover? Whether we did or not, we certainly heard it being bombed, day after day, like a recurring thunderstorm in the distance. And then, suddenly, there was no distance at all. Several times we had first-class seats at the frantic battles that took place in the sky above Belsen. As you can imagine, we children were spellbound as we watched the fighter planes dip and dive, doing their best to outwit their opponent. The roar of the engines both scared and thrilled us; it was far, far better than watching a film.

Then one day the war got very close indeed – deadly close. I was outside with a crowd of kids watching a German

Messerschmidt plane doing its best to outrun a wonderfully aggressive *Spitfire*, a British fighter plane. The German machine was easily recognisable thanks to the dreaded swastika painted on its wings. They were flying very low, almost brushing the trees and the roofs of the huts as they raced overhead. Some of the kids ran indoors because the noise of the engines was quite terrifying, plus shells were shooting out of the *Spitfire* at an alarming rate. As I stood there in the yard, neck craning to follow the lethal chasing game, one shell rocketed out of the sky, embedding itself rather deeply into the muck only a paltry few inches from my feet, such was the speed of its trajectory. It was a miraculous escape, but one I immediately forgot about when, a few hundred metres from the barbed-wire fence, the *Spitfire* succeeded in bringing down its quarry. The explosion was incredible. There was no way that the German pilot escaped, since he was flying much too low to parachute out. Well now, here was one death that could be celebrated. How we cheered and danced at the sight of the black smoke that spewed heavenwards over the tops of the trees.

Chapter 17

• • • • • •

Liberation, April 1945

Probably in response to Kramer's begging letters there was a visit, on 10 April, from SS officer Kurt Becher. He had just recently been appointed by Heinrich Himmler as the Reich Special Commissar for the affairs of all Jewish and political prisoners. Once Becher inspected the dismal conditions of the thousands and thousands of inmates, he and Kramer decided that the only practical solution was to hand over Bergen-Belsen concentration camp to the advancing British army.

Unbeknownst to us in the women and children's camp, Heinrich Himmler issued an obscene order than no inmates were to be left alive for the incoming liberators. Consequently, there was the beginning of an attempt to evacuate

Belsen. In the end, only three transports were organised, on 10 April, each totalling about 2,500 men, women and children who were herded back into the cattle carts. The trains were supposed to go to Theresienstadt concentration camp near Prague, but never got beyond the Elbe river, thanks to the advancing Allies. At this point, the train drivers and SS guards scarpered, leaving hundreds to suffocate to death in the inhuman conditions – the carriages were so packed that everyone had to stand straight, arms by their sides, one right up against another, like sardines in a can, and, of course, there was neither food nor water. Urine and faeces could only run down their legs since there was no space and no means of relieving oneself, not even the crude bucket-toilet that I had shared with so many on my own dreadful journey to Belsen.

Those three trains became know as the 'Death Trains'. One of them stopped in the small German town of Farsleben to await further orders that never arrived. Then a unit from an American tank battalion came upon it. They unlocked the doors and were understandably stunned by the cargo of hundreds of dead and dying human beings. It was yet another example of a catastrophic, stupid waste of innocent men, women and children.

I was told about the Farsleben Death Train by a survivor. A Hungarian, Robert (Bob) Spitz and his father had been arrested in March 1944 and deported to Belsen the following month. They were interned together until the guards realised that they were related. Robert's father was duly sent on to Mauthausen concentration camp while Robert remained in Belsen and was assigned to clearing the railway tracks of bombs that were regularly dropped by the British and Americans. The Nazis needed the tracks in working order since it was their way to transport ammunition and weapons. The work was very hard, with little food provided and no protective clothing for the winter months. Then, in April 1945, the sixteen-year-old Robert found himself back in a cattle cart, bound for goodness knows where. The conditions were suffocating – and lethal for many of his companions. When he had boarded that train he was already suffering from typhus and weighed 28kg, less than five stone. It was a miracle he survived. Those American soldiers must have made a huge impression on him because once he had fully recovered he joined their army as a linguist.

Back in the camp, we knew nothing about all of this, but what we did know was that on 11 April there were no guards in the watchtowers. I cannot remember who noticed the vacant towers first, but in a very short time everyone else knew about this peculiarity. Furthermore, there was no sign of any SS personnel around, male or female, and rumours began to circulate that we might be liberated soon, though nobody knew for sure – in fact, most of the guards fled the camp that day. Our hopes were understandably high in anticipation about what was going to happen next. Therefore, it was difficult to cope with the fact that absolutely *nothing* happened over the next three days. Throughout this time the same two questions were asked again and again: 'Are we free? Are the Germans gone?'

We heard that the water pumps had been bombed by the British, but had our doubts about this. It seemed much more likely to us that the pumps had been sabotaged by the retreating Germans. Whoever was to blame for it, the consequences were the same – there was no water or food for anyone in the camp for four days, from 11 to 14 April.

Margo continued to make her way, every day, to the kitchen to see if there was anything she could get to feed the children. Also, she was our contact with the rest of the camp, bringing back to us the latest whispers about our situation and the multitude of possibilities concerning it.

You might well ask why none of us actually left the camp. Surely if there were no guards we were free to walk out the gate? Yet the truth of it was that we were still afraid. Just as the rumours about liberation swept through the camp, so too did an opposing rumour that this was all an elaborate trap and that certain death awaited anyone who believed, or had the audacity to act as if they were free.

The sun shone in a bright blue sky on the morning of 15 April, a Sunday. It was about 11.00am and I was sitting with the rest of our family in our room, waiting for goodness knows what, when all of a sudden we heard an unfamiliar noise, a low rumbling coming from the middle of the camp. Next there was shouting, lots of shouting, different voices calling out the same thing: 'Come and see! We're free! We're free!' Miki, Chava, Margo, Mother and I jumped up together in complete synchronisation and charged out into a perfect spring morning; the sun was warm on our faces, the breeze was refreshingly sweet. Once we got outside we did what everyone else was doing. It seemed like the entire camp was running in their direction so we ran towards the fence too to get a better look at these victorious soldiers. All around me I heard triumphant cries: 'At last, at last. We are saved at last!'

Then something caught my attention. To my left I saw a SS officer, about 200 metres away, wave his gun in the air and shout at the runners in obvious rage. When I remember it today, I am almost sure he was quite drunk. I can see him in my mind's eye, swaying from side to side, his once pristine uniform unbuttoned to the waist. He even stumbled forward a little as if to give chase, displaying a remarkable lack of dignity for an officer of the Third Reich. It was the strangest thing to see him being completely ignored. Not one of us stopped running, not one of us even glanced in his direction. In the face of the oncoming troops he was powerless and lost. There was only one thing left for him to do. He raised his weapon and singled out one of the crowd, a woman who was running towards the foreign tanks in desperate abandonment. Perhaps it was the colour of her hair or the clothes that she was wearing that caught his eye – whatever it was, she lived only long enough to know her war was finally over before the angry guard pulled the trigger and she crumpled to the ground, causing those behind to trip over her.

Our rescuers were the 11th British Armoured Division, headed up by Lieutenant Derrick Sington. Their first task was to explain to us what was going on. For this a loudspeaker was needed, along with three sergeants who could speak several European languages between them. Their message was one and the same: 'You are liberated. This is the British army.' I think a lot of the inmates had assumed that our rescuers were Russians, since all the talk from the Auschwitz arrivals was about the Soviets pushing the Germans back. In my nine-year-old eyes, these soldiers were nothing less than heroes. I didn't care where they came from.

One of the jeeps contained a crew from the BBC led by the famous journalist Richard Dimbleby who described his visit to the camp as the most horrible day of his life. He was responsible for the first report – the first real evidence of what had been going on – to be broadcast from the camp. Years later I watched this first newsreel with our family, and, much to our shock, we found ourselves looking at the thirteen-year-old Miki standing at the barbed wire with some of the other children.

If I have given the impression that the camp was full of deliriously happy people greeting the British with open arms, that is wrong. For one thing, not everyone was capable of running to the fence. A lot, of course, just lay where they were. It is believed that there were, that day, approximately 25,000 to 30,000 unburied corpses, not to mention the thousands more who were barely alive, barely aware of what was happening. I also remember some confusion over what the words 'You are liberated' meant. Too many inmates had no energy to be jubilant, though some women did find some pine branches to throw at the British in celebration. They would have thrown flowers, but there was none to be found.

On the night of the fifteenth, however, the feeling of freedom was celebrated with a bout of looting. First the food stores − or what was left of them − were ransacked by hundreds of prisoners. Most of the available food had already been taken by Russian prisoners of war; they appeared to understand the fact that they were free much more quickly than any other nationality. In fact, our family owed them our thanks, as some bread was made available to Margo when she approached them about us children. The following day I joined in when a raid was made on the huts that stored the non-food stuffs, from SS uniforms to socks to bicycles. Unfortunately, I had not thought to grab the practical warm underwear and socks, instead I became enamoured with items like the gold-plaited tassels that were used to decorate swords and the SS insignias that were to be sewn onto garments. I leapt on these useless things as if they were plates of goulash, absolutely delighted with my scandalous treasure. Older and wiser inmates were helping themselves to the clothing and shoes, the more successful ones loading their particular finds onto the German bicycles.

In the immediate aftermath of liberation, the number of British soldiers present in the camp was kept to a minimum because of the typhus epidemic. For the first few days I hardly saw any. Rumours flew around that our camp Commander, Josef Kramer, had been arrested, along with the other SS officers who had fled just before the British arrived. It seems that the order for the arrests was actually given after the incoming troops investigated the sounds of gunfire and found an armed SS guard standing over inmates he had shot dead for taking some potatoes. In Kramer's defence, he stayed at the camp to receive his replacements. When asked by his captors why he had not tried to escape, he replied in typical fashion: 'I stayed, these were my orders.' In any case, his fleeing colleagues didn't travel very far and were easily rounded up and brought back to help deal with the mess.

One of the first things the British did was to give us food. During those early days of liberation soldiers brought around trailers containing army rations, the food that the army lived on, and people were free to take as much as they wanted which, in hindsight, proved to be an unwise course of action. Everything came out of a tin. There were sausages, bacon, Irish stew, steak and kidney pie, rice puddings, cheese and jam. Much to my mother's surprise, I enjoyed every little bit of it. My favourite was a sort of square tin that contained salty meat − it was the most beautiful thing I had ever tasted! Later on I found out it was called 'corned beef'. There were also beans, crackers and tinned fruit with jelly which, as you might imagine, was an absolute delight for me and the other children. Then, to drink, there was apple *or* orange juice. Instead of berating me for picking at my food, my mother had to tell me to slow down and carefully chew each mouthful!

Over thirteen thousand inmates died following liberation. Makeshift hospitals were set up, with British and German medical staff, but for many, gripped in the rigid claws of typhus, it was simply too late. I have read since that the British troops were completely unprepared for what greeted them in Belsen. Many of them cried openly as they took their first walk around the different huts. They handed out their army rations in their desperation to do something instantly, unintentionally killing hundreds whose stomachs and digestive systems could not accept the solid food, their first in months. It was estimated that approximately two thousand inmates died from eating the wrong food. The situation improved when the army brought in proper cooking equipment, although it took many more weeks of feeding to heal the surviving inmates.

Almost overwhelmed with the mammoth task facing them, the British army decided to break their approach down into four parts: to provide food, to stop the spread of disease, to remove the sick from the camp and to bury the dead. Each of these four parts was a massive undertaking in itself. Incoming medical staff were briefed on 17 April by Lieutenant Colonel James Johnston, who referred to Belsen as the 'Horror Camp'. His tour of the camp shook him, making him want to vomit, he said, and he strove to do the impossible, to prepare the doctors and nurses for what they were about to see: 'Half-starved, emaciated, spiritless, demented, these people roaming the camp have been reduced to animal level.'

My first real contact with our rescuers came a few days later when the male and female SS officers were despatched to collect and bury the thousands of rotting corpses scattered everywhere under the cold, watchful eye of armed British soldiers. Feeling energetic and bold, thanks to the huge improvement in our diet, all the kids and I went out to inflict what punishment we could on the scowling grave diggers. I don't suppose either the SS or the British understood what we were saying, but we kept up a rant of abuse at the Nazis as they went about their work, interjected with encouragement to the British soldiers to be as horrible as possible to their charges. Pointing at their guns we gestured that they should stab the SS with the bayonets. The soldiers nodded, but declined to follow our orders. We quickly befriended these smiling, cheerful men, despite the language barrier, especially when they introduced us to chewing gum and gave us sweets. The way they treated us reminded us once more that we were children. The only other time we had experienced this over the past few months was inside the hut of the kind-hearted Hungarian girls.

Apart from the fun of being able to curse the SS officers, it was both emotionally and physically demanding to watch them as they picked up corpses, one by one, to put on to the back of a nearby truck. Sometimes the limbs, the very bones, would come away from the body, leaving a thin sheet of flesh blowing in the spring breeze. And, of course, the smell was indescribable, thanks mainly to an improvement in the weather. When I think about those first few days, I can almost feel the sun on my face again – but also smell the awful stench.

What a change it was to see those bad-tempered SS tyrants getting their hands dirty at last. The British wouldn't allow them the luxury of wearing protective clothing or even gloves. Furthermore, they also had their belts confiscated, which made them look rather lumpy and dishevelled. The SS women no longer glowed as if they had just stepped out of a hairdresser's or beautician's shop; instead they were haggard, dirty and basically distraught over their sudden change of fortune. Some of the officers had the audacity to look enraged at having to perform such a dreadful job, while others were pale and frantic, as if they were going to be sick. As hard as I try, I just don't remember any of them looking particularly shamed or sorry. Maybe it was the first time they had to properly deal with the existence of thousands of corpses, a fact that the rest of us lived with at such close quarters. It had probably been relatively easy for them to have ignored the horror going on outside by remaining indoors, fiddling with paperwork or however else they had spent their days. I would be willing to guess that most, if not all, would not have considered themselves in any way personally responsible for the countless deaths from disease or malnutrition – but these piles of grimy limbs and broken bodies represented whole communities of Jewish men and women: parents, sons, daughters, doctors, teachers, actors, dancers, musicians, businessmen. As a result of handling, with their bare hands, these diseased bodes, many of these SS officers went on to contract and then die of typhus themselves.

Looking at photographs today of the big clean-up, I sometimes struggle to believe, to remember I was actually there, but there is one particular image that instantly returns me to that place, standing beside the other kids, flapping away the flies and barely noticing the smell of rot, as we yelled out the worst curses we could think off: there was one SS officer, a man, who was wearing a white jacket. It was so odd, that white garment, in the midst of the dirt and the stench, so wildly inappropriate, given what he was doing. Of course, it became quite muddy and grey with each passing moment, but when he first stood out there in his gleaming jacket under the blue sky, I was bedazzled. He features in a lot of photographs taken at the time. Once the camp had been liberated, we were inundated with another army – this one was made up of journalists and photographers – and I fancy that I wasn't the only one to fixate on the white jacket; it obviously caught the attention and imagination of the visiting media too.

When the attraction of harassing the SS wore off, we children exercised our newfound freedom by exploring the camp in search of adventure and interesting things. Imagine our delight when we came upon the repair shop for the armoured vehicles of the German army! It was the stuff of dreams: an unsupervised playground, filled with tanks, cars of all sizes and motorbikes. Blissful hours were spent in the turrets of the different tanks, turning them from left to right, manoeuvring the guns up and down, as we fought, and won, mighty fictional battles against innumerable Nazis.

In those early chaotic days the British army demonstrated their anger and repulsion by rounding up German dignitaries and civilians from the surrounding villages and forcing them to see exactly what had been done to Jewish families in their name.

* * *

A couple of days after the British arrived, my mother told us that Aunt Margo had typhus and needed to go to the hospital. She had been feeling unwell even before liberation. Somehow, in the midst of a full-blown epidemic, nobody in our hut had contracted this hugely contagious disease, which was nothing short of a miracle. Margo did her best to fight the weakness, wanting to do as much as possible for the women and children who were, as she saw it, in her care. Eventually, she was much too ill to get out of bed and my mother kept the rest of us away from her while tending to her sister herself. It was the first time that I saw Mother look scared and I remember the next few days as being very tense indeed. As far as our family was concerned, our British liberators could not have arrived at a more perfect time – any later and we might have lost our beloved Aunt Margo.

After the British arrived it was estimated that 70 percent of the inmates required medical attention. To try to cope with such huge numbers the nearby Wehrmacht Panzer Training School was turned into a hospital and because our hut contained mothers and children we were considered a priority. I don't think it was an easy decision for Mother to let Margo go, but she probably felt she had little choice because of the speed of her sister's deterioration. But she worried that Margo would not receive enough personal attention in the hospital since hundreds of typhus sufferers were being brought in every day. Then she came up with the idea of having me accompany my aunt. She could have chosen my older brother, but she suspected that I might be in danger of succumbing to typhus because I was so skinny and complained of feeling tired all the time. So my mother decided to tell the British doctor that I too was sick and in need of urgent medical treatment. We had come through so much there was no way she was going to take any risks at this stage.

Upon hearing that I would be going to the hospital, I felt a sudden fear about leaving my mother and brother behind. We had not been out of each others' sight for so many months that I felt immediately anxious about a separation. This feeling, however, was immediately followed by one of pure elation as I considered the awesome fact that I would actually be leaving the camp for other surroundings. The world beyond the barbed wire seemed like a dream I once had and the thought of stepping back over the threshold again made my heart race with excitement.

Someone had the unpleasant task of measuring how sick people were. There had to be a cut-off point because there were too many sick people and only a handful of doctors and nurses available. Only sufferers who stood a strong chance of recovery were looked after in those early days.

I had a few days to get use to the idea of going to the hospital before Margo and I were collected by the ambulance, on 23 April, and taken to what was called the 'Human Laundry'. This was a converted garage where German tanks had formerly been serviced and now it was human beings that were being cared for. I saw lots of metal tables; each had its own flexible hose from which wonderful warm water came. Margo and I were stripped naked, then helped up onto a table and scrubbed clean by a German nurse. As you can imagine, we were absolutely filthy after wearing the same clothes for six months and washing rarely in freezing water. Nine-year-old boys are probably not known for appreciating a good scrub, but I must say I revelled in watching the months of dirt and grime being removed from my body. The only way to describe how it felt is to use the rather plain but blatant truth: I felt human again.

Once we were clean and dry, we were sprayed with DDT delousing powder and given fresh pyjamas to wear. Because I was so small and thin and it was an adult size, the pyjama top went right down to the ground, so there was no point in putting the bottoms on me. The nurses were filled with pity for me as I stood there, my wasted frame utterly swamped by the pyjama top. These German girls were very good to us; they were gentle and did their best to reassure us that everything would be fine. I have read since that initially they were resentful at finding themselves there under the supervision of the British army, but their sulking attitudes changed as soon as their patients arrived. On seeing the physical condition of the Belsen inmates, they immediately burst into tears. Certainly, the ones Margo and I encountered were simply lovely to us.

After the delousing, we were placed on stretchers and covered with blankets, a luxury in itself, and then placed on a waiting line for the hospital. The ambulance collected us in fours. I made sure I was right beside my aunt at all times. I could see she was quite ill, but she still managed to say a few words to me. I'm sure we chatted until our ambulance arrived, but what we talked about I have completely forgotten.

The hospital was approximately a twenty-minute drive away. I remember it as a large, concrete building, three storeys, with lots of rooms inside. What I did not realise was that our building was one of twenty-seven in a large compound. We ended up in a room with eight beds, four each side. Margo was placed in a bed right beside the door and next to that was a makeshift bed made up especially for me. The soapy smell of those spotless, white sheets soothed any nervousness I may have felt. All the other beds were occupied by strange women, who looked to be barely breathing. I just remember how thin we all looked, especially in comparison with the hearty medical staff.

My aunt's condition seemed to worsen soon after we arrived, and she began to yell out random, unconnected words and obscure bits of sentences that bore no relation to her or her surroundings. She succumbed to wild hallucinations, while the doctors and nurses did their very best to loosen the grip of the disease. One time she was convinced that her husband had come to visit her and regaled me with the bizarre details of their imaginary conversation. I was smart enough to remove the jewellery that she had hidden all this time from the Nazis, knowing that she would be easy pickings, in her unconscious state, for any light-fingered member of staff. I took my Uncle Dula's watch, the one he had thrown to her from the cattle cart at Sered, along with a gold chain, and I wore them myself until I decided she was well enough again.

Meanwhile, I craved food; it was all I could think about. The hunger pangs never left me. No matter what I ate, I was still hungry, and plagued the nurses constantly for more. In fact, they doted on me because, as I found out, I was the only child in this building at the time, so I constantly had my hair tousled and my cheeks fondly stroked. Whatever I wanted they gave me. Even though I was a child, I was still touched by their embarrassed apologies over what food was available – sandwiches of ham and bacon, as far from Kosher as one could get. 'But I don't care; really, I don't. I'm just hungry,' I would reassure them.

My father's parents would have been shocked at the way I licked my fingers, searching for invisible remnants of the salty meat and craving for more as soon as I had finished. At first the nurses limited my daily consumption to tiny amounts because they thought I was sick, but then they realised that there was nothing wrong with me thanks to the improvement in my surroundings, so it was safe to feed me whenever I said I was hungry, which was often. Those small amounts had only served to awaken a raging appetite that could only be satisfied by good-sized regular meals, along with whatever the nurses would give me in between.

Aunt Margo's condition was beginning to worry me. I knew something was very wrong when she refused point blank to eat or drink. The nurses did their best, but there just wasn't the time to stand over her with so many other seriously ill patients needing their attention. My mother had been right to anticipate this. Margo wanted only one thing – and that was a cigarette. It was all she asked for. In vain I begged her to eat something. She was skin and bone, and I was watching women dying from malnutrition all around us. Nearly every day there was yet another vacant bed ready for a new arrival. I was not sure why they were dying, but I assumed it was because they weren't eating enough. In my head, food and water were the only things that could save my aunt, probably because I felt so healthy myself after receiving regular meals again.

'Please, Aunt Margo, you have to eat. You heard what the nurses said.'

'Oh, don't nag me, child. I'm not hungry. I just want a cigarette. I'd do anything for a cigarette.'

I knew I was a favourite with the nurses, with my tiny

body and blond hair. They couldn't resist me, so when I asked them for cigarettes, they would give me two, once they realised that I wasn't actually planning on smoking them myself. I had a plan, and the cigarettes were to play the most important part in it.

'Now, Aunt, I have a cigarette for you. But, see, I'm tearing it in half so it will last longer. I'll give you the first half when you eat your dinner.'

'No, NO! Give me the cigarette now, there's a good boy. Don't torment me.'

But I refused. The poor woman was forced by her addiction to allow me to slowly spoon-feed her, forcing down a few small mouthfuls and accepting a few sips of water until I was happy enough to give her what she wanted.

Somewhere beyond our ward my mother and brother were looking for us. With over two dozen large buildings, each with three storeys, in the hospital compound and absolutely no information available about the patients inside, they had to go into each every single one and search each room on every floor until they eventually found us. This took several weeks because the hospital staff were actively discouraging visitors as they wanted to combat the further spreading of disease. It was an emotional reunion. I think it must have been hard for my mother to let me leave her sight. I certainly missed her and Miki more than I had anticipated. Still hallucinating, Aunt Margo told her sister about all the visits she had received from their many relatives. I stood beside her, subtly making faces and pointing to my head to assure Mother and Miki that my hopelessly muddled aunt was making it all up.

Over the next few weeks I took good care of my patient. She managed to eat a little more every day, if only to have a puff of the cigarettes I begged from the generous nurses. I too was the one who helped her to the bathroom and stayed with her while the nurses washed her or checked on her progress. I never left her alone, and the nurses told Margo she was very lucky to have a nephew like me! It was a slow process, but slowly and surely I began to see a clear improvement in her; her temperature returned to normal and the small meals she was eating helped to rebuild her strength.

Years later, whenever I visited Margo's house, she would call out in front of everyone, particularly if she had any other visitors around: 'This here is the angel who saved my life!' Margo never curbed her addiction to cigarettes and smoked right up to the end of her life when she died, in Israel, in 1974, from throat cancer at the age of seventy-two.

Chapter 18

• • • • • •

After Liberation

Plenty was happening back at the camp while I was busy nursing Margo. Her daughter, Chava, also fell seriously ill and the British doctor recommended that she too be transferred to the hospital. However, my mother insisted on caring for her as she feared that the timid girl would be forgotten about because of the lack of nurses. (Not surprisingly, a lot of nurses themselves ended up contracting typhus from their patients. This put an enormous strain on an already stressed medical staff.) Fortunately, thanks to my mother's constant attention, Chava began to improve after two weeks or so.

There was a strange occurrence at the end of April when a large consignment of lipstick arrived at the camp. The British officers, who were trying to organise vast supplies of food and linen as quickly as they could, were much annoyed over what they perceived to be a waste of resources. However, they soon changed their minds when they saw the psychological effect the lipstick produced in the hundreds of still-skeletal women. Being able to apply some make-up again stirred up feelings of pride and interest, perhaps even hope, that had lain dormant for months, even years. Again I use the phrase: it made them feel human.

Then there was the second-hand clothes stand that was nicknamed 'Harrods'. Women flocked, once they were well enough, carefully inspecting the wide selection of dresses, coats, jumpers and blouses, revelling in the luxury of wearing something different that, more importantly, allowed them to be an individual, a real person, once more.

At the beginning of May, Mother, Miki and Chava were finally evacuated from Bergen-Belsen. Their new home was the Wehrmacht barracks, building MB22, about a mile away from the concentration camp. Because it was formerly a residence of the German army it was modern, spacious, well-equipped and built of brick instead of wood – four reasons why it was a one hundred percent improvement on Hut 207. There they were free to choose a room and they picked one that was big enough for the five of us to share eventually.

It took five weeks to evacuate the entire concentration camp. As each hut was emptied of its inhabitants, it was burnt to the ground to stamp out the typhus bacteria. This was the only solution, since all the huts were completely infested with lice and fleas. The last hut to be burnt was Number 217 – the bonfire was lit at a special military ceremony on 21 May.

As soon as Margo was well enough, about three or four weeks after our arrival at the hospital, she and I joined the others in our new accommodation. We didn't have to travel very far since the hospital too was part of the barracks. My mother collected us, bringing fresh clothes for us to wear. I was very excited at being with her and Miki again, this time under much happier circumstances. I loved the new room and my spirits soared on seeing the clean, roomy bath and toilet facilities and the great, big, airy canteen where we sat on chairs at a table to eat our delicious food from a plate. These little things were of immense comfort to me now. The world was beginning to come right again.

There was a large cinema in the camp specifically for British soldiers, but they were each allowed to bring in one inmate with them to the films. With the majority of the women on the road to recovery, wearing nice clothes and make-up, they certainly had their pick of possible escorts. I remember seeing lots of couples made up of soldiers and former inmates as they walked about the camp hand-in-hand. It was such a positive, life-affirming sight after so many months of horrors and degradation. Hoping to be chosen instead, I would line up outside the cinema with the other kids, and we would beg to be brought in to see whatever was showing. I had the good luck to be picked a few times and wish I could remember the films I saw – though I would not have understood them since they were in English, but I do remember they were all about war and I thought they were glamorous and exciting. It was with great satisfaction that I watched the Nazis being trounced again and again.

The British army continued to be very good to us. They organised plenty of activities because they not only wanted to heal us of disease and malnutrition, they also wanted to rehabilitate us and so get us used to living normal lives again. There was a library, courses in the English language, music lessons, art lessons, concerts and dances, while newspapers allowed the adults to catch up on what was happening in the rest of the world. My favourite activity was the jeep racing, where soldiers had to drive their jeeps in reverse, as fast as they could, while manoeuvring in and around obstacles. It always brought out a crowd, who were more than ready to cheer and applaud the driving skills on display. Other events included raucous football matches between the military and the former inmates, along with athletic competitions of all kinds.

So, you may think, life was good and we could laugh again. And that certainly may have been the case for the first few weeks, but then the worry began, once we were all fit enough: the desperate desire to know about our relatives. For the first time in a long time we wondered about our father. Was he still alive? Had anything happened to the house or farm? While I might have been happy and busy enough, both Margo and my mother began to grow anxious about their husbands and about Margo's son, Laco, and the rest of the family.

Because the war had only just ended – officially on 8 May 1945 – there had been little or no communication with the outside world before then. It was left to the Red Cross to compile the lists of survivors, which were then distributed to the capital cities throughout Europe, according to the relevant nationalities. Our names were added to the list of Slovakian survivors put on display in Prague. Meanwhile, notices arrived almost daily in response to the lists, with information put on the noticeboards. This became part of Mother's and Margo's day, traipsing over to these boards to see if anyone from the family had sent any messages through.

The British authorities were against former inmates leaving the barracks too soon, which was understandable since they had to be sure that we would not present any danger to Europe by bringing typhus or any other disease on our journeys home. There were still a great many sick people who would not have been welcomed back just yet. Towards the end of May, the first groups of former inmates left for their country of origin. Sweden was one of the first country to accept all their ill citizens, provided that typhus was

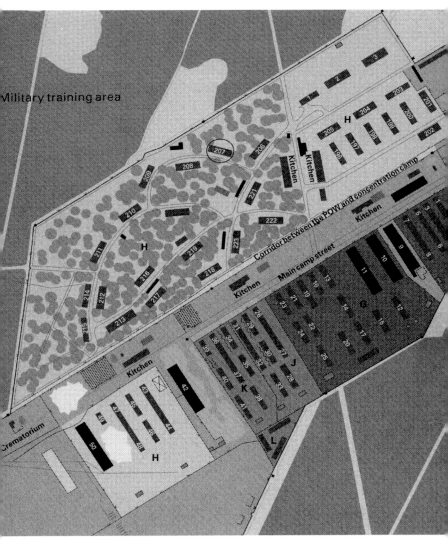

Section of a map showing the topography of Bergen–Belsen camp, reproduced by kind permission of the copyright holders: Stiftung niedersächsische Gedenkstätten/Gedenkstätte Bergen–Belsen.

We were held in Hut 207 (circled).

Left: Aunt Margo on her wedding day with her husband, Dula, on her left and her brother, Gejza. Both men died at Buchenwald.

Above left and right: A whole family wiped out: my mother's sister, Adela, on her wedding day with her husband, Bela. Their children, Kati and Agi. They all perished at Auschwitz.

Left: Three cousins who had survived Bergen–Belsen: Miki, Chava and me.

My immediate family in 1948: Myself, Miki, Mother and Father.

Above: This is me (centre front) with my Hashomer Hatzair group in Bratislava in 1947–1948.

Below: Here I am learning engineering at the works in Israel, 1952.

Above: On my
beloved Vespa,
Israel 1952–1953
Left: Miki (left) and
myself in Germany,
1958 on our great
trip around Europe.

Above: My wife, Evanne, (second from left) on her way to Israel after our marriage, 1961. Below: Miki's family. *Back, left to right*: Judith (Miki's wife), Mother, Miki, Father. *Front*: Dorit, Raya (Miki's daughters).

Above: My family in recent years. *Back, left to right:* Veronica (my son David's wife), David holding their baby, Anna; myself, my sons Gideon and Jonathan; my grandson, Jonathan (Gideon's son); my partner, Joyce.
Front: Josh and Zoe (David's children from his first marriage); Jacob, Adam (Gideon's sons); Mark (my nephew).

Right: Meeting President Mary McAleese, September 2005.

'I realised that, as one of the last witnesses, I must speak out.'

firmly under control. But not everyone was welcomed back, despite perfect health. For instance, eight thousand Polish Jews reached Poland and quickly retraced their steps back to the barracks in Belsen after finding themselves still unwanted and despised. The barracks, therefore, became their actual home, along with any others who felt they could not or would not return to where they came from. There was a new name for the barracks, the 'Displaced Persons' Camp', and it became an efficiently-run village, with its own leadership, Yiddish and Hebrew newspapers, schools and political organisations, up until 1951. Over the next few years approximately two thousand babies were born here.

Meanwhile, there was huge excitement among the larger family in our honour, only we knew nothing about it for another while. Uncle Artur, my mother's brother, had made the journey to Prague to read the lists of survivors and there he made the discovery that Mother, Margo, Miki, Chava and I had survived Bergen-Belsen. He rang my father with the wonderful news.

Maybe it was only a couple of days after my uncle's phone call that my mother and Margo made their daily visit to the noticeboard. Miki, Chava and I accompanied them, as usual, since we were all anxious for news about our relatives. Even if there was nothing for us, it could still be an exciting experience as someone always received good news while we were there. It was fun to watch the laughter and tears of joy that greeted a name, or names, on the board. And then, just like that, it was our turn. When my father heard that we were alive he sent a card to us in Bergen–Belsen – and there it was on the board! My mother screamed, making us all jump: 'Arnold! Arnold Reichental!' She grabbed Margo's arm: 'Here, read here! Tell me I'm right. He's alive. Yes?' Margo read out his name and immediately hugged her sister through her tears. Meanwhile, we three children hadn't moved a muscle. We just stared at the sobbing women, doing our best to take it all in. Mother turned to me and my brother, reaching for us both: 'Father is alive! Oh my goodness, I can hardly believe it. He's alive!' It was a magical moment. I don't know if during our stay at the camp I had really considered whether my father was alive or not; I probably didn't allow myself to dwell on it. A child only ever wants to hear good news; anything else can be put off until later – much, much later.

Our good news fired up Margo and Chava that they would soon be hearing from my Uncle Dula and cousin Laco.

The barracks began to empty out in June as the health of the majority was deemed good enough for them to travel. Since most of the main railway lines had been bombed, the thousands of inmates were being driven home in buses. We had to wait our turn. Dutch inmates left first, followed by the Poles and Hungarians (many of whom would soon be back).

Unbeknownst to me, five young orphans were on their way to a new life in Ireland (see Appendix 3). After that it was the turn of the Slovakian Jews – us.

It was 15 July before we got to say goodbye to the people we were leaving behind, and boarded our bus. It was a strange experience seeing those buses branded with our national flag and the destination of Prague on the sign. You might think that we'd jump for joy, but we didn't. For one thing, the silence surrounding Dula and Laco was, by now, absolutely deafening. Margo had received no news about her husband and son, and the strain on her was enormous as she did her best to hide her worse fears from her daughter. But, of course, Chava was more than aware of what her mother was trying to shield her from. Death was still all around us as the news of murdered relatives began to filter through to those noticeboards alongside the names of the survivors. As far as I could see, everyone that we knew in the barracks had lost somebody. No family had remained untouched. Therefore, though we were glad that the war was over, that we were no longer living in a concentration camp, and that we were finally on our way home, there was no sense of hysterical celebration, as plenty of people were too busy mourning before we even reached Prague. Thanks to our ignorance, we merely worried about Dula and Laco, having no idea, just yet, of who had died or lived from our extended families. All we knew for definite was that we would see my father again.

I remember Miki looking very smart in his Belgian army uniform as we departed! Actually it was just the jacket. The clothes we had worn in Belsen had been burnt with the rest of the camp, so we were wearing whatever was available from the second-hand clothes stall. Miki, obviously at an age where he could choose his own clothes, picked out the dark blue jacket and beret for himself. He looked so tall that day and I felt rather proud to be his little brother.

Our three buses were old and weary. Our one couldn't go very fast and every time the driver changed gear the whole bus shuddered back and forth. We had a long journey in front of us and hoped that the bus would make it there in one piece. Despite any worries that we may have had about the near future, it was still a wonderful thing to drive out of the barracks and into the countryside. For the first time in over nine months we felt properly free. We passed many villages that were dotted around the edge of the forest; I remember red tiled roofs and pleasant little gardens. Untouched by war, they made perfect little postcard images, proof to us that flowers still bloomed and that pretty little things like lace curtains still mattered. They contrasted enormously with the towns we travelled through, the damaged buildings, gaping holes and shattered glass, a stark reminder of what had been going on. I particularly remember the total devastation of the city of Nuremberg.

After driving all day, we stopped each evening in a designated town or village for food and accommodation. Wherever we ended up, we were greeted by the local mayor or authority figure, who welcomed us with a speech. The three busloads would then be split amongst the population. The five of us strove to stay in the same house together. We were treated impeccably by the German families. Each table would be beautifully set with the best china and crockery. The meals were always generous in our eyes, though I recall many apologies made for shortages owing to the war. After supper, we were given the beds of the house. We never asked questions, never asked where the hosts and their family would sleep since we were obviously taking their own beds. When we got up in the mornings, a fine breakfast would be ready for us. Lunch mostly took place in public town or village halls, where it was usually served up to us by Americans, the occupying army. Our every meal had been meticulously planned before we left the barracks.

Throughout the German towns and villages, we heard the same thing over and over again: 'We didn't know anything about the camps. We had no idea.' This was treated with suspicion by the adults, including my mother and Margo, who questioned each other: 'Could it be that they really knew nothing about what was done on *their* behalf? How is that possible?' The Germans certainly never asked us any questions about our personal experiences, only profusely apologising for their lack of knowledge as they served up the best food they could offer. On the bus afterwards I would hear the adults compliment the kindness and politeness of their hosts while asking the all-important question: 'How did it happen that this nation of well-mannered and intelligent people could inflict such cruelty and criminal behaviour on innocent human beings – men, women and children?' Nobody had an answer to this.

That's all I really remember about the trip, which took seven days. The only other thing was poor Chava's nervousness. While the Jewish adults wondered if the German civilians were telling the truth about their blissful ignorance, Chava simply did not trust them enough to eat their food, so convinced was she that they were going to poison us. She had brought biscuits from the army canteen and this is all that passed her lips until we reached Prague. No doubt the unanswered questions surrounding her father and brother's existence was taking its toll and preventing her from relaxing at all in Germany. Constantly on her guard, she fully expected us to be harmed in some way before we could cross over the German border.

It seemed to take forever in those ancient buses, with their constant creaking and straining. The trip was tiring, and rock-hard seats were uncomfortable, both on one's backside and one's nerves. But we eventually left western Europe behind, now occupied by the British and the Americans, and entered the eastern block, now occupied by the Russians.

The strange thing was that as we were coming from western occupied Europe to re-enter what was now Czechoslovakia, we were perceived to be outsiders and required special documentation in order to be allowed to return and live once again in our own country. In other words, we were coming home as refugees.

We were driven to a detention centre on the outskirts of Prague where we ended up unintentionally staying for the next two weeks. For the first few days we weren't allowed to leave the immediate area because we were basically under quarantine until the doctors were sure that we were clean and healthy. However, once we had all been tested and duly found to be disease-free, we were told we could leave Prague whenever we wished.

But we didn't go yet. Margo had reached the end of her tether. She announced that she would not return to her home in Bratislava unless she got word that her husband and son were there waiting for her. Mother refused to leave Margo and Chava behind, so all we could do was wait, hope and pray for good news. Every day of our extended stay in Prague we made our way to the Red Cross building to see if their names appeared on the lists of survivors, but they never did. It was a very tense time. Then, one morning as we walked together to the Red Cross headquarters, Margo bumped into an old friend of hers from Bratislava: 'Margo! What a surprise! What on earth are you doing here in Prague?' My aunt barely smiled, which was most unlike her. Instead of saying hello, she burst out in despair: 'I'm not going home until I know my husband and son are safe. And if they don't come back to Bratislava, I will never set foot in that city again.' To our amazement, her friend replied: 'What are you talking about? Laco is at home waiting for you and Chava.'

Chapter 19

• • • • • •

Home Again

We had everything we needed in order to take the next step in our journey. The centre provided our medical clearance documents, some more second-hand clothing, a little cash and our new identity papers. They also gave us, if I remember correctly, travel passes as we would not have had any money for train tickets. One thing that we and thousands like us did not receive was any form of counselling. Not one person spoke to us about the traumatic experience of living in a concentration camp and being surrounded by thousands of rotting corpses.

Margo had to make several attempts to get through to her brother, Artur, on the phone, telling him when we would arrive in Bratislava. Nothing worked as it should in the aftermath of a devastating world war. Finally she got through and my uncle, overjoyed to hear his sister's voice, told her that he would meet us at the train station.

We boarded the train for Bratislava on a beautiful day in the first week of August. In peace time the journey from Prague would have taken no longer than a few hours, but public transport, just like making a phone call or sending a letter through the post, was hugely inefficient during those first few months after the war. So, instead of maybe three hours the journey took almost fifteen, with the train going almost as slowly as the old bus that had brought us from Belsen to Prague. There were also a lot of stops along the way. Security was tight. Our papers were checked again and again by the Russian soldiers, who were suspicious of anyone travelling from western-occupied Europe.

For the most part we were rather subdued. The security checks were an unnerving reminder of what we had all been through even before we had been incarcerated in the concentration camp. Then there also was the looming, inevitable fact that soon we would know who had survived and who hadn't. However, that all changed when we started to recognise the scenery outside the train window. In spite of everything, we began to get very excited indeed. I couldn't wait to see my father again; it was all I could think about, though I kept my impatience to myself as I could see how worried Chava was about her own father. My mother, no doubt, was going through the same thing.

After what felt like an eternity, the four steeples of Bratislava Castle came into sight. We all jumped up from our seats, wanting to be ready to get off as soon as the train stopped, hardly believing that this journey was almost at an end. Then there was an emotional reunion with my Uncle Artur and cousin Laco. Standing closely together, we heard that Dula, Margo's husband and Chava's father, had not survived Buchenwald concentration camp. I would imagine that Margo and my mother had had their suspicions that this was the case, but it must have been a dreadful shock to have it confirmed. We mourned him there and then, in the middle of the busy train station. Laco was extremely thin and his mother fussed over him, so grateful to have him with her again, while trying not to dwell on her husband's death. Laco didn't provide any details about what had happened and no one asked. It was enough just to know that we wouldn't be seeing Uncle Dula again. Artur had more sad news to impart to his sisters: their two brothers, Osy and Gejza, had also died in Buchenwald. However, for now, what was most important was that *we* were all alive. That's what we had to cling to. He also told us that my father was on his way to collect us. It was such a mix of the worst and the best kind of news. My head was spinning.

Margo gathered herself together with typical efficiency: 'Come on, everyone, let us get out of this station.' We followed her out the door, making our way to the tram stop. In spite of her grief, Margo kept hugging her son and looking about the city in wonder. Almost a year had passed since we last saw Bratislava and it felt like a very long time indeed. Taking our seats on the tram we gazed out the window drinking in the familiar sights. It was an emotional journey. We passed the National Theatre and got off at the Carlton Hotel, which was just down the road from the house, number 6 on Polovnicky Row. We walked briskly by the shop where thirteen of us had been arrested – and now only six returned.

At Margo's house, Laco had prepared some food. We must have eaten it, I suppose. Really, the only thing I remember next is my father's arrival at Margo's door. One minute he was standing outside and the very next he, Mother, Miki and I were clustered together in one sobbing embrace. We were a family once more. When we were calm enough to let go of each other, Father was given a seat at the table and a plate of food. He stared at us with pride: 'You boys are so tall now. Miki, you're almost as tall as your father.' I was very relieved to note that he had not changed at all; he was exactly as I remembered him as we had waved goodbye to him all those months before.

We were returning to Merašice that very day, so it was just a short visit with Margo. At some stage the adults began talking in Hungarian, probably discussing the tragedies of their relatives who never came back from Poland, or maybe my mother and aunt were filling my father in on the past ten months or so. He certainly never asked Miki or me about our experience in Belsen. It was simply never referred to again, either by him or my mother. I suppose my parents just wanted us to forget it and put it behind us forever.

As soon as my father finished his meal it was time for us to leave. I think the four of us were impatient to get back to our village, to our own home. It was an emotional farewell. Margo and Chava had been with us all day every day for the past ten months and we had been through so much together, so it was quite a wrench to leave them behind as we made our way back to the train station. Margo and my mother clung to each other for many minutes, Mother making Margo promise that she'd come to Merašice as soon as she could. They both knew that once we were gone, Margo would have time and space to grieve for her husband.

The train journey to Leopoldov station took its usual two hours. It was a much more exciting journey than the train to Bratislava as the scenery meant a lot more to us. The fields, houses and trees were so familiar; I found it hard to believe that such a long time had passed since I last had seen them. Already Belsen seemed a very distant place in my mind, almost like a dream I knew I had, but could remember nothing about.

There was a friendly face waiting for us at the station – who else but Mr Duraj, with the horse and carriage. How lovely it was to see him sitting proudly there, waiting to escort us on the last leg of a long journey home to Merašice. Maybe it was only in later years that I realised how this man's actions saved our lives: if he had obeyed those soldiers at the railway crossing and allowed us to be arrested there and then, my mother, Miki and I would probably have ended up in Auschwitz, where we most likely would have been murdered. Instead, Mr Duraj charged the horse to run amid the screams of rage, risking his own life to get us on the train to Bratislava.

Thus began the most enjoyable part of the trip home. The air was so clear and the winding road through the forest never looked so captivating and green. True, there had been a forest just outside the concentration camp, but it had never seemed real. I couldn't smell the freshness of the leaves or the bark of the tree; there were no birds singing. Here, however, all was lush and vibrant, with a full chorus of birds cheering, as it were, our long-awaited return. After we passed by the little village of Galanova, we could just about make out the steeple of our local church. I was beside myself with excitement, so much so that when we finally reached the drive up to our house I leapt down from the carriage and took off on foot. At the doorway, with arms open wide, was Mariška and I flung myself at her. Once she freed me I ran through the house, anxiously checking it for any drastic changes. I was hugely relieved to find that it was all exactly the same, aside from a fresh coat of paint inside and out. The kitchen table was set for dinner; Mariška and one of her daughters, Francka, had prepared a fine meal for us. There were plenty of tears and laughter over the next few hours as news of our arrival spread through the village. Everyone turned up to greet us and drink a glass of my father's *slivovic* to our health. It was good to be home.

Among the welcoming party was the man who had managed the farm in our absence. After my father's arrest, in September 1944, the house and farm was handed over to Adjutant Michael Bojansky; in fact, it was just one of five farms he took charge of, at the instigation of the National Property Fund, which was part of the Aryanisation programme for the confiscation of Jewish property. Fortunately for us, Bojansky had appointed Pavel Polacek to manage our farm. Pavel's brother was the man who had always provided the steam engine to plough the harvest, so he knew the land well. Because Pavel was a neighbour, he was determined to do right by my family and now he approached my parents with a proud declaration: 'I looked after the farm as if it were my own and I return it to you just as you left it.' Thanks to Bojansky receiving the farm so soon after my father's arrest nothing was touched, from the furniture, carpets, ornaments to the pictures on the wall. So many other Jewish people returned home to find their houses and possessions ransacked by their neighbours.

Over the next few days my parents' immediate priority was to fatten me up. I was very weak and run down from Belsen, so they looked into sending me somewhere to recuperate. They found out about a group that was set up to help Jews in need after the trauma of the holocaust – the American Jewish Joint Distribution Committee. I was sent off for a month-long holiday, along with twenty-five other children, aged between eight and twelve years, to Štrbské Pleso in the High Tatras. Accommodation was a villa called Erika. I loved every minute of it. The mountain air was clean and pure, there was plenty of exercise and the food was wonderful. I think we all put on weight over the month and our health was vastly improved. The vacation was designed to keep us busy, with plenty of activities and games, the hope being that it would go some way towards helping us forget about our traumatic experiences. Keeping in contact with our families was compulsory and we were supervised or helped to write proper and frequent letters home. We did not once mention our war experiences to one another. We didn't exchange stories about who had died belonging to us or who had survived. The holiday was all about us enjoying ourselves, it was all that was required of us, and all our parents wanted for us.

I returned home just after the harvesting. It was a comfort to see the place full of activity again. My father re-hired the same men to work on the farm, while contact was renewed with our Jewish friends from the surrounding villages. Quite a few of them had survived and so it seemed that life returned to normal again, with weekend visits and services at the synagogue.

Over the next while my parents told Miki and me as much as they felt we needed to know. My father explained that his parents, *Omama* and *Opapa*, would not be coming back home again. We were also told about our Nitra cousins, aunt and uncles who had died in the camps in Poland and Germany. They urged us not to dwell on the sadness. What had happened could not be changed. Therefore, it was our duty to our relatives to look to a brighter future and make the best of our own lives. I couldn't help feeling very sad about my grandparents. Their house looked so empty and forlorn, with just a few bits of furniture in it, some beds and the dining table.

It was decided that Miki should go to live with Margo in Bratislava because there was no decent school for him around Merašice, and since that would have been too many people for Margo to feed, Chava was going to come live with us for a while. This was good news for me. My cousin and I were like brother and sister, and I was struggling to find my footing in the village again. Chava and I began to attend the national school, but it wasn't a pleasant experience for me. It was a small school, with only two rooms: one accommodated four stages, first to fourth class, while the second held the next stages, fifth to eighth. There were only two teachers, a husband and wife. She taught the first to fourth classes. The school principal was our great family friend, Fr Harangozo. Initially I was – unsurprisingly – years behind my peers and had to go and sit with the youngest children to begin learning my alphabet again, which I found humiliating. I had great difficulty with writing, grammar and reading, and was much better with numbers and mathematics. After a while I began to make progress, but it made no difference, I still hated the school.

Back in Bratislava, Margo had re-opened her laundry and dry cleaning business. Life was tough in the city; there were a lot of shortages and the black market was thriving. In fact, Margo got involved herself, buying and selling cigarettes. Miki was her delivery boy. It was a good business, but the risk of being caught prevented them from enjoying it. Later on, after Czechoslovakia was re-united, there was a big demand for flags. Aunt Margo showed off her entrepreneurial skills once more by getting herself a contract to make large flags. The two boys, Miki and Laco, helped her with the sewing as the flags were too big for just one person.

Before we knew it, it was winter again and I was looking forward to the Christmas holidays. Snow fell earlier than usual and my mother took us tobogganing, just like she always had, on the little hill beside the Catholic church. It was my favourite time of year; we dressed in layers of our warmest clothes and spent hours building a snowman in the garden, giving him a huge carrot for a nose and a chamber-pot hat for his head. After that we flung snowballs at one another – Chava, Mother and me – until Mariška called us in to eat her homemade soup.

Miki, Laco and our other two cousins, Juraj and Bandy, came to stay for the holiday. All the children slept in my grandparents' house. We celebrated the New Year in Galanova, at the Schlesinger's ample house. There were twelve spacious rooms, enough for all our Jewish friends to come together for a raucous party that went on until the early hours of New Year's Day. It was the only time I remember Miki and me being allowed to stay up until morning.

I reluctantly returned to school in January. My mother was still concerned with trying to fatten me up. None of our family discussed what we had been through, but the results of it still lingered with my constant ailments – I picked up whatever cold or bug was going, because my energy levels were still relatively low for a child of my age. My mother made all my favourite foods. Every morning she went outside to skim the cream from the tops of the milk churns before they were taken away to be sold; she would add the cream to my morning coffee. Throughout that winter she made me lots of dishes with a high fat content: chicken liver in fat, fatty bacon and pork sausages, all available in the village. It was lucky we lived in a rural village – if Miki or Margo fancied sausages they would have had to buy them on the black market. Mother also made me the sweet dishes I liked: noodles with poppy seeds and sugar or jam, pastry flakes with cabbage and sugar, along with plenty of homemade bread, butter and cheese. When the weather improved, Chava and I followed my mother around the farm in our bare feet, watching her feeding the geese, or else we supervised the clucking hens as they sat upon their eggs, only moving on when the eggs had been hatched.

School was still a huge source of unhappiness for me. Chava made a little more progress than I did, but neither of us made any friends; so we just played together. My problem at school was the obvious one: there weren't enough teachers. I needed someone who was free to focus on my failings in order to help me overcome them. Unfortunately, the husband-and-wife team simply had no time for us and I had long stopped asking questions or admitting when I didn't understand my lessons. After some discussion over the summer months, my parents decided that it would be best if Chava and I went to school in Bratislava. It was inevitable, anyway, that one day I would have to go elsewhere for a better education – it was why Miki had left. Education was taken very seriously in our family and since there was no decent second-level school or college in Merašice I had always known that leaving home would definitely feature in my childhood at some point.

Margo agreed and so, in September 1946, we packed our bags and took the train back there. The only problem was how would Margo have time to look after us, as she was working long hours in the laundry, not to mention her extra-curricular duties concerning the black market. Some sort of 'home help' was needed and one that was completely trust-worthy, and preferably someone we knew. This is how Mar-tuska, Mariška's daughter, came to live with us in Bratislava, to take care of Chava and me and help about the house.

PART III
AFTER BELSEN –
LATER LIFE

Chapter 20

Bratislava

I moved to Bratislava shortly after my eleventh birthday, in June. It was a big step for me, having spent all my life – aside from the previous year – on a rural farm in a small village. It was quite a squash in Margo's two-bedroomed flat. Chava and Laco slept in one room while Miki and I were given the other one. Margo slept in the sitting room, while Martuska made up her collapsible bed every evening in the kitchen.

I attended the National Gymnasium College on Grossling Street. It was a large mixed school, with three storeys and, therefore, vastly different from the little village school in Merašice. My classroom was on the third floor. Academically, I had quite a challenge ahead of me as I had had to jump four stages from where I was in my old school. Mathematics was my favourite subject while I still struggled with reading and grammar. I hated history because I could never remember the dates of battles or the places they were fought in.

Miki and I needed new clothes for the coming winter months. Before the war, Mother would have taken us shopping, but this wasn't possible now as there were a lot of shortages in post-war Bratislava. New clothes, when available, were of poor quality – and, besides, another shortage was cash. Once again the American Jewish Joint Distribution Committee came to our assistance. We went along to them and were completely kitted out with new outfits. The only problem was that they were American clothes – for instance, I was now the dubious owner of a good quality red-checked jacket. There was nothing like this available in a local store.

My cousin, Laco, was a member of a Zionist youth organisation called '*Hashomer Hatzair*' (The Young Guardsmen). In fact, he was one of their leaders, and insisted that Miki and I join as soon as possible. So we did, along with Chava too, not that I fully understood what it was all about, but once I got involved I never looked back. For the first time I felt part of something good thanks to my religion. At that stage, we, the surviving children of the Holocaust, probably needed to be reminded that Judaism was not a bad thing that would bring only trouble to one's door. In this group I was no longer the religious outsider with a yellow star or a loud, red-checked sports jacket.

The organisation was housed in a large, two-storey build-ing on Zochova Street. Before the war it had been a Jewish school, and it had a large yard where we played football and attended our roll calls. We shared the building with two other Jewish religious groups: the '*Maccabi*' and '*Bnei Akiba*'.

The group became a big part of my life. We met three or four times a week and were divided into groups according to our age. There were about twelve children in my group and I was the smallest. Each group was named after an Israelite tribe; ours was called Jehuda, and our leader was Gila Fatran. She was very popular, thanks to her intelligence and good looks. We were steeped, willingly, in the culture of our forefa-thers. I learnt Hebrew, Hebrew songs, Israeli folk dances and all about Israel and Palestine. One day Gila said to me: 'Tomi is not a Hebrew name, so I think we should give you one. How about Ezra, do you like that?' I nodded with pleasure. Ezra remains my Hebrew name to this very day – it's how all my friends address me in Israel. (In later years Gila went on to marry Duro Fatran [Friedman] from Kapince, the village next to Merašice. She studied at the Hebrew University in

Jerusalem and fulfilled her dream of becoming a writer with the publication of *Fight For Survival* as part of her doctorate.)

As a proud member of Hashomer Hatzair, I marched with my friends on 1 May to celebrate International Workers' Day, waving Israeli flags, representing the Jewish Socialist Movement. Our group even spent summer holidays together. The first time I went away with them was July 1947, to Vranov, in Eastern Slovakia, for a fortnight of fun and activities. Jewish children from all over Slovakia took part. You might find it hard to believe, but we never mentioned the Holocaust or anything about how many relatives we had lost. Our sole purpose was to look forward to a better future. Accordingly, we never talked about the past. The organisation, which was similar to the scouts, was actually preparing us for a better life in Israel, our true homeland. Over the course of those two weeks we were taught self-defence, first aid and there were plenty of lectures about Israel and the Hebrew language. At night we sang Hebrew-Israeli songs around a blazing bonfire and practised our folk dancing.

When I visited Merašice I would talk excitedly to my parents about the possibility of moving to Israel. They were already very keen about the idea as my Uncle Dusi, who had already moved to Israel before the war, was urging them to do the exact same thing. There was a deadline too, as once the Communists took over Czechoslovakia, the border would probably be closed. The Zionist movement was contacting Jewish families to advise them to start packing as it was only a matter of time before it would be made impossible for them to leave. Another reason that the move might have been attractive was that all was not as it should have been. I'm afraid that post-war Czechoslovakia was still a difficult place for its Jewish citizens. When I played out in the yard at Hashomer Hatzair Zochova Street school, my friends and I would inevitably find ourselves the target of stones and abuse from the non-Jewish kids in the neighbourhood. We had got used to picking up their stones and firing them back at them. However, more and more frequently, things would get out of hand with Jewish boys bleeding from cuts to the head and face. These battles could last for up to an hour and would only end when some of our senior boys rushed outside to chase away our attackers. Then there was the time that I was walking alone up Zochova Street on my way to a meeting. A strange boy suddenly appeared by my side, falling into step with me. 'Where are you going?' he asked. Too timid to tell him to mind his own business, I replied, 'Just up this road.' He must have known exactly where I was heading because he swung his arm behind me. It turned out he had a stone hidden in the palm of his hand, which he launched quite viciously at the back of my head and, of course, at such close proximity he couldn't fail to meet his target.

It was around this time that Margo found herself on a bit of an adventure to retrieve some personal possessions. In 1941, when Jews were ordered to hand in their valuables to the authorities, my Uncle Dula collected up precious items of sentimental value belonging to himself and Margo, like wedding gifts and presents they had given one another: a gold pocket watch, necklaces and rings. He bought a steel box for the jewellery and gave it to a Mr Skoda for safekeeping. Mr Skoda was the man who had given his holiday home to Margo's family when they were hiding out from deportation; he then cracked under interrogation, which had led to their arrest. Because he was a German, he found himself banished from Bratislava by the Soviets, only returning to Czechoslovakia after the war. Margo went to the police, who were able to give her Mr Skoda's address – he was now living in the Sudetenland, the area that had been annexed by Germany in 1942, but was now part of Czechoslovakia again. She wrote him a very nice letter asking for the box to be returned to her. Much to her surprise he replied in kind, explaining that unfortunately he no longer had the jewellery in his possession. Convinced he was lying, Margo asked Uncle Artur, the barrister, for his help. The brother and sister decided to pay Mr Skoda a visit and took the train to the Sudetenland, giving him quite a surprise when he opened his door to them. He was wearing an armband with the letter 'D', for *Deutscher*, meaning German. Margo explained she had come for her jewellery and then watched Mr Skoda squirm as he offered up various reasons as to why he couldn't help her out, ranging from the box being taken from him to his dutifully burying it 'somewhere', but exactly where he just could not remember. Artur listened to him politely until Mr Skoda ran out of excuses. Then he told him that he and Margo would be back first thing the following morning, adding a veiled threat to unmask him: 'I really hope you will have found my sister's jewellery by then, sir. As it stands, some people might feel that the Mayer [Margo's family] family's arrest, along with Mr Mayer's subsequent death, was a result of your collaboration with the Gestapo. After all, it was your house that they were removed from, so you can appreciate how easy it would be to make that assumption.'

When Margo and Artur returned the next day Mr Skoda took them, and his shovel, on a short walk to a nearby forest. There they stopped beneath a tree and he began to dig, just for a few seconds, before the box appeared in the mud. On opening it, Margo discovered that a couple of pieces were missing, but there was no way of proving it. Besides, she was delighted to have the pieces that were left. The three of them walked back to the house, where, as a gesture of good will, Margo invited Mr Skoda to come out to a café for a coffee with herself and Artur. He declined, however, explaining, 'Germans are not allowed into cafés.' How the world had changed.

Chava still has the rusty metal box with the jewellery today.

* * *

After the summer holidays, I returned to Bratislava, but not to Margo's flat. Instead, I went into a Youth Boarding House that was run by the Hashomer Hatzair and supported by the Jewish agency. Laco had already moved out of the flat and Miki was away studying, so it made sense for me to go into the hostel as if I remained in Margo's she would have needed to retain Mariška's daughter just for me. Just a short walk from the train station, it was a large, spacious building with three floors, enough for twenty children like myself, between the ages of twelve and fifteen years. The ground floor was made up of the kitchen and large dining room, and the first and second floors were the bathrooms and dormitories. We were well looked after by our Jewish cook/housekeeper, Mrs Hass. She doted on us as if we were her own children and we called her *Hass Neni* (Aunt Hass). It was she who made sure we were well turned out for school each morning.

I was very relieved to pass my first-year exams at the college and was, at long last, able to join a class of children my own age. For me, school was all about education. Because I was so wrapped up in the Hashomer Hatzair, which provided me with a full and active social life, not to mention a home from home, I had no need for non-Jewish friends. So I didn't push myself to be popular with my classmates. All my free time was spent with Jewish children. I didn't have one Christian friend.

Meanwhile, Miki had moved on. He went to live in Czeské Budejovice in order to study engineering at the technical school there. Like him, I found myself absorbed by mechanical matters. My father was a little disappointed that neither of his sons had any interest in agriculture.

On 29 November 1947, the United Nations General Assembly voted in favour of the Partition plan for Palestine (Resolution 181). We heard the news on the radio in Zochova Street, holding our breaths as we listened to the votes being read out, state by state: 33 voted for partition, 13 voted against, with 10 states abstaining. I remember us jumping up from our seats and cheering madly. Quite predictably, the Jewish population were overjoyed while the Arab states rejected it, threatening war if a Jewish state was established. Accordingly, as soon as partition was introduced, the siege of Jerusalem began, lasting from 1 December 1947 to 10 July 1948. We celebrated the result on 1 December 1947, in front of Bratislava's National Theatre. I stood with hundreds of other Jewish boys and girls, dancing and waving our Israeli flags. Everyone felt it was only a matter of time before Israel would be declared a state. And we weren't wrong. Five months later, on 14 May 1948, at 4.00pm, the leader of the Workers Party (MAPAI), who would become Israel's first Prime Minister, David Ben-Gurion, read out a statement, declaring the inauguration of an independent Jewish state of Israel, bringing an end to thirty years of British mandate. The following day, six Arab armies belonging to Egypt, Syria, Jordan, Iraq, Saudi Arabia and Lebanon invaded the fledgling state.

The war raged on between temporary ceasefires for the next two years, finally ending in January 1949, by which time Israel held an additional 2,500 square miles more than had been previously allotted to it by the UN Partition Plan. Seven months of intense negotiations ensued before Israel signed an armistice agreement in July, with Egypt, Jordan, Syria and Lebanon.

Back in Bratislava, we followed the events on our radios. Some of us fretted that the state of Israel, which seemed so small and fragile in comparison to the vast Arab area of the Middle East, might not survive. However, as the news improved, our pride in the little state grew. Not only could Israel defend herself, but she also had the strength and resources to take territory from the Arab forces. With the end of the fighting, in January 1949, the Arab states continued with their refusal to recognise Israel and the uneasy neighbours remained in a state of war. In fact, there were three further major wars to be fought in order for Israel to retain her independence. Of course, the tragedy is that, more than sixty years later, the little nation is still in a state of war with most of its neighbours; only Egypt and Jordan went on to sign a peace treaty.

Once the British mandate ended, the path to Israel was a highly attractive one for Jews from all over Europe, who took to it in their thousands. It was a dream come true for them as they continued to feel marginalised in the respective lands of their birth. My own parents' desire to emigrate was spurred on with the introduction of new Communist-led land reforms which restricted the amount of land a farmer could own. Feeling that there was no future for himself and his family in Czechoslovakia, my father put the word out that he wanted to sell the house and farm. Within a short amount of time, two brothers showed an interest and suddenly it looked like we would actually be leaving Merašice for good.

I turned thirteen in June 1948, my Bar Mitzvah year. It wasn't such an enjoyable day thanks to my failing history in my end-of-year exams. The results came out just before my birthday and devastated me. I would need to repeat the exam and if I failed it a second time I'd have to repeat the entire year again. There was no celebration in the synagogues and I didn't get to read my portion of the Torah. To be honest, it's a bit of a mystery today why there wasn't more of a fuss. I suppose, when I think about it, the Hashomer Hatzair was a socialist organisation, and there was no mention of religion or religious-based ceremonies. Certainly, no one encouraged me to go to a synagogue or attend the classes for the Bar Mitzvah. Instead, Margo made a luncheon in my honour and we all gathered in her flat: my parents, Miki, Laco, Chava and me. Before the food was served it was suggested that I make a speech. Standing up, I began to thank Margo for the food before us and then, branching out, I thanked my parents for their constant love and support. At this point, my history result got the better of me and I broke down, apologising to everyone for failing the exam. My poor parents rushed to reassure me, but it was no use. That result ruined my day, though, of course, my Bar Mitzvah was a huge improvement on Miki's in Belsen. The food was better and, more importantly, my father was sitting beside me.

The next six weeks were spent in intense preparation for my repeat exam. I worked long and hard to memorise the hundreds of battles and the names of little known kings, along with the names of famous poets and writers that I plainly had no interest in. But it was worth it when I passed. That summer I went away for the annual holiday with my friends from Hashomer Hatzair for a glorious two weeks of camping in the middle of a forest. As usual the timetable revolved around sporting activities, Hebrew lessons and learning all about Israel. When I went back to Merašice afterwards my parents told me that we would be emigrating as soon as we were able to. I was hugely excited.

In September I returned to Bratislava, back to the youth hostel, to begin my third year in school. But my heart just wasn't in it. All I could think about was going to Israel. What was the point in throwing myself into my studies here when none of these battles or poets would mean a thing in my new country? And I wasn't alone. There was a distinct fall-off in school attendance among my Jewish friends. Hass Neni did her best, but there was no controlling us. One morning we left our school bags behind and had only taken a few steps before she was bellowing at us from the upstairs window: 'Wait! Wait, your bags are still here. Stay where you are, I'll drop them down to you.' This she duly did, quickly throwing our satchels out the window before we could run away. Most days we headed off to the library instead of going to school. The thing was we felt we wouldn't be in Bratislava for much longer. Accordingly, just before the Christmas holidays we received the most wonderful news: our youth group, the Hashomer Hatzair, would be emigrating to Israel in February, as the first organised group of children to go. In other words, my last day of school before I went home for Christmas was the last day of school for me in Czechoslovakia.

All our parents had given us their permission to go. My parents agreed to let me go first and then they would follow with Miki. Chava was in the same group as me and we began to organise ourselves for the departure. Right across Europe, thousands of others were doing the exact same thing but in Czechoslovakia we were experiencing lots of unforeseen and unnecessary difficulties, thanks to the Communists. They put severe restrictions on what we were allowed to take with us.

Firstly, we had to compile a list of possessions we wanted to take. This list was sent to the customs office in Nitra and any item not cleared for emigration was struck off your list. To ensure that you kept to the new list a customs officer actually came out to your house to check through your suitcase or trunk, item by item, and it was they who sealed up the box. Valuable items like sewing machines, typewriters, cameras, musical instruments and so forth were not allowed to leave the country unless you proved beyond a shadow of doubt that you needed them to continue with your profession. To put it in a nutshell, they didn't want us taking anything we could sell for cash. Taking money out of the country was also an impossibility, so when the Jews sold off their Slovak homes and properties the money had no value – it had to be spent in Slovakia; you could not take it with you. I'm sure some people managed to buy dollars on the black market, but the risk of being caught was too much for the rest of us. We thought we had left that kind of fear behind us when the war ended. Just like when the anti-Semites took away Jewish businesses and personal valuables, so too did the Communists. And just like the last time, greedy officials made small fortunes out of accepting bribes to allow a Jew to take his own possessions to his new homeland.

I wanted to take my bike to Israel, but it was struck off my list. My father took me to Nitra so that I could plead my case in person. He thought if the official saw how young and small I was he might relent, but he didn't. It seemed that we were still hated by the bureaucrats.

My departure date was 13 February 1949, from Bratislava. It would take two weeks, including a stopover in Italy, to reach Israel. It was a strange moment. When we had to flee from the Nazis, I had always believed that I would see Merašice again. It never occurred to me that I wouldn't. But this time it was different. I was resigned to the fact that I might never see Merašice or Slovakia again and, as a result, my last day in the little village I grew up in was an emotional one. By far the hardest goodbye was to Mariška. Having known and relied on her so much since I was a very young child, it was a dreadful wrench to walk away from her. I also said goodbye to her daughter Martushka, who had looked after me in Bratislava. I remember walking around the farm saying a quiet farewell to it all and, I suppose, to my childhood. Never again would I watch the fields being ploughed, my father chatting with the men or my mother feeding the chickens. Never again would I see this particular patch of sky or smell the wild flowers in the summer breeze. I was amazed at my mixed emotions, the gladness about going to Israel conflicting with the sadness of leaving all this behind. What helped enormously was the knowledge that my parents and brother would soon be joining me. When it was time to go, my father and I hugged briefly: 'Don't worry, son. We'll see you very soon.' 'Yes, Father,' I said. 'See you in Israel.'

As usual, the ever-reliable Mr Duraj was taking Mother and me to the train station. He bade me a formal goodbye, saving his tears, I'm sure, for when he had to say goodbye to my parents. My mother and I were spending the night in Margo's, and then Chava and I would leave together the following morning. Last-minute items were added to my suitcase. We had all been told to bring several packets of cigarettes so that we could use them to barter for trifles like chocolate, sweets and oranges when we were passing through Italy.

As it happened, a lot of us were bringing a little more than was on show in our suitcases. Because we were just children, many parents thought that we mightn't be subjected to strenuous checks by the customs officers and therefore quite a bit of jewellery that had been previously deleted from packing lists, was leaving with us. Aunt Margo had added a solitaire diamond ring to Chava's list, but it was struck off by the inspector. She was very annoyed by this so I said: 'I'll take it with me, Auntie. I have a good place to hide it.' With that I whisked off my shoe and my sock, stuck her ring on my toe and put back on my footwear. 'Nobody will ask me to remove my shoes.' My heart was in the right place, but it wasn't the most practical of plans. A little while later Margo noticed I was limping. 'What's wrong?' she asked. I shrugged my shoulders, embarrassed to admit: 'It's really hurting me.' Margo smiled and thought for a minute: 'Well, since you so kindly volunteered to help me out, I'll make it easier for you in return. I'll sew the ring into the seam of your trousers, just below your belt.'

The following morning, 13 February 1949, the station was packed and chaotic. Over two hundred and fifty Jewish children, between the ages of thirteen and seventeen, were saying goodbye to their parents and relatives. There was a lot of noise and a lot of tears. My mother hugged me hard, making me promise to eat all my meals. 'We'll all be together shortly. Just remember that if you feel lonely for us.' I would imagine it was a huge relief to the two women that Chava and I would be together. As the train pulled out of the station we waved goodbye, feeling rather torn, just as I had felt the previous morning in Merašice. The goodbyes were sad, even though we knew they were only temporary. It felt very grown-up to be saying farewell to the land of our birth. Also the excitement about seeing Israel was beginning to bubble in our bellies.

Chapter 21
· · · · · ·

A New Life in Israel
and Beyond

I will merely outline my later life here but not go into detail as, thankfully, my life became an ordinary one after the traumas I experienced in childhood.

It was 24 February 1949 when Chava and I set our tired feet down in Israel. It was very emotional, but also very, very pleasant, thanks to the sun shining high in the sky. We had left behind the freezing cold of Bratislava and now it seemed that the very weather was ensuring that we felt welcomed home after our long journey. The port of Haifa looked like a military outpost, having served as the departing point for the British once their rule had come to an end. Everywhere I looked I saw barbed wire, sandbags and watchtowers, obviously built by the British in case they came under attack, as they were packing up, from some terrorist group seeking revenge.

Before we could have a decent look around the administration had to be dealt with, so we filed up for registration as new emigrants, and received our identification papers. After that we were split up into smaller groups. Some of the groups were directly allocated to a kibbutz, while the rest of us, including my group, boarded a bus for the *Kiryat Elijahu* Absorption Centre, located on the outskirts of Haifa. Now we had time to appreciate our new surroundings. For the duration of the journey every one of us gazed out the window in wonderment at the country, *our* country now. It was only a short trip, of fifteen minutes or so, to the Absorption Centre, which turned out to be a huge camp with hundreds of large tents, each one big enough to hold a family. There were lots of people around, a fantastic mixture of nationalities and languages, and all delighted to have found their true home.

We spent a week or so in the camp and then our group was split up again. I belonged to the group of younger kids, and we were sent to a youth boarding house in Kfar Sabah, called 'Onim Institute'. For the first time Chava and I had to separate when she was sent off with the older group to

Kfar Masaryk. I wasn't at all happy about this for two reasons: I was sad to be saying goodbye to her but also I was most annoyed at not being allowed to join her group. Chava was a little younger than me but she was obviously more mature, which I understand now but did not then, and better suited to mixing with the older children. So I had to bite my lip and concentrate on getting ready for my new home.

Onim Institute was built and financed by the American Jewish Joint Distribution Committee in 1948–49, and, therefore, it was a brand new building with luxurious additions like gardens with water fountains, an outdoor swimming pool, and the best of sports facilities. It was a beautiful place, very much like a busy five-star hotel. There were plenty of other kids from different nationalities. Initially, though, I spent all my time with my friends from home since I couldn't converse with the other emigrants until we were all fluent in Hebrew, the national language that would bring us all together. We also studied Israeli history and there was also plenty of time for swimming and sports.

Like thousands of others across Europe, Miki and my parents were preparing for their journey home. Thousands of Jews were also making their way to America and Canada, as far from the iron curtain as possible. The family finally arrived about two and a half months later, in May. They were sent to an Absorption Camp not far from Haifa and then on to another centre in Bait Lid. I had to wait a bit before I could see them. It was a wonderful reunion though I think I might have showed off a little, as I felt like the experienced old emigrant who was introducing young novices to their new life! I remember my father showing me the bits of furniture, utensils and pieces of carpets he had brought with him, lamenting, 'I've worked all my life and after selling off the house and farm this is all I have to show for it.' Needless to say they had to leave all the good stuff behind thanks to the government fleecing them before they left.

My parents decided to settle in Nahariya, the northern-most coastal city in Israel, not too far from the Lebanese border. They fell in love with it at first sight. The city was founded by German Jews in 1935 and then went on to become a popular holiday spot. Because of its proximity to the sea, the city had served as an entrance route for illegal Jewish emigrants during British rule. The emigrants were helped by the locals: when a ship was approaching the shores of Nahariya, the local people would gather in their hundreds on the beach and as soon as the ship docked, emigrants would quickly disembark and make their way into the centre of the jovial crowd, thus making it impossible for the British to find them.

My parents, along with Miki, were allocated a tiny two-roomed flat in a Swedish prefab hut, containing just a sitting room and a bedroom. When I visited at the weekends I slept with Miki in the sitting room. They also had to find a way to

support themselves. The first job my father found was building roads; most of his co-workers were doctors and academ-
ics, and the road they built is still called the 'Doctors' Road'.
Later on he mixed whitewash, which was neither pleasant
nor healthy. Fortunately, it didn't last too long and he decided
to go into business for himself, selling oil for small paraffin
stoves. He got himself a donkey and a barrel on wheels to
transport the oil. Meanwhile, my mother began working in
a butcher's shop, where she tended the cash register and cut
the coupons from the customers' ration books – meat was
rationed at this time. So it wasn't exactly an easy or prosperous time for either of them. I'm sure my father missed the
farm and my mother missed her pretty house and Mariška,
but, in spite of long hours and hard physical labour, they
were both happier than they had been in years. We all were.

The Kibbutz

In July 1949, after six months at the institute, my group was
told that we were going to a kibbutz called Shamir. We were
more than sorry to leave our beautiful institute and packed
our bags with heavy hearts. At least I had my fifteen Slovak
friends with me. We were about twenty-five girls and boys in
total as we waited for the bus that would take us to the kibbutz. With the bus came Surika Draverman, a tall, slim, dark-
haired woman who had no difficulty controlling twenty-five
excited children.

Kibbutz Shamir was five years old, having been established in 1944 by young Romanian Zionists from the Hashomer Hatzair movement. They chose a wonderful location; looking west I could see the green vastness of the Chula Valley while to the east were the Golan Heights which belonged to Syria at that time. We were joining about two hundred and fifty inhabitants. All kibbutzim are independent settlements, and our new home supported itself through farming, growing grapes, apples and tomatoes.

Surika led us to our quarters – two large prefab huts, each with four rooms inside. Next she divided us into groups of three and four. I would be sharing a room with two Slovak boys, which pleased me immensely, especially since one of them, Tomi Wald, was my best friend now. Tomi, who would later change his name to Jacob Yaary, a proper Hebrew name, was much taller than me and spoke with a strong Hungarian accent.

Surika informed us that we would be in her care, she was our leader. In fact she was like a mother to us, albeit a very strict one. We had a daily schedule and it was Surika who made sure that we washed ourselves, kept our rooms tidy and always had clean clothes to wear. Our mornings were spent in lessons and in the afternoons we learned a profession that we had picked for ourselves. For instance I chose to go and work in the engineering workshop while Tomi went to learn how to be an electrician. It was something I had always been interested in: back in Merašice, as a very young child, I loved nothing better than watching the blacksmith perform miracles with iron, and make shoes for the horses – plus Miki's decision to study engineering definitely influenced me too. I loved my workshop. My supervisor was very good to me and taught me how to weld and cut metal. My first big project was to make beds for the kibbutz members. The day I finished the last bed was a proud one for me. I had worked so hard and my clothes were absolutely filthy, but I found the sense of achievement intoxicating.

Kibbutz life was serene and ran like clockwork. We shared everything and the society was a democratic one. A common sight was the kibbutz chairman scrubbing dishes in the kitchen, just like everyone else. There was no hierarchy and, in my opinion, it was true communism. I also had my first proper romance here. Adult life was truly beginning for me.

But after two and a half years I was getting bored of kibbutz life and yearned to try my skills beyond its boundaries. The year was 1951, I was sixteen years old and about to make my first grown-up decision: I wanted to leave – plus, my lovely girlfriend had fallen in love with someone else! My heart was broken and I began to feel stifled in the camp. After an emotional farewell to my friends, I packed my bag and made my way to my parents' house in Nahariya.

Out of our original group there are still six living in the kibbutz today with their families. It is a very nice way of life, though not suitable for everybody. In later years the Shamir Kibbutz became one of the richest in Israel, manufacturing a variety of products, from lenses for spectacles to baby nappies and disposable napkins.

My First Job

I moved into my parents' wooden Swedish hut. It was a tight squeeze, but nobody complained. Miki was serving in the Israeli army now and came home only at the weekends. My father found me a position as an apprentice in a small work-shop with a master toolmaker, Mr Polivka, and his partner. I wouldn't be paid, except in what they would teach me.

I distinctly remember my very first job. We got a con-tract to produce several thousand small sheet metal squares, 20mm, with a hole in the middle for a nail to be put through. I was sent off to the waste dump to gather discarded metal and corrugated sheets that had been thrown away because they were damaged. When I had found enough and brought them back to the workshop I had the job of cutting up the sheets into small squares and piercing a hole into every single one of them. It took me many days to complete the task as Mr Polivka's apprentice.

I was particularly interested in tool-making and had to rely upon my own dogged determination to learn because Mr Polivaka turned out to be one of those old-fashioned masters who are very secretive and possessive about their craft. This meant that I had to peer over his shoulder to see what he was doing!

Another challenge that proved a lot easier to accomplish was regarding the lathe, the machine used to drill, cut or polish metal, wood or plastic. Neither Mr Polivka nor his partner had any interest in using it and if a customer came in requesting a job that required a lathe they were simply turned away. Determined to learn how to use it, I got myself a book on turning and told my boss that I would look after any jobs that came in, doing them in the evening when no one else was around. I received an unexpected boost of help when Stef Wertheimer, who made tungsten carbide-tipped tools, walked into the workshop one afternoon while I was work-ing the lathe. He watched me for a few minutes and then said: 'You could go a lot faster than that, let me show you.' When he demonstrated his tools it was like being shown a magic trick. I couldn't believe the speed at which he worked the machine. In time, with plenty of studying and hours of practice, I became a very accomplished turner indeed.

I quickly grew to love Nahariya and made good friends there, one of whom I would later link up with again, Uri Honigsberg – we embarked on a friendship which is still going strong over sixty years later. While I was busy learning about the lathe, Miki had finished his army service and returned to Nahariya. He got a job in Mifratz, an industrial area north of Haifa, for the Transmisia Company, operating metal machines in their factory. Six months after he started working there, he suggested that I join him as a lathe operative. I was very happy to be receiving a wage packet at long last.

Then I was lucky enough to pick up a job with Stef Wertheimer. He had recently set up his own company ISCAR, in Nahariya, and I became one of his first employees. My job was to repair the drilling heads that were used to drill for oil in the oil wells of southern Israel. I worked alongside master engineer Chajim Lilienfeld. He had studied engineering in Germany and was a perfectionist. The machines we built together ran smoothly, doing double shifts for many years after, without a single hitch − although, I admit to finding his attention to detail just a little wearying, sometimes. Stef also gave Miki a job. So we both earned good money that we turned over to our parents, only keeping some pocket money for ourselves.

Back to Europe

Like all Israelis, I had to spend two years in the army. Thus in 1953, the year I turned eighteen, I received my call-up to report to Camp Sarafend and from there I was assigned to an armoured brigade, south of Tel Aviv near Beer-Sheba. Here I learned many things, the most important being that I was trained as an army driver, which meant I also had to know how to repair the vehicles, of course. When I left the army in 1955, at the grand old age of twenty, I felt that I had entered as a child but I was now a man.

As soon as I was released from the army I contacted Iscar to see if they would take me back to work for them. And they did, which is not too surprising considering that Miki had been promoted to the position of works manager. Like me the company had grown a little more sophisticated over the previous couple of years. It was no longer located in a little shed; instead it had moved to the industrial area in the north of Nahariya, into a large building that was big enough to accommodate the large number of machines required to meet the orders for tungsten carbide-tipped tools.

I began working on the lathe but soon progressed to other machines. I was hungry to learn as much as I could. My old friend Stef began work on a new project – to produce the tungsten carbide himself. The process was a lot like making a cake; several metallic powders were mixed together and baked in an oven, at an extremely high temperature, until it had turned into a hard metal, that is, the tungsten carbide. A special oven was ordered and I helped Stef assemble it. Today Stef is one of the wealthiest men in Israel. A supremely intelligent and clever businessman, he built an emporium of factories throughout Turkey, Jordan and Israel. Iscar became an internationally recognised company, supplying tools all over the world. I stayed with Iscar until 1957, and, thanks to Stef, I became an expert in tungsten carbide tools.

Meanwhile my parents had also moved into a new house

with two bedrooms, a kitchen and a sitting room, a veritable palace compared to the prefab. My father went into business with a friend of his and they opened a small hardware shop. It really was very small, especially after they filled it with stock, including paint, screws, rope, wire and so forth. If there were three people in the shop, a fourth would have to wait outside until someone left! As usual, Father worked very hard. I'm sure he must have thought back to *Opapa*'s shop in Merašice. How long ago that seemed now. He worked long hours, no mean feat in the summer months in the unbearable heat. Disaster struck when he had a heart-attack. Fortunately he survived, but the doctor was adamant that he give up the shop. The pressure was just too much for him and, with my mother's help, he was obliged to give in and sell his share of the business. Mother worked for a laundry, ironing men's shirts. Every morning a basket of shirts arrived to the house and she got to work immediately. I loved watching her; she was the fastest ironer I've ever seen. Well, she had to be fast because she was paid per shirt, and she did earn a very good living indeed. Her employers were so pleased with her that they suggested my father set up a collection service whereby he would collect people's dirty clothes, bring them in to be washed and ironed, and then return them to the customer. It was a thriving business.

My military days weren't over, however; I was in the reserve army now, spending an average of thirty days a year on manoeuvres, updating myself with new equipment and weapons. During one of these manoeuvres my friend Uri lost most of his arm when a grenade exploded in his hand. I was shocked and distressed by this, having managed to ignore, I suppose, the potential killing power of the weapons I was so familiar with. It took a long time for the wound to heal and Uri had to learn how to live with a prosthetic arm. His parents decided to move back to Germany, sometime in 1956. The German government was offering financial packets to any Jews who would be prepared to return home. Uri eventually followed them back but we kept in touch for many years afterwards.

My only brush with war in the army was when I saw action in the reserve army in 1956, when Egypt, Jordan and Syria unified their armies under one Arab commander. Egypt's president, Abdul Nasser, then decided to nationalise the Suez Canal, thus offending the British and the French. He also blocked the Straits of Tiran, preventing Israeli ships from using the Red Sea.

Tension was high and everyone expected war. I received a call to report to my unit. Things were happening very fast. As soon as I reached my unit I was immediately given a uniform and gun, and instructions to take up my position as personal driver for the camp commander. A couple of anxious days followed as we awaited further orders and then, on the evening of 29 October, we were on the move. A long column involving several hundred jeeps and trucks, carrying men, supplies and ammunition, set out on the road to Beer Sheba, the largest city in the Negev Desert, in southern Israel. My car was at the front of this military procession, alongside the half-track troop carriers. With me were the commander and several other high-ranking officers from the different companies. We drove all night. At one point I heard someone shouting, 'We have just crossed the border into Egypt.' Ahead of us the regular army already had the Egyptians on the retreat, while Israeli paratroopers were parachuting into the Mitla Pass in the Sinai of Egypt, to block the enemy's escape. We were heading to central Sinai, to take Abu Agella, a large fortified military camp.

At about one in the morning we were ordered to halt and the soldiers in the half-tracks were instructed to fire their weapons in the air to make sure that they were all ready for action and in full working order. When all guns had been successful discharged we took off again, for about another hour, until we reached a hill. My passengers joined their respective brigades and I was told to drive to the side of the hill and wait.

The noise was terrific. Behind me large field guns were spraying bullets into the sky above me. As I sat in the jeep I could feel the ground actually shaking. Two kilometres away from us, on the other side of the hill, was the Egyptian stronghold of Abu Agella, our goal. There was no movement from the reserve soldiers; they and their commanders could only wait until they were told what to do. It was after three in the morning and I'm sure the commanders fretted about the strong possibility of losing the cover of darkness to the imminent rising sun. The order was given to proceed without any further delay, desperate to attack while it was still dark. The half-tracks took off with speed, disappearing behind the hill. I remember an eerie calm, a few spare minutes while I wondered what was going to happen. Suddenly, I had my answer. The sky lit up with umpteen massive explosions that seemed to shred the darkness of night into something bright and supremely dreadful. Was the world ending? The air was hot and heavy; I guessed that maybe there were thirty large guns propelling bullets just over my head. They whistled past me and I tried to drown out the noise with the pathetic gesture of clamping my shaking hands over my ears. Flinging myself on the ground I rolled myself under the vehicle, the very earth beneath me jumping with every crash. Maybe thirty minutes passed as I lay there, thinking it would never ever be quiet again.

Half-tracks began to arrive back to where I was waiting. There was panic all around me. The planned surprise attack had failed. Our men had expected to surprise a camp of two or three thousand Egyptian soldiers, according to our intelligence. Unfortunately, however, when the Egyptians started to retreat before the full-time Israeli army, they made their way to Abu Agella, therefore, instead of a couple of thousand, our soldiers met with three times that, all fully armed, with plenty of tanks. Our reserve army, on the other hand, had no tanks and was completely overwhelmed. Now on retreat ourselves, the road in front of me was filling up with wounded and dying comrades. Everywhere I looked were bleeding and limping Israeli soldiers. I could only wait where I was until I received an order. A decision was made to bypass Abu Agella and head towards the Suez Canal. A path of destruction greeted us, with burnt-out tanks, trucks and military hardware of the Egyptian army that had been bombed by the Israeli forces.

The Abu Agella camp surrendered not twenty-four hours after we left, without a single shot more being fired. The Chief of Staff of the Israeli Defence Forces, Moshe Dayan, brought about a tremendous victory against an Egyptian army that was superior in numbers and weapons. The Israeli campaign, which had begun on 29 October, was finished by 1 November, when the reserves were ten kilometres from the Suez Canal. I was discharged a few days later but it took me a long time to get over the sad sight of injured and dying colleagues.

I returned to work, happy to be doing something normal again. And so life continued on until Uri wrote to ask me to join him in Germany, explaining that there were plenty of jobs, plenty of college places and I could live with him and his parents. There was no better country than Germany to pursue my education in engineering and this was the dominant reason for my writing back to Uri to tell him I was packing my bags. My parents and Miki were typically supportive, seeing my decision as a practical one regarding future employment. Others, however, amongst my neighbours and friends, were a little shocked or bewildered at my wanting, first of all, to leave the homeland and, secondly, for Germany, of *all* places. The question I heard repeatedly over the next few weeks was: 'Why would you want to go THERE after all you went through?' My reply was confident and maybe a little cheeky: 'When David Ben-Gurion goes anywhere he is accompanied by his guards of honour on their BMW motorbikes. If the President of Israel is happy to be accompanied by German-made motorbikes then I am happy to go to Germany to study engineering!'

Germany to London, then Italy – and Ireland

Uri and Suzy, his mother, were waiting for me in Dortmund. I was very fond of Suzy; she was a gentle little woman who doted on her son and thought the world of me. Her husband, Heinz, was the complete opposite; he was big, loud and chain-smoked cigars. The three of them lived in a spacious rented flat on Leuthard Street, not far from the train station. In fact they lived just beside the railway bridge. I was slightly appalled when I entered the flat to hear a dreadful noise. The others laughed and told me that I'd soon get used to it. Trains raced by every few minutes, on a tight schedule, shaking the building from top to bottom. It took me a couple of weeks before I could successfully ignore this.

Heinz asked me what kind of job I was looking for, 'Or perhaps you would like to work for me?' A builder by trade, he has secured a contract for Purfima Company and was building petrol stations along the motorways. That suited me just fine, especially as it meant that Uri, who was a plumber by trade, and I would be working together. He drove the truck with all our equipment and we went from station to station, connecting the petrol containers to the pumps. I learnt all about plumbing and was hugely grateful for the experience.

I also enrolled for evening classes so that I could accumulate some German qualifications. The course I chose to do was called '*Arbeitsvorbereitung*' (work preparation). I was studying to be a project manager so that I could manage an entire engineering job, including planning all the elements, the material and the equipment to enable a smooth flow of production.

You might wonder how I got on in Germany, as a Jew. In fact I got on extremely well *because* I was a Jew. The year was 1957 and many Germans were filled with guilt and shame over what had happened and so I had plenty of people more than willing to help me, whether it was in relation to my work permit or my application to study.

At some stage I decided to try and get a job in the engineering field. After some searching I found a large workshop called Lumer. It had three departments: one floor handled the repairs of machines, one floor was a shop that sold large machines and the third floor developed machines that could cut trapeze thread. I started work in repairs. It was a dirty and smelly job but I used the opportunity to keep an eye on what machines they were developing on the other floor. Two days after I started working there I got a chance to prove myself when I spotted a problem in connection with the tungsten carbide tools and mentioned it to the manager. He asked me how I knew about the tools, allowing me to give him a brief history of my experience with Stef, explaining that I was a bit of an expert. The bosses decided to implement my suggestion and discovered that I had been exactly right. To my great pleasure I was immediately transferred from repairs to the development floor, where I worked on a spinning device called the '*Wirbelgerät*'. My work served me well over the next few months, achieving top results which led to a promotion. I was now the person making the quotes on the jobs that were brought into us and also, when the boss wasn't around, I would personally deal with the customers.

Then Miki and his wife Judith arrived on holidays. I decided to join them even though I had been left in charge while the boss was on holidays. I explained the situation to the boss's daughter who said that he wouldn't be pleased but to make up my own mind about it. I left everything in order, but when I got home there was a letter waiting for me from Mr Lumer. He was most upset and would no longer be requiring my services. It was my very first sacking, but I could understand his anger. With no job and my evening studies at a successful end, I began to prepare for a return to Israel.

Then, suddenly, everything changed again. A few days later I received a letter from a Mr Koppell. It contained an open airline ticket to London and an invitation to come and see him in London as he thought he might have a proposition that would interest me. He pointed out that I had nothing to lose, either I would like his proposition or I could just enjoy an all-expenses paid trip to London. Indeed, just like Uri's invitation to Germany, it was an offer that I couldn't refuse. Another added attraction was the fact that my Uncle Robert lived in London, so it would be an opportunity to meet up with him too. Well, that was it.

It was sad saying goodbye to Uri and his mother. Suzy had made me feel like an important part of her family, and I had become very fond of her. I hugged them both goodbye, promising to stay in touch and that I'd come back for a visit as soon as I could. It would be my last time to see Suzy as I didn't make that visit for another forty-six years, in 2007.

There was a pleasant surprise waiting for me in the airport in London when I was met by my second cousin, Chava Weis. I was delighted to see a friendly face amongst a sea of strangers. A couple of years older than me, she came from Hlohovec in Slovakia and had also moved to Nahariya with her family. Now she worked in London as an *au pair* while studying graphic design. It was her job that had led to my invitation, as it was Mr Koppel's children that she cared for. Mr Koppel was involved in various manufacturing businesses and one was in zip manufacturing. One day Chava was reading a newspaper when she noticed an advertisement for a production manager for a zip-manufacturing company in Ireland. Chava immediately went to Mr Koppel and said: 'You know you will have competition in Ireland?' But he replied: 'No, I will not have a competitor, I put in the advertisement myself! I am looking for a production manager for a factory in Ireland.' And so Chava told him about me. He got straight down to business when we met. I felt a little anxious, as I didn't know anything about zip manufacturing, but he assured me that this wasn't a problem. 'I'm going to send you to Italy,' he told me, 'to the company that is supplying me with all the equipment I need. They'll teach you everything you need to know. You're an engineer, it won't be difficult.'

It all sounded rather fantastic but I wasn't ready to answer just yet. Fortunately, Mr Koppel understood this. 'Look, the decision is entirely yours,' he said. 'If you do agree to work for me then I need you to commit to staying for the next three years. That's my only condition. Oh, and, before I forget, your starting wage will be £15 a week.' Considering that the average industrial wage in England, at that time, was £12 – and £10 in Ireland – this was a very generous offer indeed. We chatted some more and then Mr Koppel told me to go away and think about it, 'Come back to me in a couple of days, and we'll see where we are.'

Robert was my father's brother, and was born in Merašice, in 1912. He trained as an accountant and got his first job with a firm in Bratislava when he was eighteen years old. Three years later he enlisted with the army for his two years national service. After his discharge he returned to Merašice, to help out in his parents' shop. When he was twenty-seven years old, with the rise of Fr Tiso and his anti-semitic ilk, he guessed that life would become very difficult for Jews. A member of the Zionist movement, he decided to emigrate to Palestine. He made it out of Bratislava on the last ship, the *Pentcho*, on 18 May 1940, just before the Nazis arrived. The proposed month-long journey was to involve sailing down the River Danube, into the Black Sea and then on to Palestine. You might think his adventure ends here, but in fact it was only beginning. The ship was hopelessly overcrowded, with 520 passengers on board, plus the crew. Due to the overcrowding, where passengers had to be frequently rescued after falling into the sea, there was a serious shortage of food and disease was rife. It was a hazardous journey, with the captain overdosing on morphine and the ship being shot at to prevent its mooring anywhere near Bulgaria and Romania. Then, allegedly, the ship was sabotaged by its crew who had been promised – but denied – a slice of the pie from an insurance claim. It made it into the Aegean Sea before a boiler exploded, shipwrecking everyone onboard.

Robert survived this and ended up, in October 1940, interned with fellow survivors on the island of Rhodes. In March 1942 the survivors were transported to the Italian concentration camp Ferramonti. Life was very harsh and many succumbed to illness, including my uncle who developed malaria, the consequences of which would be lifelong, leaving him with a considerably weakened heart.

Upon liberation by the British, in 1944, Robert rejoined the Slovak army in Bari, Italy, and from there he was posted to London. He visited Merašice when I was about eleven years old, in full army uniform and laden with gifts like chocolate, cocoa, chewing gum, cigarettes and lots and lots of needles and thread. Miki and I came to the conclusion that he must be very rich.

When he was discharged from the army in 1946, he chose to stay on in London where he met L.J. Newman, an old school friend who gave him a job. He quickly worked his way through various jobs to becoming a chartered accountant, and eventually a senior executive at Apal Travel.

The last time I had seen Uncle Robert he had looked every inch the fighting soldier so I was not prepared for the grand gentleman who greeted me at Piccadilly Circus. There wasn't a trace of his continental mannerisms. Instead, my uncle was impeccably dressed in a smart suit and carrying a black umbrella, looking like the perfect Englishman. By now he was fluent in English; in fact, it was just one of four languages he could speak, the others being German, Slovak and Hungarian.

I filled him in on Mr Koppel's proposition and he confirmed my own beliefs, that it was a very good offer indeed and that I should take it. That made up my mind beyond any shadow of a doubt.

The family had often worried about Uncle Robert as he had never married. They feared that he must be very lonely and instigated a bout of match-making that Robert always found a way to avoid. He did have some girlfriends during his internment, but never wanted to marry any of them, or anyone else for that matter. I supposed he liked his independence but there was another reason too: it seems that he was rather fixated on not being a burden to anyone. This was also the reason for his never attending family weddings or Bar Mitzvahs; he just chose to stay away, which naturally caused some hurt in my father's family. I suppose our war experiences affected us in different ways and this was Robert's, that he constantly imagined that he would be a burden on his family and friends. Everyone was kept at a polite distance.

So he lived alone in a small, rented one-roomed flat and there was also, for me, the troubling matter that he wasn't, I felt, earning a proper amount for his executive position. However, money wasn't important to him. He said he had enough to live on and that was enough for him. His hobbies included the theatre, swimming, reading, walking, attending concerts and good restaurants, so it wasn't an extravagant lifestyle.

The following day I made my way back to Mr Koppel's house to tell him that I accepted his proposition. We shook hands on it and Mr Koppel's smile as broad as my own: 'So, Tomi, from today you are working for me!' And, indeed, my wage packet began from that very day.

In Italy I learned everything I needed to know about zip manufacture. Sure enough, by the end of the two months I felt confident that I could now put a system in place in Ireland for Mr Koppel. But there was a delay. Mr Koppel was experiencing huge difficulties in getting me a work visa for Ireland, due to the country's high unemployment figures. As a result, foreigners were not allowed to work there. Mr Koppel persevered, but it took eight months, with lots of emphasis on the jobs he would be providing to the people of Ireland to arrange the visa.

Ireland was to be my future. Here I settled into work at the zip factory. Then I met my wife, Evanne Blackman. We met at a film in the Jewish club, and after the film that night

I invited her to meet me again, to have dinner at the Paradiso restaurant on Westmoreland Street. An intense courtship followed, involving lots of lovely walks in the woods of Wicklow or at Dun Laoghaire pier. We fell in love very quickly and after six months I went to seek her father's consent to ask her to marry me. Her father, Jack, ran a small jewellery business on Anne Street. Jack had guessed my reason for seeing him, and he raised the issue of a suitable ring. Being in the jewellery business, he would, of course, want the best for his daughter. I knew very little about jewellery at the time, so when he pointed to a particularly beautiful ring and asked me how much I could afford, I said forty pounds. The ring was duly purchased – and it was many years later that I discovered it was worth well over a thousand pounds at the time! Evanne and I were married on 12 March 1961. She was twenty-one years old and I was twenty-five; it seemed the perfect time to get married. The synagogue in Terenure was booked and we held our reception in the synagogue's hall. It was a small wedding, but I was particularly delighted that Uncle Robert came over from London, the only relative of mine present, and it meant so much that he was there for me as it wasn't his habit to attend family celebrations.

On proposing to Evanne I had asked her to emigrate to Israel with me, so we duly set off – by boat and train. The journey took four days, but finally we were hugging my parents and Miki in the sunshine. I was overjoyed to see the three of them again and proudly introduced my pretty wife. They seemed instantly taken with her, and embraced her as warmly as they did me.

Miki had left ISCAR in 1960 and set up his own business, DIMAR, and naturally he offered me a job that I accepted on the spot. I relished the idea of us working together again. He had set up a small workshop supplying the surrounding industries with specialised precision tools. Miki and I worked hard, from 7.00am sometimes until 9.00pm every day, building a future for ourselves and our families. We gained some coveted contracts from the Israeli Defence Forces. We had other big projects too, including producing lead rawl plugs, which was hard work since we did it by hand, melting down the lead and pouring it into forms. Using my experience from the zip fastener factory, I designed a machine to do the job, allowing us to improve production tenfold and do the work at a gentler pace. A little later I made forms for the manufacture of plastic and rubber rawl plugs. We went on to sell these in the thousands. In fact, my main input to the company was in developing the possibility of mass production. We also won a contract to manufacture a patented attachment to cars that reduced air pollution on heavy diesel lorry engines. So you can understand how we found ourselves working eleven-hour days.

Everything we earned went straight back into the business.

But it wasn't all work even in those early years. On the morning of 18 January 1964 Evanne gave birth to our first child, David. When I saw my son for the first time, in his mother's arms, I could only think of one word to describe the scene: 'miracle'. That summer Evanne's parents and sisters came out for a holiday. I spent a lot of time with her father, Jack, throughout this visit and he talked about his worries, the main one being that he felt he had no one to look after his business when he retired. He tentatively suggested that it would be great if I came back and took it over, but I was absorbed in my own business with Miki. This tentative suggestion became a constant reminder in the letters that Evanne received from home, her mother writing about how thrilled Jack would be if I would only return to Ireland to work for him.

Then I changed my mind. It wasn't a sudden decision; it was more like a flowering realisation. I kept my feelings from Miki and did my best to ignore them but, over the next coming months, that became harder and harder to do. Evanne thought that we might have a better future in Ireland. I knew in my heart of hearts that she had never stopped missing Ireland and her family since the day we arrived in Haifa – and I felt that it must be harder for a daughter to be away from her parents than for a son. So it was, about the middle of 1965, that I found myself looking towards Ireland for a better future. I discovered that I had, for some time, felt that our return was inevitable, it was merely a matter of *when*.

My parents and Miki took the news rather badly – the worse part was Miki's stunned belief that I was betraying us both by leaving. My parents were bitterly disappointed, but they didn't try to change my mind. And so, after four years in Israel, Evanne and I returned to Ireland with our son in 1965. Miki's company, DIMAR, became a very successful business in later years, specialising in wood-working tools and exporting about 80 percent of its production. Its enormous success was all down to Miki's vision and planning. Much later – in 1981 – DIMAR was named 'exporter of the year', a very high achievement indeed. I watched the progress over the years and a few years ago Miki bought a German factory – he visits every year and has very good relations with his employees there.

Because I was now married to an Irish citizen, I no longer had to make that nervous three-monthly visit to the Aliens' Office in the grounds of Dublin Castle. It had never been something I liked, since I could never assume that my work permit would be extended for another three months. As soon as I could, I applied for Irish citizenship. I suppose I must have known that I was going to stay in Ireland now, come what may. On 16 March 1977 I finally received my citizenship.

I worked with Jack in the jewellery business again applying my systems knowledge and helping increase the productivity rate, especially in the making of bracelets — with new systems and machinery we increased our production hugely. I also set up my own distribution company, representing ISCAR and Miki's firm, DIMAR, distributing engineering items. I was busier than ever. This involved me visiting engineering companies, presenting myself to the bosses and then visiting the workshops to personally demonstrate the tungsten carbide tools to their staff. At the time there was very little known about this technology in Ireland and, therefore, sales poured in. I made these visits during my lunch-breaks, sticking to firms in Dublin. Every sale meant paperwork and accounting, and this I did at home, in the evenings after the family went to bed.

The good news was that business took off at an impressive rate; the bad news was that this meant both more administrative work and preparation for each visit. Those working nights got later and later as my hours of paperwork increased over the next few months.

This company became very successful but also very stressful — I was working day and night — so in the end I had to sell the company.

Evanne and I had two more sons: Gideon on 25 August 1966 and Jonathan on 15 June 1970.

Chapter 22

• • • • • •

A Generation Passes Away

Losing My Father, 1966

Our son, Gideon, was born in August 1966, and unfortunately not three months after that Miki rang me to tell me that our father was dead. I don't remember much about that conversation now, only that I went to pieces after I hung up the phone. At only sixty-four years of age he had suffered a massive heart attack. He and Mother had gone to the cinema to see a western, his favourite type of movie, when his head suddenly drooped onto her shoulder. Thinking he had fallen asleep, she pushed at him and knew immediately that something was wrong when he didn't respond. He was rushed to hospital, but pronounced dead on arrival. Two years later I received a letter my father had written to me that morning. We used to send each other long letters every single week since I returned to Ireland and now here was his last one, strangely delayed. Among the usual family news he wrote to tell me how, following his most recent examination, his doctor had found him to be in perfect working order. He admitted that he was told to relax more for the sake of his blood pressure and heart, but apart from that he was enjoying life.

I couldn't make it to the funeral. Jewish law dictates that a person must be buried within one day of death, unless a post-mortem is necessary or all the children are abroad; the family can insist on the funeral being delayed until at least one child makes it back home. Well, Miki was there for both of us. I don't expect everyone to understand why I decided against going back to Israel immediately after that to be with the family. Evanne and her father tried their best to encourage me to get a plane ticket, but I couldn't bring myself to do it. Sunk into my own shock and misery, the only thing I knew for certain was that I definitely could not handle seeing my mother and brother's grief. Miki wrote me a letter the day after our father's funeral, describing to me how crowded it was, surmising that Father was more popular and well known than either of us had realised.

The Death of Uncle Robert, 1981

I had stayed in regular contact with Uncle Robert; we talked on the phone once a week and whenever I visited London, on business, I also made a point of meeting up with him. Determinedly independent, he never accepted my many invitations to come and visit me again in Ireland. He could never escape his fear that should something happen to him during a visit to us, or anyone else, he would instantly become a burden.

He rang me early December 1980, and mentioned that he hadn't been able to shift a heavy cold, even after buying more heaters for his flat. I remember a brief reference to a pain in his chest before he told me he was feeling much better now. That was the last time I spoke to him. Four days after Christmas, Robert became sick at work and was taken to the Royal Free Hospital where it was discovered he had had a second heart-attack, a mild one this time. It must have been a warning for the fatal attack he suffered on 8 January. I had to organise the funeral and made arrangements with the Burial Society of the United Synagogue; we decided on Bushey Cemetery, the Jewish cemetery. Mrs Liverman, Robert's landlady, assured me that she would accompany me. Knowing how quiet and contained my uncle's life was, I fretted that there would be nobody else around to mourn him at his funeral. To my relief a couple of his work colleagues contacted me for the arrangements, so now there would be five of us, including the rabbi. At the cemetery the rabbi approached another funeral party, who were just finishing up, to ask them if they would join us — Jewish tradition requires that there be at least ten men, a *Minyan*, present for public prayer where the Torah is being read. The lack of mourners added to the wretchedness of the cold, grey afternoon.

There were a lot of papers in his flat and, when I got home, I used them to write about his life for the rest of the family who had felt so distant from him in the latter years. Today his breakfast-room table and chairs sit in my breakfast room and not too many days pass without my thinking of him.

The Death of My Mother, 2003

My ninety-six year old mother believed in enjoying life to the very full, no matter how old she was. She visited me three times over the years, including turning up at my surprise sixtieth birthday party in her eightieth-eighth year. She led an active life in Israel, continuing to cycle everywhere on her three-wheeled bike even after turning ninety. However, following a fall and a mild stroke, she was obliged to have twenty-four hour supervision. Miki hired the wonderful Erzi, a Hungarian who had recently arrived in Israel for a holiday, fallen in love with the landscape, and immediately looked for a job so she could stay on. Lucky for us, she moved in with Mother, fell in love with her and devoted herself to caring for her seven days a week. She became an important member of our family. In fact, I rang her every day to see how my mother was.

We celebrated our mother's ninety-fifth birthday with all the family around her. She was in a wheelchair, but still smiling and full of chat. Of course, I couldn't deny that her health was deteriorating. I visited her once a year, sometimes twice, but over the last few years of her life I couldn't help thinking this might be my last goodbye to her – so much so that I started to leave without saying goodbye because it was upsetting for both of us.

My wife Evanne became seriously ill with cancer in January 2002. Her last fourteen months were very difficult and she suffered terribly. I was heartbroken and looked after her as well as I could. She suffered panic attacks as well as physical pain. Her tumour just got worse and worse, and nothing could be done to cure it. In the last three months she was unable to stand up and I had to do everything for her. It was so hard on her. I was still working so I found it all very demanding too. It gradually became clear that the end was near. After some very difficult months we lost her in June 2003, just before her sixty-third birthday. I was devastated and exhausted. Then, not too long after Evanne's death, Miki rang me to tell me that Mother had been taken into hospital and that it would be best if I came to see her as soon as I could. As you can imagine, it was an awful blow, just as I was trying to pick up the pieces after Evanne's death. I packed my bags and went to Israel, where I immediately went to the hospital, with Miki warning me that she might not recognise me. On entering her room, Dorit, my niece, said to her grandmother: 'Look who has come to see you.' Not terribly prepared to have my own mother stare blankly at me as if I was a stranger, I was hugely relieved when she opened her eyes, looked at me for a split second before saying, 'Tominko.' It was the last time she spoke to me.

Not wanting her to be alone, we worked shifts to ensure that one of us was with her twenty-four hours a day. I lasted five days and then found myself in a bit of a state – it was all just too much after the months of tending to Evanne, far too soon for me to watch another loved one die. I told Miki that I would go to Prague and he could call me there when things got bad. He rang four days later and I took a midnight flight back to Israel. But my mother wasn't ready to leave us yet. Days passed without any change in her. We asked the doctor for his prognosis. He complimented her strong heart, telling us that she could last for many days or many weeks yet, he just couldn't be sure. I decided to fly to London to visit Gideon before returning home to my empty house in Dublin. But I wouldn't be there for long. The very next day Miki rang to say that my Mother was gone. The date was 13 August 2003. As soon as I put down the phone I booked a flight and flew back to Israel for the funeral the following day. It was a horrible, horrible time.

Mother was the last of a generation in our family. It was a huge, huge loss.

Quite naturally, I had thought that I should get back to work as soon as possible. I needed to be busy and I needed a routine. So, for the next twelve months I went to work, and then, in the evenings, cooked my supper, cleaned the house, did the laundry and ironed my clothes for the next day – I had learned to iron very well in the army. However, with the passing of each new month I began to question my choices. Always a sociable person, I joined classes, made new friends, and when my cooking skills improved, invited people over for dinner to repay the invites that came my way. Determined to do my utmost not to dwell on the past with all its sadness, I began to think about my future. The biggest question I asked myself was why I was working so hard when there was no need to, now that it was just me. I had had great success with my businesses. All my years of hard work had paid off and I had more than enough money to pay the bills. Therefore, about a year after Evanne's and my mother's deaths, I decided to retire. Life was short; it could end at any moment, and shouldn't be wasted.

Then, one day Kim, my daughter-in-law, asked me if I would be prepared to give a talk in the Zion school in Rathgar about my experiences in the Holocaust, explaining that my grandson, Josh, had mentioned me to one of his teachers. Up to that point, I had never spoken about my war-time experiences. All Evanne and my sons ever knew was that I was a Holocaust survivor; they knew absolutely nothing about what that involved for me, what I had actually been through, basically because I never wanted to tell them about it. So this unexpected request was a bit of a jolt. But in the end I agreed to do it for Josh.

To be honest, I couldn't understand why they would want to hear *my* story. But I wrote down a few notes, without really thinking too much about it, and presented myself to the school on the appointed day.

I was nervous, having never done anything like this before. On being asked if I wanted to stand up during the morning assembly and introduce myself to the entire school, I said no, feeling capable only of talking to the class I had been specifically engaged for. There were about fifteen of them, between the ages of eleven and twelve. I hadn't thought to ask anyone for advice in dealing with this age group and I certainly wasn't prepared for what happened. As I started to recount what I had been through as a young child, first in Merašice, and then in Bergen-Belsen concentration camp, I broke down, upsetting the students, who began to cry too, along with their teacher. When I managed to pull myself together and finish the talk, I felt thoroughly ashamed of myself, believing that I had been a complete disaster as a speaker. Therefore, it was a pleasant if bewildering surprise to discover that the teacher and students felt the complete opposite, and I was fervently thanked for coming in to talk to them.

A Future Based on the Past

One evening, towards the end of 2004, I was having dinner with some friends and found myself talking again about the Holocaust, 'my' Holocaust. One of the people present, Michael Colman, told me that he knew someone who would be very interested in my story. A few days later I received a phone call from a woman who introduced herself as Lynn Jackson, a founding member of the Holocaust Memorial Day committee. I invited her out to my house and there she asked me about Bergen-Belsen and living in Slovakia as a hated Jew. When I finished talking, she asked: 'Tomi, would you be prepared to read something at the Memorial Day, at the end of January?' My reply was an instant: 'Oh no! I couldn't. I'd be too emotional to read anything.' Unable to persuade me to change my mind, she suggested that I light a candle instead. Well, that was fine; I could certainly do that much.

Lynn also showed me the brochure that the Memorial Committee publish annually and invited me to write an article for the brochure. I was very flattered. This was probably the first time that I allowed myself to think seriously about what I had been through. It was an emotional few days. At some point I panicked about not describing things properly, so I rang Miki. We were surprised to find that our memories, in some places, varied and, in the end, he told me to just write what *I* actually remembered. I called the finished piece: 'One Morning in Bergen-Belsen'. Lynn was very pleased with it and suggested that I read it at the Holocaust Memorial Day, but I declined, knowing that it would be too emotionally demanding. Instead, I suggested that David, my son, read it in my place, which he kindly did.

Lynn's founding partner in the Holocaust Memorial Day committee was Oliver Donohue. Years earlier he had worked for Radio Telefís Éireann as a producer, and had also been a researcher for the hugely popular chat show *The Late Late Show*. Oliver contacted RTÉ, suggesting they interview me on radio, and this resulted in a phone call from RTÉ's Religious Affairs Correspondent, Joe Little, who gave me my very first interview. I remember being very nervous, but also excited at the prospect of being on the radio. The programme was pre-recorded, so that took some pressure off me. I spoke for ten minutes or so, about the conditions in Bergen-Belsen, in our hut, and about the starving and dying all around us. It was broadcast an hour later and I couldn't help feeling rather proud as I listened to myself. I thought I sounded rather well, considering it was the first radio interview I had ever done!

Of course, I couldn't have known what that kind of exposure would lead to. Within days I found myself the subject of newspaper articles, including one written on 15 January 2005 by Kim Bielenberg for the *Irish Independent*, which was followed by a feature in the *Irish Examiner*, written by Colette Colfer, and the *Evening Herald* also followed suit.

Meanwhile, Lynn was receiving requests from lots of schools who wanted someone to come in and talk to students about the Holocaust, and two other survivors, Suzi Diamond and Zoltan Colis, took up the offer to visit schools whenever they could. It was inevitable that Lynn would ask me whether I would be interested in doing the same thing. If she had asked me years before, I would probably have said no, convincing myself I was much too busy and also I just would not have wanted to talk about the past. Perhaps losing Evanne and Mother had something to do with it, but it suddenly occurred to me that this was something I *had* to do. As one of the last survivors, I had a moral duty to tell my story, to ensure that the Holocaust would never, ever be forgotten.

Not that it was easy. In fact, I found it quite traumatic at first, and broke down many times in front of students and teachers. To combat this I tried leaving out particular details, thinking that it was just certain matters that made me cry. Very quickly I discovered that it made no difference what I chose to leave out or include – I continued to break down, no matter what. Releasing my memories about Belsen after pushing them to the back of my mind for so many years was a highly emotional ordeal. I probably always knew it would prove difficult, which is why I never wanted to think about it before, but now, ordeal or not, I had to remember and recount, and the more I recounted, the more I remembered. I felt honoured to be invited to come and tell my story, and everyone I met, both young and old, was so very welcoming. I suddenly found myself very busy, lecturing in schools, universities and private societies, basically to whoever invited me to come and speak to them. On 21 September 2005 the Holocaust Education Trust was established, its inauguration taking place in the Mansion House with a rousing speech made by the President of Ireland Mary McAleese. Lynn became the chief executive and driving force of the Trust; she was also responsible for the immensely popular programme, 'Meeting a Holocaust Survivor', in which I play a major part today.

My personal life changed dramatically too. In 2006 I was introduced to Joyce Weinrib — well, re-introduced, really — as she used to live around the corner from us, and Evanne and I would often bump into her when Jonathan was still in his pram and Joyce had her little daughter, Joanna. We arranged to meet at the Berkeley Court Hotel. It happened to be Valentine's Day so I arrived with a little bag of special chocolates for her, tied with a nice red ribbon! We really enjoyed each other's company and we both wanted very much to meet again. We have been together ever since. I consider myself a *very*, very lucky man to have her in my life.

Chapter 23
• • • • • • •

Reunions and Revisits

When we left Czechoslovakia back in 1949, Artur Scheimovitz and his family decided to stay. Artur was a successful lawyer so the thought of moving to a country where he would have to learn a new language and, undoubtedly, start all over again, did not appeal to him. Plus, his son, Bandy, was getting on well in medical school, while Klara, his wife, could not leave her mother. Even if they had fantasised about changing their minds in the future, any thoughts of following us or going elsewhere were thoroughly banished once the Communists came to power. In the beginning, we made sure to stay in regular contact, with frequent letters home to keep them up to date on how we were doing. But even this wasn't allowed to continue and they had to ask us to stop sending so many letters because the authorities were suspicious of anybody receiving post from the west. So my parents were reduced to merely sending and receiving birthday and New Year cards. And, of course, the very idea of us westerners, and Israeli westerners in particular, visiting Czechoslovakia was out of the question.

The years passed by in quiet isolation and Artur died in 1963. It wasn't until 1987 that we found our solution in the shape of a more liberal Hungary: arrangements were made for the family to meet up in Budapest after thirty-eight years. I first went to Israel to spend some time with my mother, and Miki and his family, and then from there we all flew to Hungary to spend two days with Artur's family. As you can imagine, it was a very emotional reunion. The biggest absences were my father and Uncle Artur. My eighty-year-old mother and Aunt Klara, who had last seen each other as two vibrant women in their early forties, faced each other now as two elderly widows. They brought plenty of family photographs so that the gap of thirty-eight years could be bridged through sharing the memories of the past few decades. The advance of age, though expected, was still a shock. It was a small reunion, just Mother, Miki and me on our side, with Klara and her sons, Bandy and Juraj, Bandy's wife Zuzka and son Palo, but it was a most enjoyable one, with tasty meals and long walks throughout the streets of Budapest. My two cousins had done very well for themselves. Bandy ran a children's clinic in Piešťany, while Juraj was a camera man for Czech television; he was also an outstanding artist and photographer, having exhibited many times throughout Slovakia and the Czech Republic.

The following year, 1989, marked an important occasion for me. It was forty years since I had moved to Kibbutz Shamir in Israel, and I found myself wanting to commemorate that move with a reunion. I contacted my friends, some the remaining few from that very first group of settlers who still lived on the kibbutz, and they agreed that a reunion was a wonderful idea. Over the coming weeks we worked hard to trace as many of our other friends as possible, those who had left the kibbutz like me to forge their own path in the world. We eventually found a good number of people available to meet up to celebrate and the date was set for June.

What an unforgettable experience it was to meet again with so many friends after such a long time. We had been children, and now here we were, fully grown, most of us with fully grown children of our own. Naturally, there were some who had not changed much in forty years, and then there were those who had changed so much that even after introducing themselves I struggled to place them. It seemed I was one of the ones who had not changed much, which was nice. People approached me easily, hands held out as they greeted me by name – although this meant the pressure was on me to remember who they were! I was dumbstruck when a woman stood in front of me and asked: 'Well, Tomi, I hope you know me?' I didn't, at first, but after staring hard for a few seconds, I recognised her smile; it was Tamar, my first true love, who had broken my heart all those years ago and was one of the reasons for my leaving Shamir. She was a grandmother now, but looked just as good as she had in her teens, I thought.

It was a lovely day. There were approximately sixty of us. I didn't know everybody as some of the crowd were people who would only have arrived at the kibbutz after I left. The camp was unrecognisable, with new buildings, fancy sports facilities, a luxurious indoor swimming pool, and even new roads and paths. Our huts – the ones we had lived and slept in – were due to be knocked down, but not until after our reunion, which was considerate. Our old classroom, with the corrugated sheet roof, was also to be demolished after our get-together.

I found it interesting to discover what kind of adults my childhood friends had become. We were a diverse group, with professors, scientists, company directors, teachers, amongst other things. What was most fascinating was that it seemed to me that the ones I had always considered to be the smartest and most confident were often the ones who were struggling most with life! There were lots of photographs taken and the noise was tremendous, with everyone talking excitedly at once. The unforgettable day ended with many refrains of, 'Goodbye until the next time', but, no further reunion has been organised yet.

Going Home to Merašice

I suppose all these nostalgic gatherings began to stir up my emotions because that same year, 1989, I started to seriously think about visiting Czechoslovakia. The country was Communist at this time, which was just before the 'Velvet' or 'Gentle Revolution' of December 1989, leading to the democratic republic of Czechoslovakia, and, in 1993, the split into the Czech and Slovak republics. Unsure about the feasibility of a visit at this time, I enquired about a visa at the Czech offices in Dublin. When I mentioned that I had been born in the country, I was told that I didn't need a visa, just a Czechoslovak passport. But actually I wanted to visit my native country as a tourist and not as a citizen, because I was worried I might be arrested for never having served in the Communist Czechoslovak army. When I insisted on this, I was told that I would have to renounce my Czechoslovak citizenship.

Well, that was no problem, or at least it wasn't emotionally – but it certainly was financially. A huge pile of forms arrived in the post to do with proving that I had been born in Czechoslovakia and about renouncing my citizenship.

Bandy, my doctor cousin in Piešťany, had sent me over my birth certificate. Then came this strange form to do with assessing my education in Slovakia and wanting me to pay for my schooling! I couldn't believe it. Of course I objected, claiming – indeed, reminding them – that my education had been disrupted from 1941 to 1946, and that my remaining time in the country, before I left for Israel in 1949, had been concerned only with trying to make up for those lost years. They didn't care and demanded an impressive sum of £300. It was a lot of money and I had no option but to pay it.

That was the first expense. Next I was told I would have to get myself to London to see the Czechoslovak ambassador in person. There was no embassy in Dublin and it turned out that my meeting with the representative in Dublin would not satisfy the authorities. So I had to fly over for a meeting – a brief encounter that took no more than five minutes, including my introduction and one or two questions. Yet, maybe it was worth it as I was promised a visa with the proviso that I would report to the local police in each city I intended to visit.

There were five of us: Gideon and Karen, his wife, and our youngest son, Jonathan. One city I was anxious to see on the way was Nuremberg – I had last seen it in July 1945, when it had been in ruins. How different it was now, with hardly a trace of war wounds. We went to see the courthouse where the Nuremberg trials had been held and then I went to a fruit market to buy oranges to bring to Prague because I knew they were so expensive in Czechoslovakia.

We weren't too far away now, only about 95km from Czechoslovakia. At the border we handed in our passports and waited. The guard addressed me in Czech, asking me what the purpose of our visit was. I answered him without think-ing – and then it hit me: I was really here, back in Czecho-slovakia, speaking my mother tongue for the first time in so many years. As I listed off the places we intended to visit, I felt a rush of emotion and nostalgia. The guard, a pleasant man, reminded me about having to get a stamp at a police station in every city where I intended to stay overnight, and then handed back the passports, wishing us a pleasant stay.

As we drove further into the country the road was narrow and in poor condition, with dozens of pot-holes that forced us to drive slowly. The Communist presence was everywhere. Each village we passed carried banners with slogans such as, 'All Workers Unite', 'Capitalism Is Our Enemy' and 'We Will Be Victorious'. It was a different world to ours. There were absolutely no advertisements for brands or products, only the Communist philosophy. We also saw large loudspeakers fixed to high poles in every village, no matter how small it was. They played music in between providing information about meetings or communal activities.

The first days of our homecoming were all about meet-ing relations. We were to spend two days in Prague with my cousin Juraj and his wife, Jana. Then we drove to Brno, from where we would take the road to Sloup to visit Professor Mrazek who had taught Miki in technical college, they had remained good friends. He gave me my first reminder of my home village. During a wonderful banquet he and his wife had prepared for us, Professor Mrazek made a short welcoming speech, telling me he had a surprise for me. He picked up an intriguing large roll of canvas and handed it to me. I opened it out to find a painting of Merašice, with the family house in the background. He had found a photograph of the village and given it to a good friend who was a famous painter. The painting has pride of place in my dining room today.

We headed to Piešťany, where we met up with my other cousin, Bandy, his wife, Zuzka, and my Aunt Klara. It was another joyful reunion. They lived in the centre of the town, in a large three-storey house. Unfortunately, however, the Communists had confiscated most of the house and then put in five strange families, and even their own flat was split in half by a wall they were ordered to erect, as the authorities insisted that they needed only two bedrooms. After the fall of communism, the house would eventually be returned to them, but for years they were unable to remove their tenants, and the rent they received from each family was so small it didn't cover the maintenance or cleaning expenses. Plus the post-Communist government forbade them from raising the rent, and therefore, for a very long time their home was more a burden than anything else.

It was at this stage of the trip that I began to feel very excited about seeing Merašice again. The last time I had travelled this road, I was a little boy in the back of a horse-drawn carriage and it had taken almost half the day, so naturally I had assumed we would be driving for a few hours — so you can imagine my shock at spying the church steeple fifteen minutes after saying goodbye to Bandy! I had never known how close the two places were.

It was a beautiful warm summer's day and the fields were in full bloom and decorated with colourful flowers. The familiar twists and turns of the road, the dips and hills ambushed me with nostalgia. Had I really been gone so long? I didn't expect to remember everything so keenly. Unable to speak, I could only soak up the sights and atmosphere. On seeing the sign for Merašice, I stopped the car to take photographs. We passed where the road used to be that Miki and I took to get our illegal school lessons after the Jewish schools closed in 1942. Both the road and the farm were long gone.

The first house of the village belonged to the Trebichalsky family. I stopped and got out of the car, with the family following me. The entrance to the yard was at the side and a small path along the house led to the front door, where I could see an elderly woman sunning herself. As I neared her, I realised it was Mariška, our old housekeeper. She looked up in surprise at our approaching group. I greeted her, asking, 'Do you remember me?' She stared in confusion until I said, 'It's me, Mariška, Tomi Reichental.' Jumping up, she shouted out, 'Jesus Maria, Tominko!' We threw our arms around each other as tears of happiness flowed. I was overcome with emotion; I think I had forgotten how much this woman meant to me. When my parents, Miki and I returned home after the war, Mariška was the one person I was anxious to see. She turned to hug my family one by one and then gestured for us to follow her inside, her face still wet with tears. Her daughter Francka, hearing the commotion, appeared suddenly, mystified at the strange group in her mother's kitchen. As soon as I introduced myself to her, she too began to cry. Mariška, however, didn't allow her to indulge herself for too long, typically ordering her to make sandwiches for the guests!

Next, Mariška's son, Jano, came in. We had played together as children, but unfortunately life had not been good to him and it showed in his lined face. His mother snatched up the whiskey we had brought and hid it away out of sight. Nevertheless, he was delighted to see me again and announced that he would take us around to all the neighbours who would remember me. And that's what we did. We went from house to house: Jano would knock on the door, introduce me and immediately we were brought in for a *slivovic* in my honour – only I couldn't touch it because I was driving. I was thrilled to meet the wife of Mr Duraj, my father's most trusted worker, who had chauffeured me so many times, including that time when he had got Mother, Miki and me to safety, galloping us away from the screaming soldiers on the hunt for Jews. Sadly, I had arrived too late to see him again. She was very old and living alone in her house and, not surprisingly, didn't recognise me, but once Jano said: 'It's Tominko Reichental', she threw her arms around me in delight.

Finally we came to our own house. The first thing that struck me was the narrow entrance to the tiny yard. I had remembered it completely differently. In my head the entrance was wide and the yard was massive; I suppose everything appears bigger to a child. It was a little depressing and I was filled with conflicted feelings. The garden and the fruit trees were all gone and everything was in disrepair. My father had painted the house before we left and the paint had all but disappeared in the intervening years, though I spotted traces of it on the window frames. The place was now owned by a woman and her son. They lived where my grandparents used to live, while our part of the house was locked up. The woman explained that she rented it to a student and he only came home at weekends. We took hundreds of photos from every angle. It was very strange, a mixture of elation at seeing it again and sadness over the state of the place, hardly recognisable as the home I grew up in. Nevertheless, I raced around excitedly telling Evanne and the others where everything had been. Gideon's response to my childhood place delighted me. As he stood watching some geese waddle by, he suddenly said: 'Dad, you came from this tiny village, lost out on most of your education, yet, against all kinds of odds and obstacles, you travelled across half the world and achieved so much.' It was a very proud moment for me.

We decided to head for Karol Hloben's house then – apart from anything else, the women wanted to use a toilet. We went via the little bridge that Uncle Oskar had built over the village stream, which was only a pitiful trickle now, but at least the bridge was still standing. I turned around to see the Pankovy Breh (Sir's Hill), the hill behind the church where we used to toboggan with my mother. I remembered it as a tough climb, involving lots of huffing and puffing. How amazing it was to see not an imposing hill, but a small incline!

I led everyone to Karol's house. The last time I had seen him, he was a twenty-year-old man who worked the farm with my father. Jano, our guide, had gone ahead to announce the arrival of visitors and Karol came out to us, but he met my eye without recognition. Smiling, I said, 'Ah, Karol, you don't know who I am?' He struggled to remember and then thought he had it, 'Miki Reichental?' I laughed. 'You are close. I am his brother, Tomi.' Leaping forward, he grabbed me in a hearty hug. 'Welcome, welcome! This is a surprise;

we have to celebrate with a drink.' As a successful member of the Communist Party, and Merašice's representative, Karol had a car and his house was newly built and modern – and he had a modern toilet! We had a lot to talk about and got down to it immediately, reminiscing about old times. Meanwhile news had spread through the village that Tomi Reichental was in Karol's house and people whom I hadn't yet met began to arrive at his door to say hello. I didn't remember most of them, but they knew me, and remembered my parents and even my grandparents.

On our way home, we were to go through Austria, but I wanted to spend a little time in Bratislava first, where Aunt Margo and Chava used to live. Instead of taking the motorway from Piešťany, where we stayed for a few days, I drove one more time through Merašice, very slowly, soaking up a last look at everything. I followed the road, the one I had walked many times in my childhood, to the neighbouring village of Galanova, whose synagogue we had attended. The Communists had destroyed the synagogue, but only because there were no Jews left in the area. Then I took the winding road up through the forest, I was immersed in nostalgia, remembering every turn. This was the same road that Mr Duraj had driven us, back in 1944 when we were very nearly caught. In fact, I now drove across the same railway crossing where we had had no time to say goodbye to Mr Duraj before jumping on the train. This part of the railway line was no longer in service, so I was free to slow down and tell my family what had happened to Mother, Miki and me, at this very spot, forty-five years before.

Bratislava is about 90km from Piešťany and, once we got back on to the motorway, it took no more than fifty minutes or so to get there. Again, this considerably shortened journey made me feel peculiar; it used to take over half a day when I was a child. We headed to the centre of Bratislava where I managed to park the car right in front of the shop at 6 Polovnicky Road, where Aunt Margo used to live. We peered in at the yard that I knew so well – the three apartments were still there, but Margo's building was now an office block. We soon headed on to do a quick a tour of the old city. I was disappointed to see the houses were neglected, just like those in Prague. They were grey and dirty and I itched to paint them. The park in front of the National Theatre was full of weeds and in a sad state. It was depressing to see what this regime had done to the country. All the property belonged to the state and the people didn't care. I wanted to show Evanne and the boys where Miki and I had been picked up by the SS, but the old shop was gone and a bank now stood in its place.

Not wanting to arrive too late in Vienna, we left Bratislava in the afternoon. The border was only twenty minutes away and there weren't many other cars around. The border-guard asked me to step out of the car and open up the boot. He wanted to know if we had bought anything valuable, and whether I was carrying Czechoslovak currency, which could not be brought out. The only thing I was worried about was the professor's present, as it was also expressly forbidden to take art works out of the country, but I had it well hidden behind our cases. I told him we only had our clothes and toiletries, and he was satisfied with that. He took our passports away to check them and when he came back he asked, as a matter of form: 'So, where were you? Where did you stay? What cities did you visit?' I started to list off the places we had been only to have him heatedly cut me off: 'What? Where are the stamps from the police?' Out of the corner of my eye I saw my wife's face pale with anxiety. This was the moment I had been dreading, but I was surprised to find that I wasn't scared now, only suddenly very angry. Determined not to cower down in front of him, I found my voice: 'Look, I was a Czechoslovak citizen. I am visiting my home town after being gone for more than forty years. I am *not* a criminal. I expected a welcome from my country, but if *you* feel that I should be punished for not reporting to the police, then so be it, I'll pay the fine.' My voice was trembling with rage. It was foolhardy – but a deliberate decision; I could have been fined severely for my insolence alone. The guard looked stunned. A second or two passed and then, quite unexpectedly, he shook my hand and told me to continue on with my journey. My legs were shaking when I opened the door of the car, which was filled with tension, and Evanne, beside herself with fear, practically screamed at me: 'What happened?' Settling myself gingerly into the seat I could only say: 'He let me go.'

Thinking over the previous few days, I couldn't help experiencing a smugness or satisfaction. Czechoslovakia couldn't get rid of us Jews quick enough. The government had stripped us of everything before shipping us off to be killed. Well, I had returned, with my head held high, having lived a productive and prosperous life. Now it was Czechoslovakia that was in a shambles, completely backward and neglected. Yes, I couldn't help it, I was very proud of myself.

Four months later, on 17 November 1989, the Velvet Revolution blew up in Czechoslovakia. This was the bloodless revolution that saw the overthrow of the Communist regime and brought back democracy, after fifty long years, to Czechoslovakia. Two years later Evanne and I made a second trip there, this time with David, my eldest son, and his wife Kim. It was quite a trip; so much had changed in just two years of democracy and private enterprise. I was lucky enough to see Mariška one more time, as she passed away several months later.

Over the coming years I visited Slovakia many times. It has changed dramatically since my first visit in 1989. Bratislava is now a very beautiful city – the old part is revamped, the houses repainted and the roads have been re-tiled. The opera house is magnificent once more and there is also a new concert hall. That's the good news; the bad news is that the once terrifically low prices have caught up with the western world, and the hotels, in particular, are pricey. Also there is a lot more traffic too. No matter what the reason was for my trip, I always visited Merašice, for two reasons: to look at our old house and to see Karol. Every time I would hope that this would be the time that I could get in to see our part of the house, but it was always locked. It was a sorry sight, just an empty ruin now, its previous tenants long gone.

There were plenty of sentimental reasons for me wanting to get inside but there was also a practical one: I wanted the coat dresser – at least, that's what we called it. Basically, it was a wooden board, 1.7 metres wide and 1.9 metres high, divided into three parts. A framed mirror sat in the centre and beneath it was a little wooden drawer for brushes, while at the top were the hooks to hang coats. This was a very special to me because it had been in our house for as long as both Miki and I could remember. It was hand-painted in a cheerful blue with lots of Slovak patterns, and I was determined to bring it back to my own house in Dublin.

When I visited in 2005, part of the wall of the house had collapsed, allowing me to climb up and, for the first time in over fifty years, see the coat dresser which was still fixed to the wall. Determined to have it, I tried to prise it off, but it was firmly stuck, and I was afraid I'd damage it. Instead, I asked Karol to find somebody who could take it off the wall without wrecking it. He assured me he knew the perfect person, and also offered to store it until I could arrange to have it collected and taken to Ireland.

This wasn't easy, but a good friend finally came to my rescue. Another good friend, Shirley Haringman, used to have foreign students staying with her and some time in 2004 she rang to ask if I would like to meet some Slovak engineers who had come over to learn English. Of course I was delighted and arranged to take them on a drive around Dublin. And this is how I met the wonderful Oskar Baranovich, a highly intelligent and simply lovely guy. I remember driving him and his colleagues around the Dublin mountains, and somehow I ended up telling them how the Slovak government had treated my family and the Jewish population during the war. I don't know who was more shocked – them at my story or me at the fact that they had never heard it before. These were men who had studied and graduated from college under the Communist regime which left them totally ignorant about the Jewish suffering at the hands of the Catholic fascists. The Communists wiped these historic events from the school curriculum to hide the crimes of the Slovaks against the Jews.

When I visited Slovakia after that I always made time to meet Oskar. Thanks to on-going dental treatment I had there, we met up quite regularly. During a visit in 2006 I happened to mention the difficulty I was having in trying to bring the coat dresser back to Dublin. He inquired about the size and weight, and, when I gave him the figures, he surprised me by saying: 'That's no problem; I'll contact my despatch department and we'll sort something out.' All it took was one short phone call and a couple of months later I finally received this huge box which contained the superbly packed coat dresser! Today it is in my hall, just as it had been in our house in Merašice. Over eighty years old, older than me, we don't dare hang coats on it because it is much too beautiful and fragile. I did a lot of restoration on it myself and I hope it will last for many more years.

Chapter 24

Return to Bergen-Belsen

In July 2007 I gave a talk about my experience in Belsen and the loss of so many of my relatives at a teachers' seminar in Dublin. Afterwards there was the usual 'meet and greet', where Lynn introduced me to a young man, Gerry Gregg, who was an award-winning film director. Gerry was there with cameraman Seamus Deasy, one of Ireland's top directors of photography, and Oliver Donohoe, producer and creative communications consultant. As we shook hands, Gerry looked me straight in the eye and said: 'Your story is incredible and I would very much like to make a film about it. Would you be interested?' I was taken aback but said yes, not really believing that anything would come of it. Apparently while I was talking, Seamus had nudged Gerry in the ribs and said: 'Even if I don't get a cent, we have to make a film about this.'

In the following weeks we began to formulate some plans. Gerry wanted to make an initial promotional piece about my story, of maybe fifteen or twenty minutes in length, which he would show to RTÉ and the Irish Film Board in order to get the money to make the film. In the meantime I had received an invitation to participate in the opening of a new Memorial and Documentary Centre, at the former Bergen-Belsen Concentration Camp, on 28 October 2007, and suggested to Gerry that this might be part of the film. I also felt that Miki and Chava should be involved. Gerry readily agreed and we decided to meet up in Hanover on 26 October, the day before the ceremony: Gerry, his film crew, Miki, Chava, her daughter Limi, Joyce and me.

Even with the date in place I put off booking my flight because I couldn't really believe that this was actually going to happen. I have been asked many times if I have gone back to see Bergen-Belsen and, up to that point, my answer was always the same: 'No, and I never will.' It is very hard to convey how I feel about the place, and about what I saw there as a child – in fact, I doubt that anything can properly portray those horrific months I spent in the camp. How could anyone today *truly* understand what it was like to play amongst rotting bodies, the remnants of what were once human beings? So perhaps some part of me was unsure about the expedition too, and that's why I put off finalising my arrangements. It wasn't until Gerry rang me and exclaimed, 'What? You haven't booked your flight yet?' that I finally got myself and Joyce tickets.

In Hanover we met up with the other groups of survivors who had been invited to the memorial. There were groups from England, Canada and France in our hotel, and I remember being slightly shocked at how elderly they were. Miki, Chava and I were in our seventies, but I didn't think we looked as old as they did! We searched around to find anyone who would have been in our hut. I approached one woman who appeared much too young to be survivor and asked her: 'Were you in Bergen–Belsen?' She nodded. 'Yes, I was born there.' 'But that's impossible,' I gasped, 'no babies survived the camp.' I tried desperately not to picture the dead infants that bobbed up and down in the cesspit that passed for the camp toilet. 'Ah, but I was born in Bergen-Belsen Displaced Persons' Camp that was set up after the concentration camp was liberated.' She went on to tell me that she was one of two thousand babies born between 1945 and 1950. I had had no idea.

Sunday, 28 October 2007 was a difficult day – a day I will never forget. At breakfast I tried to keep control of the fear that was sending shivers all the way through me. Was I really going to walk around that place today? I did my best to hide my emotions from the others, though I'm sure all the survivors were doing exactly the same thing. We looked like such an ordinary bunch of people in the dining room, buttering toast and milking our coffees, and yet we were bound to one another by something that was extraordinarily hideous and evil. Then Hetty Verolme introduced herself to me – she wrote the book, *The Children's House of Belsen*, about her own experience of the camp. She greeted me like an old friend, even though we had never met before, but we had both been in Belsen sixty-three years ago, and that was enough to establish a genuine and immediate friendship.

After breakfast we filed out to board the bus that was taking us to the centre, a journey that would take a mere forty-five minutes or so. A few people attempted to chat, as if we were normal holiday-makers, but they couldn't hide the tension that was on the bus. The air was heavy with dread, I'm sure of it. As we approached the camp and the bus passed over the threshold where I read the sign 'Bergen-Belsen', my chest tightened; it felt like somebody was slowly piercing it with a blunt knife, and I had quite a struggle to breathe properly. Miki and I sat side by side in complete silence. Chava was behind us with Joyce, and behind them was Limi. All was quiet. What was there to say?

I'm trying to work out what was the strangest part of this first sighting. Not wanting to dwell on the visit, I had prevented myself from forming any expectations of what I would see or how I might feel. And the fact is, to my bewilderment,

I found it beautiful. What I saw was a large, grassy meadow surrounded by a dark, thriving forest. Miki and I agreed that you could easily mistake it as a perfect location for a camp site, with plenty of room for kids to run about and enjoy the freedom of the land and the forest. Only we and our fellow travellers would have remembered this gorgeous scenery bearing witness to an open grave, the air thick with the smell of thousands and thousands of rotting bodies. Yet those bodies were still there, still part of the landscape, beneath the umpteen mounds of earth that snaked about the site. For those innocent-looking grassy mounds were the mass graves that our liberators had the SS men and women dig. When I worked out what they were, it took all my strength to read the concrete plaques that told how many were buried within. Some held up to 2,500 bodies. I think I went into a sort of shock. Miki, Chava and I trudged around in complete silence, followed by Gerry and the film crew, our faces grey from our memories.

As we walked around the site it struck me that even now, all these years later, there were no birds. It was the same when we lived here – not one bird, despite the forest of trees. We saw the grave of the Franks, Anne and her sister Margot. They had actually lived in the block next to ours, though I never met them. Anne had died from typhus just weeks before liberation.

We joined the crowd at the Jewish memorial monument

where *Kaddish*, which is part of the mourning ritual, was recited. I can't describe the emotion. All around me people were breaking down in tears as we remembered those we had lost and what we, ourselves, had been through.

The three of us wanted to commemorate our grand-mother, *Omama* Rosalia. Chava had bought a bronze plaque, which would not rust, and had had it engraved in Israel. This was her resting place and we had returned to say a final and proper farewell. We placed the plaque on a prearranged concrete block.

In memory of our grandmother
Rosalia Scheimovitz
Died in Bergen-Belsen 7/3/1945
Grandchildren, great-grandchildren, great-great-grandchildren and
all the descendants of Scheimovitz for generations

Chava recited the wonderful poem by Avraham Shlonsky (1900–1973), called 'The Vow' which includes the line:

I contracted the vow to remember all,
to remember and forget nothing
till the tenth generation.

The poem inspired Gerry to name the film *Till the Tenth Generation*. We must not forget until the tenth generation, in other words, we must never forget.

After saying goodbye to *Omama* Rosalia, we slowly made our way to the new memorial museum and documentary centre. It is a big building, filled with evidence of the gruesome past, including hundreds of photographs, films and even some archaeological finds. The exhibition is divided into four parts: the first section is about Belsen as a Prisoner of War Camp (1939–1943); the second section deals with the suffering and death of over 50,000 inmates in the Concentration Camp (1943–1945); the third section deals with the prosecution of the camp staff, including the 'Butcher', Joseph Kramer, and Irma Grese; and the final section deals with Belsen as the Jewish Displaced Persons' Camp (1945–1950). Of course, the second section was the one I was most familiar with.

It was a lot to take in. Gerry and the cameraman accompanied Joyce and me around the exhibition. I felt strangely detached for most of it, stopping infrequently to point out SS women that I recognised in some of the photos. At one stage I saw a picture that had been taken just in front of our block, of the bodies piled up on the open ground. It was almost easy to imagine that this was something apart from me, which, I suppose, is the consequence of not talking about Belsen for over fifty years.

After an hour, when we had our fill of the centre, we got a taxi to take us to the train station, that infamous station where we had arrived sixty-three years ago, 9 November 1944. It looked the same and there was even an old cattle cart there, an ever-present reminder of that horrific week-long journey before we were hounded by the SS and their mad dogs into walking for two and half hours through the forest, in the dark and the torrential rain, until we reached our dreadful destination. I found this a more difficult place to be than Belsen itself. When you think about it, what happened here was, for me and my family, a lot more frightening than the camp, where we had no choice but to get used to the conditions because we lived with them for so long. Perhaps nothing we experienced in Belsen equalled the confusion and terror that besieged us when the train stopped and its doors slid open.

Gerry and the crew followed us everywhere. We were hardly aware of them until we left Belsen behind. I don't know what we revealed of ourselves on camera. As we walked about, my only thoughts, as I remember it, were of the ones who didn't make it, the ones beneath the lolling man-made hills. Man-made indeed.

We returned to Ireland with a couple of hours of film that Gerry turned into a compelling twenty-minute film, which he then showed to RTÉ and the Irish Film Board. RTÉ loved it, but needed the IFB to put the money up for it, and that was a decision that couldn't be made lightly, or quickly. Eventually, in January 2008, Gerry rang me: 'Tomi, start packing. We got the money!' Once the decision had been made, Gerry and I discussed what we both wanted to do. The film would have to involve a lot of travel as there were several locations required to explain the history of the Reichental and Scheimovitz families, and then what befell them during the Holocaust.

I was very friendly with the Slovak ambassador to Ireland, Jan Gabor, and, at some point, I got the idea to ask him to arrange an interview, in Slovakia, with some high-ranking Slovak government official, who just might take the opportunity to apologise, on camera, to the Slovak Jewish for what the government did during the war. Gerry and I went to meet Jan – I don't think he actually agreed with my view of events, and instead spoke about how the Slovaks were victims rather than perpetrators. However, he promised to arrange a meeting for us and, a couple of days later, we were informed that we would meet with Dušan Čaplovič, Vice-Premier of Slovakia. I told the ambassador that we only wanted a brief interview, involving me asking just four questions, and he asked me to send the questions before I left Ireland.

I made several points and followed them with my questions:

I devote my time to lecturing in schools and universities about my experience in the Holocaust.

Question: What is the government of the Slovak Republic doing to inform the youth of Slovakia about what happened to Jews during the Tiso era?

In my lectures I describe Slovakia as willing perpetrators in persecuting the Jews during the war. But Slovakia considers itself a victim.

Question: How come Slovakia was the only state in Europe in 1942 that paid the Germans for each Jew deported?

The Slovak government claims that Germany initiated and pressurised Slovakia to deport the Jews. But Slovakia was an independent state, not occupied by Germany. Slovakia stopped the deportation in October 1942.

Question: Does that not prove that the Slovak government had the power to refuse or delay the deportation?

Question: What is the government of the Slovak Republic doing today to stop and counteract the rise of anti-Semitism?

On 1 March I flew to Bratislava to meet up with Gerry and the film crew. We were going to cram as much as we could into the next two weeks. For the interview with Vice-Premier Caplovic, I put on my best suit, feeling rather excited. We were meeting him in the presidential palace, from where Fr Josef Tiso had ruled in the 1940s. We were granted permission to film in the palace, so, as a prelude to the all-important interview, Gerry filmed me walking through the corridor of this magnificent Austro-Hungarian structure. Mr Caplovic was most polite. I put my questions to him one by one, and he answered them readily enough, but not in the way I had hoped. Each answer was long, with plenty of twists and turns. I was glad we were recording it because I felt overwhelmed by all the information coming at me. When the last question had finally been answered, the Vice-Premier presented me with several books about

Slovak history. We thanked him and left.

As we walked outside Gerry asked me, 'So, what did he say?' I shrugged my shoulders: 'Well, he spoke a lot but I honestly didn't have a clue what he was talking about.' Back at the hotel we played the tape and I translated the interview, word by word. The disappointing conclusion was that we had nothing significant. It appeared that the Vice-Premier kept his answers as general as possible, regretting but greatly justifying why the Slovaks behaved the way that they did. It was useless as far as the film was concerned. I suppose to have apologised would have meant an admission of guilt, which would possibly have proved unpopular with voters.

As you might imagine, it was quite an emotional journey for me to make this film about the tragedies that beset my mother and father's family. One of the more shocking episodes was when we went to Poland to film the prison where my uncle, Desider Reichental, was held. I had contacted the authorities before we arrived, asking for permission to film in the yard, where the executions took place, but hadn't received either a solid 'no' or 'yes'. When we arrived and introduced ourselves, the staff was not exactly helpful and suggested that we come back in two days. They told us that the governor was not around and they could not make the decision to allow us inside. I tried to explain myself: 'But we only want to film the place where my uncle was hanged.' The lady turned to me in surprise: 'Your uncle could not have been hanged. In this prison the prisoners were guillotined.'

Since we couldn't get into the yard, Gerry took me back outside, to film me talking about Uncle Desider beside the prison walls, but I kept breaking down. I can't explain how I felt. Not that death by hanging would be any more pleasant, but *guillotined*? It sounded so coarse and barbaric; to have believed that a person died one way, and then, in a split second, to hear something completely different, it was very distressing.

We visited Buchenwald where my Uncle Julius (Dula), Chava's father, had died. She put a plaque down in memory of him. Gerry asked me to read the inscription aloud but, again, I kept breaking down as I remembered my gentle uncle, another good man who had never caused anyone pain, murdered because of his religion.

Auschwitz was the worst. It was here that I had lost eighteen of my relatives, four from my mother's side and fourteen from my father's, including my beloved grandparents. The memory of them taking leave of us, and their house, that night of 15 August 1942, rushed over me. They must have been so afraid when they arrived here, and were probably separated for the first time since they married, before being herded towards the gas chambers. It was something I had managed not to think about for decades, and now here I was, looking at the place where those gas chambers used to stand. I couldn't stand beside them. It was just too much.

We returned to Bergen-Belsen where it was raining hard, making it impossible for Gerry to do much filming. However, I did manage to find where our block had stood. The British had burned all the wooden huts to the ground after they liberated the camp, to stop the spread of typhus, so there was little left of the original camp. Nevertheless, there had to be a reminder, something to show people today the way we had lived. Accordingly, the centre had built a roofless shell that provided an outline of the height of the wall and the length of the floor. It was quite a jolt to see that the replica was of our hut, number 207. I was able to stand on the spot where my bed was. Gerry couldn't film me, because of the rain. I can't imagine the expression on my face as I pictured my bed, the room, the hut and the block.

After fourteen days of filming we returned to Dublin, where Gerry found a nephew of Reverend Morrison, the chaplain in the British army that liberated Bergen-Belsen. You can see him in a film made in 1945 – he's praying over the bodies that are being placed in the mass graves. His nephew, Bill Morrison, presented me with a letter (dated 11 May 1945) that his uncle sent home from Belsen, and I thanked him on behalf of my family for his uncle's prayers, because my grandmother was one of the bodies he prayed over. Gerry filmed our meeting which was very emotional. Today I use his uncle's letter in my lectures:

I Was a Boy in Belsen

When we got here there were some thousands of naked bodies lying about the place. In one pile alone there were over a thousand women's bodies and it was quite common to see people crawl on their hands and knees because they were too weak to walk, while other just dropped to the ground and remained there.

It is not uncommon to find three people in one bunk – one of more of whom were dead. Huts which could accommodate thirty were made to hold five to seven hundred.

The death rate for the first few days we were here must have been nearly a thousand a day. Typhus was raging, but starvation accounted for most deaths. The food for the internees was half a litre of turnip soup a day and a loaf of bread between six once a week.

So far I have buried over fifteen thousand and I have not been able to attend all funerals, as I considered the dying to be more important than the dead. Those fifteen thousand did not take up much of my time as ten graves held up to five thousand bodies each.

Epilogue

Writing my memoir was a long journey. One thing I learned in my life is that you don't achieve your aims without working hard and devoting your energies to them. Right from my childhood my parents gave me the guidance to be polite, honest, respectful and fair. This always paid dividends, especially in my adult life. I have met a large variety of people – this required a good judgement of behaviour. Fairness, once you reach a position of being in charge, is very important – it is no good trampling on somebody to advance your own position. But one thing that my parents couldn't prepare me for was the time we spent in Bergen-Belsen.

I have tried to describe the horror we lived through there, but words don't exist to describe the suffering and the conditions we lived in. The starvation, cold, lack of hygiene, the stench and the death all around us were such that we still wonder today how we survived. Seeing the body of my grandmother being taken away to be thrown on a pile of corpses will never leave my memory. What kept our spirits up was the support and the togetherness of the family. The encouragement of my mother was especially important. Her optimism and smile in the most horrible times gave us hope.

On the day of liberation, the camp was an open graveyard. There were over twenty thousand corpses lying all around us and thousands of human skeletons were walking aimlessly, not knowing if they would survive another hour or day. It was hell on earth.

The years that followed were all about learning – learning and learning. We had lost our childhood and we had lost our basic education, but eventually we were able to build our futures. I started out as a mechanical engineer, then became a tool maker, plumber, electrician, a works manager and eventually company director. In later years, after forty-two years of marriage I lost my wife to cancer. My wonderful companion, Joyce, changed my life and I can enjoy happiness again. When I began a new career lecturing about the Holocaust, I realised that this was something I had to do. I feel I owe it to the victims that they are not forgotten. My dedication to this cause has earned me quite a bit of recognition, and a film about my life, *Till the Tenth Generation* was made.

After all the horror, I am doing my best to keep the memory of those lost ones alive.

We – you, me, your children, my children – must never forget.

Appendix 1

Members of My Family Who Perished

From My Mother's Side:

Rosalia Scheimovitz (grandmother), perished in Bergen-Belsen, 7 March 1945

Julius (Dula) Mayer (Margo's husband), perished in Buchenwald, 3 February 1945

Gejza Scheimovitz (uncle), perished in Buchenwald, 1945

Oskar (Osy) Scheimovitz (uncle), perished in Buchenwald, 1945

Adela Fried née Scheimovitz (aunt), perished in Auschwitz, June 1944

Bela Fried (Adela's husband), perished in Auschwitz, June 1944

Katarina (Kati) Fried (cousin), perished in Auschwitz, June 1944

Agnes (Agi) Fried (cousin), perished in Auschwitz, June 1944

From My Father's Side:

Jecheskel Reichental (grandfather), perished in Auschwitz, 1942

Katarina Reichental (grandmother), perished in Auschwitz, 1942

Kalmar Reichental (uncle), perished in Auschwitz, 1942

Ilona Reichental (aunt), perished in Auschwitz, 1942

Gita Reichental (cousin), perished in Auschwitz, 1942

Oto Reichental (cousin), perished in Auschwitz, 1942

Max Shön (uncle), perished in Auschwitz, 1942

Ibojka Shön née Reichental (aunt), perished in Auschwitz, 1942

Dita Shön (cousin), perished in Auschwitz, 1942

Ferdinand Alt (uncle), perished in Auschwitz, 1942

Erna Alt née Reichental (aunt), perished in Auschwitz, 1942

Ferko Alt (cousin), perished in Auschwitz, 1942

Renka Alt (cousin), perished in Auschwitz, 1942

Mr Elbert (uncle), perished in Auschwitz, 1942

Renka Elbert née Reichental (aunt), perished in Auschwitz, 1942

Marta Elbert (cousin), perished in Auschwitz, 1942

Desider Reichental (uncle), executed in Wroclaw, 29 April 1943

Appendix 2

Joseph Kramer Begs for Help

In a letter dated 1 March 1945 to Gruppenführer (General) Richard Glücks, head of the SS camp administration agency, Commandant Kramer reported in detail on the catastrophic situation in Bergen–Belsen and pleaded for help.

If I had sufficient sleeping accommodation at my disposal, then the accommodation of the detainees who have already arrived and of those still to come would appear more possible. In addition to this question a spotted fever and typhus epidemic has now begun, which increases in extent every day. The daily mortality rate, which was still in the region of 60-70 at the beginning of February, has in the meantime attained a daily average of 250-300 and will increase still further in view of the conditions which at present prevail.

Supply. When I took over the camp, winter supplies for 1,500 internees had been indented for; some had been received, but the greater part had not been delivered. This failure was due not only to difficulties of transport, but also to the fact that practically nothing is available in this area and all must be brought from outside the area ...

For the last four days there has been no delivery [of food] from Hanover owing to interrupted communications, and I shall be compelled, if this state of affairs prevails till the end of the week, to fetch bread also by means of truck from Hanover. The trucks allotted to the local unit are in no way adequate for this work, and I am compelled to ask for at least three to four trucks and five to six trailers. When I once have here a means of towing then I can send out the trailers into the surrounding area ...The supply question must, without fail, be cleared up in the next few days. I ask you, Gruppenführer, for an allocation of transport ...

State of Health. The incidence of disease is very high here in proportion to the number of detainees. When you interviewed me on Dec. 1, 1944, at Oranienburg, you told me that Bergen-Belsen was to serve as a sick camp for all concentration camps in north Germany. The number of sick has greatly increased, particularly on account of the transports of detainees that have arrived from the East in recent times — these transports have sometimes spent eight or fourteen days in open trucks ...

The fight against spotted fever is made extremely difficult by the lack of means of disinfection. Due to constant use, the hot-air delousing machine is now in bad working order and sometimes fails for several days ...

A catastrophe is taking place for which no one wishes to assume responsibility ... Gruppenführer, I can assure you that from this end everything will be done to overcome the present crisis ...

I am now asking you for your assistance as it lies in your power. In addition to the above-mentioned points I need here, before everything, accommodation facilities, beds, blankets, eating utensils – all for about 20,000 internees ... I implore your help in overcoming this situation.

Five Belsen Orphans Come to Ireland

In 1945 a paediatrician at Dublin's Rotunda Hospital, Dr Bob Collis, joined the British Red Cross and St John's Ambulance Brigade, along with a couple of his colleagues, wanting to be of service to the innocent victims of war. After hearing eyewitness accounts about the conditions in Bergen-Belsen, they immediately volunteered to go there.

On arrival, Dr Collis took over a block that contained a large number of orphaned children who were still in recovery from malnutrition. Five of these children would become very important to him. Brother and sister Zoltan and Edith were from Slovakia. Zoltan was four years old and in a critical condition with tubercular pleurisy. Suzi and Terry were Hungarian – all of their family had been murdered by the Nazis and their mother died in Bergen-Belsen. Suzi, who was very weak after surviving typhus, wasn't even two years old. Evelin was a German Jewish girl.

Once the children in Belsen had been restored to good health they were usually repatriated to their country of origin. However, no one came to claim any of these five children, so Dr Collis decided, with his assistant nurse, Han, to bring the children back to Ireland with them. There, the doctor and his wife adopted Zoltan and Edith. He also arranged for Suzi and Terry to be adopted by a Dublin Jewish couple, while Evelin was adopted by another Dublin couple who later emigrated to Australia. Bob and Han were the first Irish people to be honoured with the title 'Righteous Among the Nation' by the Holocaust Martyrs and Heroes Authority in Israel.

Justice for Belsen Survivors

An investigation into the conditions at Bergen–Belsen camp was launched almost immediately after liberation by the British army. Evidence was collected from the inmates in an attempt to establish who was behind the callous neglect of the camp's population. Of course, Josef Kramer and his administrative colleague, Doctor Fritz Klein, were deemed ultimately responsible, but there were plenty of others – SS officers and capos – who were guilty of abusing, starving and terrorising the hapless prisoners. Quite a number of these ended up in the dock alongside the camp commander.

A trial took place in Lüneburg, which isn't too far from Belsen. Sentences were passed on 16 November, with eleven people sentenced to death by hanging, including Josef Kramer, Doctor Klein and Irma Grese. Forty-four others stood trial; of these, fourteen were acquitted and the other thirty received prison sentences of varying lengths, according to their crimes.

Two hundred other SS officers, many of whom had blood on their hands, pleaded Not Guilty, claiming that they had only carried out orders. They never stood trial.

References

Fatran, Gila, *Fight for Survival*, Slovak National Museum – Museum of Jewish Culture, Bratislava 2007.

Shephard, Ben, *After Daybreak, the Liberation of Belsen 1945*, Pimlico, London 2006.

Laqueur, Renata, *Diary of Bergen Belsen March 1944–April 1945*, Stiftung Niedersachsische Gedenkstatte 2007.

Verolme, Hetty, *The Children's House of Belsen*, Politico's publishing, London 2005.

Bergen-Belsen Memorial, Stiftung Niedersachsische Gedenkstatte.

Internet: Google, Wikipedia.

Postscript

For the past twelve years, Tomi Reichental has been on a very public voyage of personal recovery from the searing embers of the Holocaust. Six million European Jews were annihilated during World War Two; among them were most members of Tomi's extended family. How, Tomi wondered, could so much hate take root at the heart of Europe? The thirty-five members of his family who perished were farmers, shopkeepers, lawyers, doctors, mothers and children.

In 1935, the year of Tomi's birth, they had every reason to hope for the future. Within a decade, their neighbours and fellow countrymen would betray them and send them to a hellish death at the hands of Adolf Hitler's genocidal killing apparatus.

The RTÉ/Irish Film Board feature documentary *Till the Tenth Generation* (2009) took Tomi back to the most traumatic days of his life. It was he said 'the time of the devil' as he retraced the last steps of his loved ones who were gassed, worked to death, starved or guillotined by reason of their race, religion and political views.

The RTÉ documentary *Close To Evil* (2014) took as its starting point Tomi's quest to meet one of Hitler's willing executioners: the convicted SS war criminal Hilde Michnia Hilde Lisiewicz, as she was in 1945, was on duty in Bergen-Belsen during the period that Tomi, his brother Miki and his mother Judith were incarcerated and slowly starving. Tomi's grandmother, Rosalia Scheimowitz, perished from hunger on Hilde Lisiewicz's watch at Bergen-Belsen in March 1945.

In the multi-award-winning *Close to Evil*, Hilde Michnia made a number of incriminating statements. Frau Michnia openly admitted in interviews she gave in 2004 that she was also involved in the forced 'evacuation' from the Gross-Rosen network of camps in what is now Poland to the town of Guben in January 1945.

We know that the word 'evacuation' was a euphemism for a manic, lethal commitment to persecute and kill Jews right to the bitter end of the Third Reich on what became known as 'death marches'. We know from the accounts of survivors such as Luba Varshavska, who spoke to Tomi in her home near Tel Aviv, that hundreds of female prisoners died on the cruel trek from Grünberg to Guben in the middle of winter. Many were shot for failing to keep up with the forced pace of the slog through snow and ice and biting winds. In her recorded testimony, Hilde Michnia claims she witnessed no ill-treatment of prisoners; indeed, she asserts that they were fed and cared for as well as could be expected by her and her SS comrades.

Now Tomi has set himself the task of bringing this unrepentant SS guard to account, not only for her complicity

...crimes but for her public distortion of the truth and ...al of the Shoah.

Ironically, Tomi's generosity of spirit has helped to heal others with a Nazi past. From Germany to Australia, those prepared to confront both the actions and the shame of their forefathers have found Tomi to be an inspiration and a source of support.

In January 2015, following a public screening of *Close to Evil* in Lüneburg, Hilde Michnia's admission that she was a participant in the Grünberg to Guben 'evacuation' in January 1945 prompted the German authorities to open an investigation into the then 93-year-old Hamburg woman. After the German premiere, a formal complaint was filed by Hans-Jürgen Brennecke, the son of a Nazi policeman whose father had justified the slaughter of Jews on the basis that 'it was them or us'. Brennecke is a man who has faced up to the skeletons in his family cupboard. He believes many more Germans have still to come to terms with what their fathers and mothers did during the Third Reich. In the case of Hilde Michnia, Brennecke submitted that her claims that there was no maltreatment of prisoners on her watch at either the Gross-Rosen–affiliated camp or Bergen-Belsen amounted to 'Auschwitz Luge' – Holocaust denial, a criminal offence in Germany.

Whether or not Hilde Michnia eventually faces trial is not the point of the process initiated by Hans-Jürgen Brennecke and supported by Tomi Reichental. Their aim is to confroi the legally uncontested claims of an SS guard that under he care frightened, famished and frozen slave labourers were fed cocoa and hot soup – when those who survived this ordeal can recall only fear and loathing and the sound of gunfire directed at those who could not keep up with the pace of the retreat from the advancing Soviet Red Army.

This book, first published in 2011, is a bestseller. It is, however, not the end of the Tomi Reichental story. Anything but. In 2015, two Irish universities, NUI Maynooth and Trinity College Dublin, bestowed on Tomi honorary doctorates for his 'mission of remembrance'. Soon Dublin City University will confer a similar honour on Tomi. But it is the affection of ordinary people that is most striking. Tomi is often stopped in the street or on trains and trams by strangers eager to shake his hand and wish him well in his work.

Every week Tomi speaks to students at schools all over Ireland. Close to 100,000 Irish second-level students have heard Tomi describe 'the indescribable'. Wherever he goes, he is received as a valued, special citizen of the Irish Republic.

In 2014 Tomi won a Rehab People of the Year Award. A frequent contributor to high-profile TV and radio shows, Tomi's commitment to truth and reconciliation is regularly the subject of sympathetic media coverage. He is now a national figure whose actions are reverberating beyond Irish shores.

...rkably, in June 2015, on the occasion of his eighti-
...thday, Tomi was invited to speak about the Holocaust
...e congregation of a large Dublin mosque. The Imam
...the West Dublin–based Islamic Educational and Cultural
...entre, Dr Shaykh Umar Al-Qadri, pointed out that this was
'a unique event in modern Europe, if not the world'. The
Imam hopes that the example of Tomi reaching out to, and
being embraced by, Irish Muslims will be a beacon for the
rest of Europe to follow.

Far from putting his feet up and taking it easy, Tomi
Reichental is starting a new chapter in his remarkable life.
He is embarking on new adventures and taking on fresh
challenges. Long may he continue to inspire with his big
heart, his open mind and his generosity of spirit.

The journey continues. The man who was a boy in Belsen
is still restless, and has 'miles to go before he sleeps'.

Gerry Gregg, producer/director of the feature documentaries
Till the Tenth Generation and *Close to Evil*